Homer's *Iliad* and the Trojan War

Bloomsbury Studies in Classical Reception

Bloomsbury Studies in Classical Reception presents scholarly monographs offering new and innovative research and debate to students and scholars in the reception of Classical Studies. Each volume will explore the appropriation, reconceptualization and recontextualization of various aspects of the Graeco-Roman world and its culture, looking at the impact of the ancient world on modernity. Research will also cover reception within antiquity, the theory and practice of translation, and reception theory.

Also available in the Series:

Ancient Magic and the Supernatural in the Modern Visual and Performing Arts, edited by Filippo Carlà and Irene Berti

Ancient Greek Myth in World Fiction since 1989, edited by Justine McConnell and Edith Hall

The Codex Fori Mussolini, Han Lamers and Bettina Reitz-Joosse

The Gentle, Jealous God, Simon Perris

Greek and Roman Classics in the British Struggle for Social Reform, edited by Henry Stead and Edith Hall

Imagining Xerxes, Emma Bridges

Julius Caesar's Self-Created Image and Its Dramatic Afterlife, Miryana Dimitrova

Ovid's Myth of Pygmalion on Screen, Paula James

Victorian Classical Burlesques, Laura Monrós-Gaspar

Homer's *Iliad* and the Trojan War

Dialogues on Tradition

Jan Haywood and Naoíse Mac Sweeney

BLOOMSBURY ACADEMIC
LONDON • NEW YORK • OXFORD • NEW DELHI • SYDNEY

BLOOMSBURY ACADEMIC
Bloomsbury Publishing Plc
50 Bedford Square, London, WC1B 3DP, UK
1385 Broadway, New York, NY 10018, USA

BLOOMSBURY, BLOOMSBURY ACADEMIC and the Diana logo are
trademarks of Bloomsbury Publishing Plc

First published 2018
Paperback edition first published 2020

Cover image: *Aristotle with a Bust of Homer* by Rembrandt Harmensz van Rijn, 1653.
Metropolitan Museum of Art, New York. Photo by VCG Wilson/Corbis via Getty Images.

A catalogue record for this book is available from the British Library.

A catalog record for this book is available from the Library of Congress

ISBN: HB: 978-1-3500-1268-4
PB: 978-1-3501-2941-2
ePDF: 978-1-3500-1270-7
ePub: 978-1-3500-1269-1

Series: Bloomsbury Studies in Classical Reception

Typeset by Integra Software Services Pvt. Ltd.

To find out more about our authors and books visit
www.bloomsbury.com and sign up for our newsletters.

Contents

List of Illustrations

Note from the Authors

This book began with a conversation. In 2014, we were both involved in teaching an undergraduate module on 'Troy and the Trojan War' at the University of Leicester, which led to friendly debate about what aims such a module might have and what potential material it might cover, given the widespread and multifarious responses that this tradition has generated. This resulted in a broader discussion about the traditions surrounding the Trojan War, and, inevitably, about receptions of the *Iliad* and Homeric poetry more broadly. Both traditions and reception, we felt, were essentially constructed through engagements, interactions, and, ultimately, dialogue; it was from this point on that the concept of dialogue became core to the project. We hope that the structure of this book goes some way towards capturing this, allowing our individual authorial voices to be heard and retaining something of the fundamental multivocality of classical receptions.

We are very grateful to several people who have read and commented on parts of the book, including: Tom Harrison, Johannes Haubold, Greta Hawes, Fiona Hobden, Gregory Nagy, Robin Osborne, Nicholas Postgate, Seth Schein, and Martin Worthington. Where this book is successful we owe these individuals a great debt; but we claim sole credit for the flaws and weaknesses that remain. Thanks are also due to Harvard's Center for Hellenic Studies (in particular to Lanah Koelle and Gregory Nagy); both of us were fortunate to spend some time at the centre during the researching and writing of this book. We are also grateful to the wonderful editorial team at Bloomsbury, including Alice Wright and Clara Herberg, for their patience and good counsel. Finally, we would also like to thank Craig Cipolla and Ollie Harris, who have been both friends and colleagues of ours at the University of Leicester. Craig and Ollie's new book (Harris and Cipolla 2017) was conceived and written at broadly the same time as our own and also makes use of the dialogic form. We have enjoyed and benefitted from our conversations with them over the years, and from reading their own innovative concluding dialogue.

In the spelling of proper nouns, we have been consistent only in following convention. In the majority of cases, Latin spellings have been used in preference to Greek. All translations are our own, unless specified otherwise.

Jan's Note:

Many individuals have contributed to this book over the period of its gestation. I am grateful to audiences at the University of Leicester, the University of Manchester, and The Open University, who listened to, and offered a number of instructive comments on, earlier versions of my sections in Chapters 4 and 5, as well as the Conclusion. I am also thankful to numerous friends and colleagues for their encouragement and advice along the way, notably: Tom Harrison, Fiona Hobden, Jason Wickham, Tao Ziyuan, Andy Merrills, Dave Edwards, Neil Christie, Graham Shipley, and Mary Harlow. A special debt of gratitude on my part is also due to Naoíse for initiating the conversation that eventually led to this volume. Lastly, I am indebted above all to my parents and other loved ones for their unfailing support.

Naoíse's Note:

I am grateful to participants of a research seminar at the Department of Classics in Nottingham in 2016, where an early version of my section in Chapter 2 was presented. Your ideas helped to push the argument in new directions. I also would like to thank Greta Hawes, Virginia Lewis, Nikos Papadimitriou, and Jason Harris for all the straight talking, laughter, perspective, and cake. I also owe a great debt to my husband John, whose support and hard work kept the whole family going while I had my head in this book. Finally, I am grateful to Jan for his patience, good humour, and friendship throughout this process.

Introduction: Dialogue

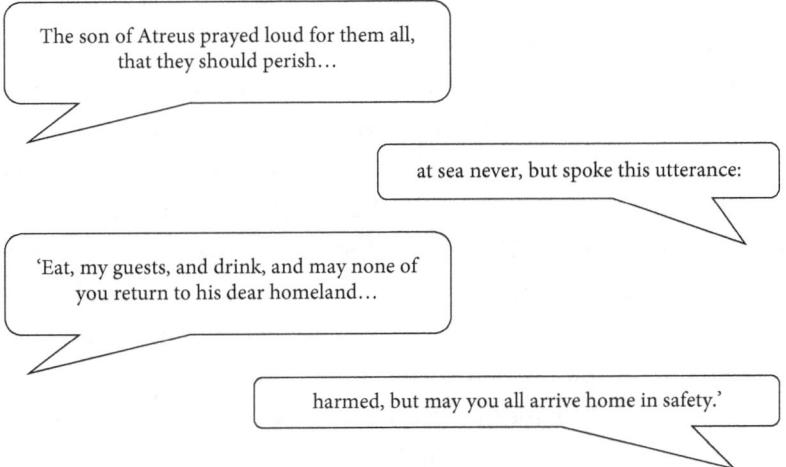

The son of Atreus prayed loud for them all, that they should perish...

at sea never, but spoke this utterance:

'Eat, my guests, and drink, and may none of you return to his dear homeland...

harmed, but may you all arrive home in safety.'

The Contest of Homer and Hesiod 9

In the second century CE, an unknown writer composed *The Contest of Homer and Hesiod*, a playful text in which the two poets try to outdo each other in wit and wordcraft. In the section quoted above, Hesiod (on the left) offers his opponent a series of freshly composed lines of hexameter verse, to each of which Homer (on the right) must improvise a continuation. In every case, Homer's response is robust; his unshakable gravitas counters Hesiod's snares to comic effect. But it is Hesiod who was eventually judged the victor by the assembled crowd, with his peacetime poetry elevated above Homer's songs of war. The text has much to teach us concerning ancient ideas about poets, and particularly on later conceptions of Homer and Hesiod at the forefront of the epic tradition.[1] But it also reminds us that no poet, poem, or work of literature ever stands alone. Homer here appears in dialogue with Hesiod, and both the composition and the reception of Homeric poetry are represented as embedded within a much wider poetic tradition.

This book is concerned with this idea of Homeric epic as set within a broader tradition – specifically, the place and role of the *Iliad* within the tradition of myths, stories, and representations of the Trojan War. We have chosen to think about this in terms of 'dialogue' because of the way that such traditions work. They are not passively received, or simply handed down from one generation to the next. Rather, they are in a continuous process of construction and development, with each new intervention adding to, but also fundamentally transforming, the tradition itself. Indeed, the dialogue between new and existing elements is what creates a tradition – the engagements, interactions, borrowings, subversions, and transformations. Yet within the Trojan War tradition, the *Iliad* occupies a central place. For the best part of three millennia, any representation of the tale of Troy entailed some kind of response to Homeric epic. While in some cases this response was direct (i.e. to the text of the *Iliad*), in others it was indirect (e.g. to expectations and patterns established by the *Iliad*, through the complex mediations of intermediary texts, or even more loosely to the *idea* of the Homeric). In this book, we set out to explore more fully the dialogical workings of the Trojan War tradition, but also the place of the *Iliad* within them.

As dialogue is our subject, it is also our method. The main body of the book consists of paired case studies. Each case study focuses on an individual work (e.g. an Athenian pot, a Hollywood movie), and considers that text's engagement and dialogue with the *Iliad*.[2] But each pair of examples also constitutes a dialogue. Linked by a common theme and comparable medium, they have been taken from different historical periods and/or cultural contexts, with one analysis undertaken by Jan and the other by Naoíse. We hope that this juxtaposition of examples, time periods, and authorial voices will bring

---

[1] For a discussion of the *Contest of Homer and Hesiod*, see Graziosi 2002, 165–80; for competitive poetic performance in Greek culture more generally, see Collins 2005. On (ancient and modern) receptions of the lives of classical poets and artists, see Fletcher and Hanink 2016.

[2] In this sentence, the word 'text' is used in the sense of Bal (1985, 5), and our assumption is that source text (or hypotext) and the receiving text (the hypertext) speak to each other reciprocally: see Gadamer 1975; Iser 1978; Martindale 1993, 29–34.

each chapter's central theme into sharper relief. Over the course of the book, it is intended that the interchange between our two distinct perspectives will lead to a more nuanced appreciation of the Homeric dialogues that we explore. In other words, for us the enactment of a dialogue is a crucial heuristic, and our own dialogue on Homeric dialogues forms a kind of metadialogue on the contexts of Iliadic reception.

We have no pretensions in this volume of charting the totality of Iliadic receptions; nor of covering the range of relevant themes and concepts. Much of this is already discussed in the existing scholarship, which offers many rich insights into Iliadic receptions specifically, Homeric receptions more generally, and the broader Trojan War tradition in both antiquity and the post-classical world.[3] This project hopes to add to this existing literature in three distinct ways. First, we aim to shed light on specific case studies from a range of cultural contexts, as well as highlighting several important themes in receptions of the *Iliad* and the wider Trojan War tradition. Secondly, we hope that our dialogic method – an experiment in historiographical methodology – makes a contribution to the study of classical receptions by capturing something of reception as process. Finally, this book aims to offer new insights on our central subject – the *Iliad's* place within the wider Trojan War tradition over the last few millennia.

There are five main chapters in this book, encompassing ten detailed case studies. By way of framing the book as a whole, the first of our chapters focuses on the medium of poetry, and the theme of positioning oneself within a broader poetic and literary tradition. Jan begins, arguing that the *Iliad* acknowledges the existence of this broader tradition. The poem makes deliberate references

---

[3] In the interests of brevity, only some of the literature can be cited here. This existing literature includes studies of Homeric receptions in antiquity (e.g. Knauer 1964; Neitzel 1975; Barchiesi 1984; Rengakos 1993; Knight 1995; Sotiriou 1998; Graziosi 2002; Hunter 2004; Nagy 2009; Kim 2010); studies of post-antique Homeric receptions (e.g. Bloom 1991; Dué 2005; Graziosi and Greenwood 2007; Winkler 2007b, 2015b; Hall 2008; Flack 2015; Goldwyn 2015; cf. also contributions in *College Literature* 2007: 'Reading Homer in the 21st Century'; and contributions in *Classical Receptions Journal* 2017: 'Homer and Greek Tragedy in Early Modern England's Theatres'); studies that adopt a comparative approach to explore issues in Homeric reception that cut across chronological and geographical contexts (e.g. Fowler 2004b, section 5; Clarke, Currie and Lyne 2006; Latacz, Greub, Blome, Wieczorek 2008; Efstathiou and Karamanou 2016); works that aim to offer overviews of the Trojan War tradition over the span of history (e.g. Young 1948; Scherer 1963; Thompson 2004; Solomon 2007; Kelder, Uslu and Şerifoğlu 2012); and studies that focus on specific elements within the wider Trojan War tradition, such as the figure of Helen (e.g. Suzuki 1989; Gumpert 2001; Roisman 2006; Maguire 2009; Blondell 2013).

to the performance of heroic song, signalling metapoetic consciousness though its reflections on poetic practice. Naoíse then considers contemporary poetry from Mesopotamia, focusing on the depiction of authorship, storytelling, and narration in the poem of *Erra and Ishum*. The pairing of the *Iliad* and the *Erra* brings together two examples from a similar time period (the eighth century BCE), but produced in very different cultural contexts and poetic traditions. And yet, in both we find similar concerns with the practice of poetry and the positioning of each poem within a broader tradition.

Chapter 2 centres on visual culture and a theme that echoes across the *Iliad* – the construction of social roles. Naoíse begins by discussing a red-figure amphora from *c.* 510 BCE, which depicts Hector arming for battle on one side, and a group of drunken revellers on the other. The deliberately 'peri-Iliadic' nature of the Hector scene and its juxtaposition with the revellers, Naoíse will argue, played with ideas about male social roles and status, and would have been politically subversive in the context of late archaic Athens. Jan then offers a contrast by examining *Helen of Troy*, a painting created by the Pre-Raphaelite artist Dante Gabriel Rossetti in 1863. In this image, Rossetti confirms Helen's ambiguous status as a dangerous yet attractive figure, who raises questions concerning female social roles and power. And yet, as Jan argues, Rossetti gives his Helen an unusually Iliadic form of agency. The pairing captures something of the diversity of artistic responses to the *Iliad* at different stages of its canonical status. During the late sixth century BCE, the *Iliad* was still newly emerging at the epicentre of the Trojan War tradition, while during Rossetti's age, the text had long held a central place in that tradition.

Chapter 3 focuses on drama as a medium and considers another theme that characterizes the *Iliad*: conflict. The examples chosen, however, do not depict martial combat but rather dramatize conflict through words, using the Trojan War as a backdrop for exploring the limits of debate, disagreement, and argument. Jan's analysis of Euripides' *Troades* ('Trojan Women') foregrounds this by exploring how the sophistic arts are deployed by Euripides' characters, and by considering how the power of debate is both celebrated and undermined in the play. Naoíse's discussion of Shakespeare's *Troilus and Cressida* discusses a similar concern with both the power and the weakness of words, highlighting a similar dramatization of failed political dialogue. By bringing these two cases together, we have sought to offer the opposite view from that of the previous chapter. We present an example from an ancient Greek context – Athens at the end of the fifth century BCE – where the *Iliad* occupied a privileged cultural position. This is presented alongside an example from a post-antique context – Early Modern England – where knowledge of the *Iliad* was limited, but on the verge of expanding.

In Chapter 4, the two examples chosen are drawn from 'historiographical' works, and centre on a theme that runs at the heart of many Iliadic receptions – the question of historical truth and the 'facts' concerning the Trojan War. Herodotus, in Book 2 of his *Histories*, sought to compare Homer's version of the Trojan War with that of the Egyptian priests, who shape so much of his narrative on earlier historical traditions. As Jan argues, Herodotus subjects the Homeric poems to an elaborate form of inquiry, not to deny the historicity of the Trojan War, but rather to elevate the distinctiveness and authority of his own chosen genre, historiography. Naoíse argues that the archaeological adventurer Heinrich Schliemann adopted a similar approach in his 1874 book, *Trojaner Alterthümer* (Trojan Antiquities). In it, he presented a key piece of evidence to support his argument that the site of Hisarlık was the location of ancient Troy – the so-called 'Treasure of Priam'. Schliemann's description of the treasure and his account of its discovery were calculated to appeal to both professional and popular audiences, using the authority of Homeric epic as well as that of modern science. Both of these authors claimed to set down the 'truth' concerning the Trojan War, acting as a corrective to the poetic inaccuracies of the *Iliad*. And yet each confirms the absolute centrality of Homer in the Trojan War tradition at their time of writing, further calcifying the *Iliad*'s canonicity.

Chapter 5 features two works presented in 'composite' media. The *Speculum Regum* (Mirror for Princes), written by Godfrey of Viterbo *c.* 1183 CE, presented a history of the world that combined both poetry and prose; this is paired with the Hollywood film *Troy* (first released in 2004) in the composite medium of cinema. Both works deal with another important theme in Iliadic receptions – the cultural ownership of a Trojan War heritage. In the *Speculum Regum*, this took an explicit form, with the presentation of a genealogy that linked the survivors from Troy to the noble houses of twelfth-century Europe. In the film *Troy*, as well as in the critical discourse surrounding it, the question of cultural ownership focuses on a more abstract claim concerning the 'heirs' of classical antiquity and the perceived 'clash of civilizations' between the

East and the West. This final pairing consists of two examples from historical contexts where the text of the *Iliad* was not strictly relevant to the process of reception. In the twelfth century, Godfrey had no access to Homeric poetry and so engaged with his own perception of what was Homeric; and in the case of the film *Troy*, popular ideas about what was Homeric drove both artistic and marketing choices. This fifth chapter is therefore an inversion of Chapter 4, which presented two cases from periods where the text of the *Iliad* was central to the tradition. In these cases, by contrast, the *concept* of the poem was more important than the poem itself.

These ten case studies illustrate that the *Iliad* forms just a small part of a much wider set of traditions concerned with the Trojan War. Yet they also underline the distinctive role played by the *Iliad* in shaping this tradition in a range of different time periods and historical contexts. While it might be possible to represent later Iliadic receptions as 'slices from the great banquet of Homer',[4] for the authors of this book they are better regarded as sinuous creatures, participating in complex dialogues that adapt, refract, translate, and ultimately transform their source text. For while it is impossible for us to imagine the Trojan War without taking some kind of recourse to the *Iliad*, it is no less difficult to imagine the *Iliad* bereft of the monumental, tentacular series of cross-cultural dialogues that have emerged from this wider tradition.

---

[4]   Athenaeus, *Deipn. 8.347e.* The comment is applied to the plays of Aeschylus.

1

Navigating Tradition

The first of our dialogues focuses on the Homeric poems in the context of the contemporary poetic traditions of their own day. While the *Iliad* and *Odyssey* may be the only surviving accounts of the Trojan War story from the period of their composition,[1] as we have already noted, these poems never stood alone. Rather, they emerged out of an interconnecting set of rich and sophisticated poetic traditions: some dealing with the Trojan War, others treating different subjects; some conforming to the generic conventions what we might consider to be 'epic', others drawing from different genres such as ritual lament or praise poetry; some in ancient Greek, others in a variety of different languages.

In this chapter, we seek to understand the Homeric poems in this broader poetic context. In the first section, Jan will explore how the Homeric poems situated themselves within the wider tradition, through their treatment of the theme of poetry itself and their representations of poetic practice. Naoíse will offer a comparison in the second section of the chapter, considering the Mesopotamian 'epic' poem of *Erra and Ishum*, and its treatment of similar themes.

The two poems are roughly contemporary. The *Iliad* is thought to have been composed some time in the eighth century, although it evidently drew on oral traditions that were significantly older. Similarly, the final form of the *Erra and Ishum* also dates to the eighth century, although the core of the poem may first have appeared some centuries earlier. The two poems, therefore, would have circulated in roughly the same time period, although they emerged from very different contexts of production and performance. While the *Iliad* is firmly rooted in the Anatolian and Aegean world of small, localized polities and a

---

[1] Aside from the fragments of the 'Epic Cycle' (for which see below).

nascent sense of Hellenic identity,[2] the *Erra* belongs to the Mesopotamian world of the Neo-Assyrian Empire.[3] Equally as important as the difference in social and cultural context, however, is the difference in the immediate literary context of the two poems.

The *Iliad* was composed in a particular dialectal form of ancient Greek and emerged from several centuries of oral tradition, perhaps not just in Greek but also in the indigenous languages of Anatolia. Indeed, evidence from the Late Bronze Age suggests that this tradition drew both from Mycenaean Greek practices of storytelling and song (most likely oral)[4] and from the literatures (both oral and written) of Bronze Age Anatolia.[5] From these traditions Greek 'epic'[6] was born – not only the *Iliad* and the *Odyssey*, but also the Hesiodic works,[7] and the poems collectively known as the Epic Cycle.[8] It is particularly significant that the Homeric poems were not the only compositions to relate myths of the Trojan War in this broader tradition. Several poems of the Epic Cycle also dealt with Trojan War themes,[9] and a fragment of Anatolian poetry demonstrates that Troy was already the subject of song in the Late Bronze Age, some five centuries before the composition of the *Iliad*.[10] Archaeological evidence from the site of Troy itself also indicates that myths of the heroic

[2] For this period in the Aegean, see Osborne 2009, 131–52.
[3] For the Neo-Assyrian Empire, see van de Mieroop 2004, 207–69.
[4] See Morris 1989 and Bennet 2007 for epic and poetic performance in the Bronze Age Aegean; see Ruijgh 1985 for a discussion of scansion in Homeric and Mycenaean Greek; and Horrocks 1980 for elements of Homeric Greek that may predate Mycenaean Greek.
[5] For Bronze Age Anatolian epic traditions, see Beckman 2009. See Bachvarova 2016b for a discussion of the contributions of Anatolian epic to Homeric epic. Relationships between Bronze Age Anatolian poetry and the Hesiodic corpus have also been much discussed in the scholarly literature; see West 1997, 276–306, Rutherford 2009, Van Dongen 2011.
[6] The definition of the term 'epic' in relation to ancient Greek poetry has been extensively discussed; see Martin 2009.
[7] The authorship of some works attributed to Hesiod is still debated. See Cingano 2009 for the Hesiodic corpus.
[8] West 2013 has suggested a possible range of dates for several works in the Epic Cycle. For the Epic Cycle more generally, see Fantuzzi and Tsagalis 2015.
[9] These were: the *Cypria*, which recounts the events in the run-up to and the early years of the war; the *Aethiopis*, which describes battle and the deaths of several major heroes including Penthesilea and Achilles; the *Little Iliad*, in which we hear of the deaths of Ajax and Paris; the *Ilioupersis*, which tells the tale of the wooden horse and the eventual sack of Troy; the *Nostoi*, which laments the troubled homecomings of the Achaean heroes; the *Odyssey*, focusing on Odysseus' particularly difficult return; and the *Telegony*, recounting Odysseus' later adventures and his eventual death. Yet more poems in the Epic Cycle treated subjects unrelated to the Trojan War: the *Titanomachy*; the *Oedipodea*; the *Thebaid*; and the *Epigonoi*.
[10] Specifically, the fragment refers to 'Wilusa', which was the name used for the city of Troy by the Hittites, who dominated most of Anatolia in the Late Bronze Age. This has prompted discussion of the possibility that a *Wilusiad* existed as a Late Bronze Age Anatolian epic, which would have been a direct precursor for the *Iliad* (Watkins 1986).

Trojan past were important around this time. From the ninth century BCE onwards, new cultic structures were erected and new ritual practices begun that incorporated the physical remains of the Bronze Age city, which at this time remained not only visible but impressively monumental.[11] The *Iliad* was composed in the context, therefore, not just of a rich and complex oral tradition of song, but also out of a pre-existing tradition of Trojan War stories – which found expression not only in poetry, but also in the social practices of the community living at Troy. In the first part of this chapter, we will begin to explore how the *Iliad* acknowledges this wider tradition, and how it uses poetics as a means of locating itself within a tradition that it would eventually come to dominate.

The context of the *Erra* was markedly different. It was written in the language of Akkadian, and emerged out of a continuous literary and scribal tradition that stretched back well over a millennium.[12] Although oral traditions continued to circulate in Mesopotamia, the surviving corpus of Akkadian literature has been crucially shaped by the existence and practices of scribal schools, and by the processes involved in the written transmission of texts. Indeed, scribal traditions in Akkadian themselves drew from pre-existing scribal practices in Sumerian, which can be dated back to the mid-third millennium BCE.[13] The *Erra* is often considered to be an 'epic' poem, in that it deals with the great deeds of heroes and gods set in a distant and legendary past.[14] Perhaps the best-known Mesopotamian example of the genre is the *Epic of Gilgamesh*, a poem codified into standard form in the late second millennium BCE which tells of the wondrous deeds of a mythical king of Ur. The written nature of the *Erra* and its emergence from a long-standing writing tradition were both crucial in shaping the poem's metapoetics. While the *Iliad* needed to position itself in relation to a tradition that was diffuse and lacking a central core, the *Erra* had to situate itself within a tradition with set norms and parameters, which had already developed canonical versions of key texts.

---

[11] Aslan 2002, 82–86 and 2011, and Aslan and Rose 2013, 11. This should perhaps be seen in the wider context of 'hero cult' elsewhere in the Aegean around this time: Antonaccio 1995.

[12] See Foster 2005, 1–47 for an introduction to Akkadian literature.

[13] See Jakobsen 1987 for Sumerian literature.

[14] For an introduction to Mesopotamian epic, see Noegel 2009. For the difficulty of defining 'epic' as a genre in Near Eastern poetry, see Westenholz 1997, 20–21 and Sasson 2009. For the classification of the *Erra* as an 'epic', see Cagni 1974, 7–11 and George 2013, 47.

The evident differences between our Homeric and our Mesopotamian examples do not necessarily mean that the two poems circulated in entirely separate cultural contexts. It has long been argued that Mesopotamian epic was influential in shaping many of the themes, motifs, and characters of Homeric epic. One case that is often discussed in this context is the *Gilgamesh*, which bears several notable similarities to the *Iliad*.[15] The many parallels between Greek and Mesopotamian epic have led to discussions about how the two traditions might be related, and the nature of interactions between them.[16] Such questions are beyond the remit of this book, but it is relevant that the Aegean and Mesopotamia were becoming increasingly interconnected at the time that the *Iliad* and the *Erra* were composed.

The eighth century was a time of heightened connectivity across the Mediterranean and Near East, driven by a range of different factors including the interaction stimulated by the expanding Neo-Assyrian Empire; the spread of Phoenician and Greek trading networks; and the Greek and Phoenician practice of founding new settlements in far-flung locations.[17] Perhaps coincidentally, the eighth century is also the time when the Greeks first appear in Mesopotamian documents. Referred to collectively as the 'Yawanaya' (Ionians), the Greeks are recorded as seaborne raiders *c.* 730 BCE in the reign of the Neo-Assyrian king Tiglath-Pileser III.[18] The social and cultural contexts of the *Iliad* and the *Erra* might well be distinct, then, but they were not entirely separate. The two poems were composed at roughly around the same time, in a period characterized by interaction and connectivity. They emerged not just out of their own immediate literary traditions, but also from a wider pool of interconnected traditions that spanned the eastern Mediterranean and Near East. In this chapter, we argue that the *Iliad* and the *Erra* were both concerned

---

[15] For a detailed treatment of the specific parallels between the *Iliad* and the *Epic of Gilgamesh*, see West 1997.

[16] See Haubold 2013 for a more nuanced discussion of the possible interrelationships between Greek and Mesopotamian literature.

[17] For the eighth century, see Sommer 2007 and Osborne 2009, 66–130.

[18] Thereafter they appear again in several texts of Sargon II (721–705 BCE), who claimed to have defeated them 715 BCE (Sargon *Annals*, lines 117–9). Sargon's successor, Sennacherib (704–681 BCE), claimed to have defeated them again in 694 BCE, according to the later historian Berossus (Berossus *FGrHist* 680 F7.31). Some years later, Esarhaddon (680–679 BCE) once more claimed that the king of Ionia was sending him tribute (Leichty 2011, no. 60 line 6). For Near Eastern sources documenting interaction with various Greek groups, see Rollinger 2001, 237–43, 2007, 2009, 2011, and Luraghi 2006, 30–33.

with placing themselves within this same interconnected world, and that they used comparable metapoetic strategies to do this.

Jan: The *Iliad's* poets

The first of our texts is the *Iliad*, and the first of our close readings considers the poet's treatment of poetry itself. Much excellent scholarship is already available on speech, performance, and the representation of poetry within the Homeric epics,[19] as well as the relationships between the Homeric poems and other contemporary epics.[20] I do not seek to replicate this work, but rather to offer an analysis of the representations of poetic practice within the *Iliad*. The discussion falls into two main parts: the representation of poetic activity and the representation of the functions of poetry. In the first part, I consider the poet's self-presentation; the poetic activities of key characters in the story; and the representation of bardic figures, or poetic specialists. In the second part, I begin by discussing the celebratory function of poetry, which plays a central role in the transmission of glory or *kleos*, and then consider its role in lament and mourning.

Poets and poetic practice

'The wrath, sing, goddess, of Peleus' son Achilles' (μῆνιν ἄειδε θεὰ Πηληϊάδεω Ἀχιλῆος, 1.1). Thus, the poet begins the *Iliad*, clearly setting out his task as being the divinely inspired preservation of past events: Achilles' inhuman anger (*mēnis*) and its destructive effects on his fellow Achaean comrades.[21] While Homer (and/or any other poet responsible for the creation of the poem) is never named in the text,[22] the poet draws a clear sense of his status as an

---

[19] Amongst which are the seminal works by Martin 1989 on the *Iliad* and Segal 1994 on the *Odyssey*. There has also been there considerable scholarly activity focused on the unique qualities of Homeric language and the Homeric poet's determination to challenge epic tradition. See variously Braswell 1971, Griffin 1977, Richardson 1987, Morrison 1992, and Finkelberg 2011; cf. further references listed under Russo 1992, 385, n.14.

[20] Scodel 2002, 99–114 shows that the poet expects his audience to have a sound grasp of the Troy saga. On the poet's necessary selectivity, see Ford 1992, 70–79.

[21] On the proem of the *Iliad*, see Redfield 2001; cf. the nuanced discussion in Halliwell 2011, 59–61.

[22] Saïd 2012, 30 with n.5. Foley 2010, 20–21 demonstrates succinctly the problems that surround any attempt to uncover a single ancient poet named Homer; cf. Nagy 1992. For discussion of the authorship of the Homeric poems, see variously Kullmann 1984, Graziosi 2002, 13–18, Fowler 2004a, b, Montanari 2012, Foley 2010, West 2011, and Saïd 2011a, 20–44, 2011b.

author, and of his enterprise as the creation of poetic song. The key word in this first line is perhaps the imperative 'sing!' (ἄειδε), signalling a clear interest from the very outset in the process of performing poetry. The voice of the self-effaced poet comes to the fore at a few other points in the poem, though it remains hidden for the bulk of the narrative.[23] In Book 2, as he prepares to enumerate the different groups supporting the Achaean effort (the Catalogue of Ships), the poet summons forth the Muses, daughters of the goddess Mnemosyne ('memory'):

Ἔσπετε νῦν μοι, Μοῦσαι Ὀλύμπια δώματ᾽ ἔχουσαι[24]– ὑμεῖς
γὰρ θεαί ἐστε, πάρεστέ τε, ἴστέ τε πάντα,
ἡμεῖς δὲ κλέος οἶον ἀκούομεν οὐδέ τι ἴδμεν

Tell me now, Muses, who have your homes on Olympus;
for you are goddesses, and you are present and know everything,
but we only hear a rumour[25] and do not know anything.

Iliad 2.484–6

Having invoked the Muses, who act as a repository for all knowledge, the poet reinforces his own impotence in the face of an overwhelming tradition:

πληθὺν δ᾽ οὐκ ἂν ἐγὼ μυθήσομαι οὐδ᾽ ὀνομήνω,
οὐδ᾽ εἴ μοι δέκα μὲν γλῶσσαι, δέκα δὲ στόματ᾽ εἶεν,
φωνὴ δ᾽ ἄρρηκτος, χάλκεον δέ μοι ἦτορ ἐνείη,
εἰ μὴ Ὀλυμπιάδες Μοῦσαι Διὸς αἰγιόχοιο
θυγατέρες μνησαίαθ᾽ ὅσοι ὑπὸ Ἴλιον ἦλθον·

I could not state nor name the multitude,
not even if I had ten tongues and ten mouths,
an unbreakable voice, and a heart within me made of bronze,
unless the Olympian Muses, daughters of aegis-bearing Zeus,
should call to my mind how many men came beneath Troy.

Iliad 2.488–92

---

[23] Scholars have tended to remark on the modesty of the Homeric poet; de Jong 2006, however, emphasizes the narrator's desire to acquire glory for himself. As the discussion below demonstrates, it is significant in relation to the character of the Homeric narrator that other internal poets such as Demodocus are specially praised for their poetic outputs.

[24] For invocations to the Muses, cf. 11.218; 14.508; 16.112.

[25] The term 'κλέος' is a complex one, although it has been translated as 'rumour' in this passage; in other places I have translated it as 'glory' or 'reputation': see further LSJ s.v. κλέος.

This passage clearly signals the poet's awareness of a rich and broad tradition, comprising more stories and songs than he could ever hope to master. It also highlights the poet's consciousness of his own art as involving not just his tongue, mouth, and voice, but also his heart (ἦτορ; 490).

There are other, additional points in the *Iliad* where the poet makes explicit reference to his own actions in the production of song, often introduced in the form (as with the passage quoted above) of invocations to the Muses.[26] At the close of the Catalogue of Ships, for instance, the poet asks the Muse to tell him who was the best of the Achaeans (2.761), while in Book 16, he asks the Muses to disclose how it was that the Trojans first set fire to the Achaean ships (16.112–13).[27] Much has been written about the way that these invocations to the Muses reinforce the poet's indebtedness to the divine (even though, in reality, his ability to sing must have derived from some kind of formal poetic training), thus helping to collapse the spatial and chronological gap between the heroic age and his own time.[28] And certainly, such moments underline the poet's special relationship to the poetic matter that the Muses channel through him, just as they underline the point that trustworthiness is an important element of his particular, Muse-inspired account.[29]

In addition to the occasional appearance of the poet of the *Iliad* in his own voice, other characters in the poem are also depicted as creating/singing poetic narratives.[30] One of the most extended metapoetic passages – instances of self-conscious reflection on poetry within a poem – comes from Book 3, when Helen is weaving a tapestry that speaks of the war between the Achaeans and the Trojans. This is Helen's first appearance in the poem, and it is significant that in her debut appearance, she is engaged in a quasi-poetic activity.

τὴν δ᾽ εὗρ᾽ ἐν μεγάρῳ· ἡ δὲ μέγαν ἱστὸν ὕφαινε,
δίπλακα πορφυρέην, πολέας δ᾽ ἐνέπασσεν ἀέθλους

---

[26] Finkelberg 1990, 295: 'the ancient Greek poet sees himself as a mouthpiece of the Muse'.

[27] Nagy 1979, Ford 1992, 78–79, and Saïd 2011a, 67.

[28] See especially Ford 1992, 60–89 and Purves 2010, 7–8. On the Homeric poems and their relationship with the heroic age, see Grethlein 2009.

[29] This is not to say, though, that the poet is at pains to present a narrative that is hyper-factual, scrupulously wedded to the evidence. As Halliwell 2011, 42 points out, the *Iliad* presents no divine voice to corroborate its aspiration to present a more-than-humanly true account.

[30] For poets and poetic activity in the *Iliad* and *Odyssey*, see Macleod 1983, 1–15, Ford 1992, 57–130, Saïd 2011a, 125–31, and Halliwell 2011, 36–92.

Τρώων θ᾽ ἱπποδάμων καὶ Ἀχαιῶν χαλκοχιτώνων,
οὓς ἕθεν εἵνεκ᾽ ἔπασχον ὑπ᾽ Ἄρηος παλαμάων.

She [Iris] found Helen in the hall. There she was weaving a great web,
double fold and purple, on this she was pattern-weaving many contests
of the horse-taming Trojans and bronze-clad Achaeans,
which for her sake they had suffered at the hands of Ares.[31]

Iliad 3.125–8

Like the poet of *Iliad*, Helen actively contributes to the memorialization of the Trojan War story, though her poetic creation is reified in the form of a woven tapestry,[32] rather than an orally disseminated poem.[33] Helen's quasi-poetic status in this scene has long been recognized, of course, as witnessed by the comments of one ancient scholiast: 'the poet has created a worthy archetype of his own poetic art' (ἀξιόχρεων ἀρχέτυπον ἀνέπλασεν ὁ ποιητὴς τῆς ἰδίας ποιήσεως).[34]

Helen will continue to act as a surrogate for the poet elsewhere in the *Iliad*, notably in the Teichoscopia ('viewing from the wall') episode later in Book 3, where she relates to the Trojan king Priam stories of the Achaean heroes that can be seen at a distance (3.177–242).[35] She regales Priam with various personal and biographical details, for instance remarking on Agamemnon's abilities with the spear (3.179) and Odysseus' many wiles (3.200–02). Helen is portrayed as a master of conversation in this episode, delighting the aged king, who praises her for the true words that she utters in speaking of these different individuals: 'Lady, really you said that account truthfully' (ὦ γύναι ἦ μάλα τοῦτο ἔπος νημερτὲς ἔειπες, 3.204).[36] Helen's status as a kind of poet within the poem can also be discerned elsewhere. To note one significant example, when in conversation with the Trojan hero Hector in Book 6, Helen informs her brother-in-law that 'because of the dog that I am and the folly

---

[31] For Helen's concern about the consequences of her actions elsewhere in the *Iliad*, see West 2011, ad. 125–28, who suggests that this sympathetic portrait of Helen may be 'untraditional'.

[32] On the connections between weaving and poetic composition in Greek thought, see the references listed under Clader 1976, 7. For the contrast between Helen's weaving and that of Andromache in Book 22, see Roisman 2006, 9–10. For weaving as a metaphor for literary composition in the Mesopotamian world, see p.29 below and especially n.77.

[33] So Clader 1976, 8, Kennedy 1986, Taplin 1992, 97–98, Austin 1994, 38, 41 Pantelia 2002, 26 Roisman 2006, 10–11, Bergren 2008, 46, 55, Purves 2010, 11, Blondell 2013, 68, and Nappi 2013.

[34] Schol. *Il.* 3126–27 bT.

[35] For a rich analysis on Helen as 'internal commentator of the [epic] tradition' (113) in this episode, see Tsagalis 2008, 112–34, cf. Suzuki 1989, 39–42, focusing on her Achilles-like liminal status.

[36] On Helen's authority in this scene, see Blondell 2013, 6.

of Alexander, Zeus has set up an evil fate, so that in days to come we may be worthy of song amongst men in future generations' (εἵνεκ' ἐμεῖο κυνὸς καὶ Ἀλεξάνδρου ἕνεκ' ἄτης, | οἷσιν ἐπὶ Ζεὺς θῆκε κακὸν μόρον, ὡς καὶ ὀπίσσω | ἀνθρώποισι πελώμεθ' ἀοίδιμοι ἐσσομένοισι, 6.356–8). Although critical of her own role in the war, Helen is nonetheless certain that it is her unfortunate relationship with Zeus that will guarantee the everlasting fame of Paris and herself (and presumably Hector) amongst future generations, a fame that is in turn preserved in Homer's account of the war.[37]

Another important character in the *Iliad* who is depicted as engaging in poetic activity is: Achilles. Insulted by Agamemnon's seizure of Briseis, Achilles skulks wrathfully in his tent, refusing to participate in the battle against the Trojans. Accompanied solely by Patroclus, Achilles sings of epic heroes: 'He was delighting his heart with this [lyre], and singing of tales of the glories of men. Patroclus alone sat opposite him in silence, waiting for Aecus' grandson to cease his singing' (τῇ ὅ γε θυμὸν ἔτερπεν, ἄειδε δ' ἄρα κλέα ἀνδρῶν.[38] | Πάτροκλος δέ οἱ οἶος ἐναντίος ἧστο σιωπῇ, | δέγμενος Αἰακίδην ὁπότε λήξειεν ἀείδων, 9.189–91). On the one hand, Achilles is found temporarily away from the battle, foregoing his own personal glory.[39] But like Helen, he is conscious of the glory that awaits those individuals who are the stuff of epic poetry, and he is depicted enjoying precisely the kind of story that he is in fact the principal figure of. This brief episode thus not only reinforces the lasting value of epic song, but it also helps to forge an inextricable relationship between poetry and epic hero.

As these examples illustrate, therefore, key characters in the *Iliad* are represented as engaging in different kinds of poetic activity. But Homeric poetry also features a number of bards, whose poetic activities are described in slightly different terms to those of non-bardic characters. In particular, one distinction between the poetic practice of bards and that of other characters is the ambiguous relationship between bard and Muse. We have already seen how the Homeric poet constructs his own privileged relationship to the Muses, representing his poetic prowess as the combined result of both his own skill

---

[37] Suzuki 1989, 40, Martin 1989, 136–37, Taplin 1992, 119, Graziosi and Haubold 2010, ad 358, and Blondell 2013, 54 ('[Helen's song] is, in fact, the *Iliad*').

[38] For the recurring theme of *klea andrōn* – the glorious deeds of men – see the main text below, as well as: *Il.* 9.524-25; *Od.* 8.73.

[39] Murnaghan 1987, 150 and Halliwell 2011, 76.

and the Muses' input.[40] Another clear illustration of this comes from Book 22 of the *Odyssey*, when the Ithacan bard Phemius (a speaking name that derives from the verb φάναι, to speak) sings 'I am self-taught, and god has nurtured my heart with all ways of song' (αὐτοδίδακτος δ᾽ εἰμί, θεὸς δέ μοι ἐν φρεσὶν οἴμας | παντοίας ἐνέφυσεν, 22.347–8). Similarly, in Book 8 Odysseus praises the blind Phaeacian court singer Demodocus (whose name literally means 'he whom the people welcomes')[41] for his account of the Achaeans' struggles, clear evidence of his divine tutelage:

Δημόδοκ᾽, ἔξοχα δή σε βροτῶν αἰνίζομ᾽ ἁπάντων·
ἢ σέ γε Μοῦσ᾽ ἐδίδαξε, Διὸς πάϊς, ἢ σέ γ᾽ Ἀπόλλων.
λίην γὰρ κατὰ κόσμον Ἀχαιῶν οἶτον ἀείδεις,
ὅσσ᾽ ἔρξαν τ᾽ ἔπαθόν τε καὶ ὅσσ᾽ ἐμόγησαν Ἀχαιοί,
ὥς τέ που ἢ αὐτὸς παρεὼν ἢ ἄλλου ἀκούσας.

Demodocus, truly above all mortals do I praise you.
Whether it was the Muse, daughter of Zeus, that taught you, or Apollo;
for how exceedingly correctly you sing of the fortunes of the Achaeans,
all that they did and suffered, and toiled over,
as if perhaps either you had yourself been there, or you had heard the tale
from another.

Odyssey 8.487–91

Preceding these remarks, Odysseus offers a choice piece of boar meat to Demodocus, observing that 'the Muse has taught them [singers] the ways of song, and she loves the tribe of singers' (οὕνεκ᾽ ἄρα σφέας | οἴμας Μοῦσ᾽ ἐδίδαξε, φίλησε δὲ φῦλον ἀοιδῶν, 8.480–81; cf. 8.62–63).[42] And a few lines later, the narrator relates that after being 'moved by the god' (ὁ δ᾽ ὁρμηθεὶς θεοῦ ἄρχετο, 8.499),[43] Demodocus begins to sing of the elusive Trojan horse and the rout of the city of Troy. Throughout this episode, then, the poet emphasizes the confluences between bardic activity and divine inspiration.

---

[40] Finkelberg 1990, 296.

[41] On Homer's blindness, see Graziosi 2002, 125–63 and Saïd 2011a, 19.

[42] Homer similarly refers to the divine bestowing the poet with his art at *Il.* 13.730; *Od.* 8.64, 498. Cf. Aristotle *Poet.* 23.1459a30–4, describing Homer as 'divine in speech' (θεσπέσιος).

[43] Cf. Odysseus' reply to Lord Alcinous at the beginning of *Odyssey* 9: 'truly this is a good thing, listening to a singer such as this man [Demodocus] is, resembling the gods in speech' (ἦ τοι μὲν τόδε καλὸν ἀκουέμεν ἐστὶν ἀοιδοῦ | τοιοῦδ᾽ οἷος ὅδ᾽ ἐστί, θεοῖς ἐναλίγκιος αὐδήν. *Od.* 9.3-4).

The portrayal of bards as having divine connections and an ability to enchant results in their privileged status.[44] They are most deserving amongst men of honour and praise, according to Odysseus (8.479–81; cf. 9.3.11)[45] – an individual who too functions as a kind of poet in Books 9–12 by regaling his Phaeacian audience with his adventures *en route* to Ithaca. The privileged relationship between bard and Muse was also potentially dangerous, however, as we see in the Iliadic episode involving the poet Thamyris. In this brief narrative, embedded in the Catalogue of Ships, the poet relates that Thamyris proudly boasted that even if he were in competition with the Muses, he would still win (*Iliad* 2.594–600). In response, the Muses mutilated Thamyris and deprived him of the gift of song. This excursus sits rather cumbersomely at this point in the narrative, particularly since the Muses have already been evoked just a hundred lines earlier,[46] but there is little doubting the passage's import. In contrast to Thamyris, the Homeric poet is well aware of the gap between singer and Muse, and he will not presume that his account oversteps that of the divine. Even so, the various reflections on poetic activity in the *Iliad* and *Odyssey* build up a striking picture in which the poet is envisaged as an authoritative source, exclusively connected with the goddesses of memory. It is this connection with the Muses that seems to distinguish the poetic practice of bards, from that of other characters in the *Iliad*.

The functions of poetry

The *Iliad* not only portrays a range of characters engaging in poetic activity, it also reflects on what this poetic activity was *for*. The most obvious function of poetry was the commemoration of great deeds, and the transmission of glory or *kleos*. The poem's interest in *kleos*, as well as that of its characters, has often been recognized. Much of the poem comprises extended battle scenes and the *aristeia* of key figures,[47] and at various junctures, individual heroes claim that the purpose of all this fighting was to create undying glory. In Book 6, when the Trojan prince Hector is afforded a rare moment away from the battlefield with his wife Andromache, he states that warfare is a necessary evil in order for him to acquire renown.

> ἀλλὰ μάλ᾽ αἰνῶς
> αἰδέομαι Τρῶας καὶ Τρῳάδας ἑλκεσιπέπλους,

[44] *Od.* 1.337; cf. Hes. *Th.* 55, 98–103.
[45] See further Saïd 2011a, 126–28.
[46] Macleod 1983, 5.
[47] Schein 1984, 80–82.

αἴ κε κακὸς ὣς νόσφιν ἀλυσκάζω πολέμοιο·
οὐδέ με θυμὸς ἄνωγεν, ἐπεὶ μάθον ἔμμεναι ἐσθλὸς
αἰεὶ καὶ πρώτοισι μετὰ Τρώεσσι μάχεσθαι,
ἀρνύμενος πατρός τε μέγα κλέος ἠδ᾽ ἐμὸν αὐτοῦ.

… I terribly
fear the Trojans, and Trojan women with trailing robe,
if, like a bad man, I avoid war from afar.[48]
Nor does my spirit command me, since I have learnt to be excellent
always, and fight with the Trojan front rank,
winning my father's great glory and my own.

Iliad 6.441–46; cf. 22.305

So too, in Book 9, the *Iliad*'s most illustrious warrior Achilles displays a hunger for glory. He declares that his mother, the goddess Thetis, advised him that he would either live a long, inglorious life or that he would fight and die at Troy, winning for himself a 'glory that will be unwilting' (κλέος ἄφθιτον ἔσται, 9.410–16; cf. 18.95–96).[49] Later in the poem, after Achilles has accepted his tragic fate, that Zeus and the immortal gods will cut his life short, he maintains: 'But now may I win great glory, so as to make some of the deep-breasted Trojan and Dardanian women, with both hands, wipe the tears from their tender cheeks, and groan without stopping' (νῦν δὲ κλέος ἐσθλὸν ἀροίμην, | καί τινα Τρωϊάδων καὶ Δαρδανίδων βαθυκόλπων | ἀμφοτέρῃσιν χερσὶ παρειάων ἀπαλάων | δάκρυ᾽ ὀμορξαμένην ἁδινὸν στοναχῆσαι ἐφείην, 18.121–24). Although less explicit than Achilles' remarks, Hector similarly acknowledges the great deeds that he must accomplish in order to achieve a great fame before his own death:[50] 'But, at any rate, may I not die ingloriously, without a struggle; but rather performing some great deed, for future generations to learn about' (μὴ μὰν ἀσπουδί γε καὶ ἀκλειῶς ἀπολοίμην, | ἀλλὰ μέγα ῥέξας τι καὶ ἐσσομένοισι πυθέσθαι, 22.304–05). Perhaps most instructive of all in the hero's quest for fame is the programmatic speech of the Trojan Sarpedon in Book 12, in which the warrior expands on the honours duly afforded the leading figures of Lycia.

---

[48] Cf. 22.105. War in the *Iliad* is clearly envisaged as the domain of men, see, e.g., 7.236; 8.161-66.
[49] Finkelberg 2007 argues that the phrase κλέος ἄφθιτον is not a traditional formula stemming from a shared Indo-European poetics, but rather a Homeric modification. For the opposite view, see the works listed under Garcia 2013, 257, n.29.
[50] On the interconnectedness of the *Iliad*'s two main heroes, Achilles and Hector, see Martin 1989, 130–45.

οὐ μὰν ἀκλεέες Λυκίην κάτα κοιρανέουσιν
ἡμέτεροι βασιλῆες, ἔδουσί τε πίονα μῆλα
οἶνόν τ' ἔξαιτον μελιηδέα· ἀλλ' ἄρα καὶ ἲς
ἐσθλή, ἐπεὶ Λυκίοισι μέτα πρώτοισι μάχονται.

Certainly not without glory are those who rule in Lycia,
our kings; they consume both fat sheep
and choice wine, honey-sweet. But their strength is
good too, since they fight with the foremost Lycians.

Iliad 12.318–21[51]

Speeches like those of Sarpedon and Hector clearly appear to reflect an aristocratic set of ideals, equating future acclamation with services rendered to the community.[52] Indeed, an indissoluble relationship is built up between martial skill and social success throughout the poem. In Book 9, one of the Achaeans' most successful warriors Diomedes delivers a robust personal defence in response to Agamemnon's criticisms earlier in the poem (cf. 4.365–400). 'My valour you first reproached among the Danaans; you said that I was unwarlike and without valour; and all this know the Achaeans both young and old' (ἀλκὴν μέν μοι πρῶτον ὀνείδισας ἐν Δαναοῖσι, | φὰς ἔμεν ἀπτόλεμον καὶ ἀνάλκιδα· ταῦτα δὲ πάντα | ἴσασ' Ἀργείων ἠμὲν νέοι ἠδὲ γέροντες, 9.34–36). Diomedes assumes here that Agamemnon's reproach is public knowledge – amongst both young and old – and so he purposefully chooses the context of a public assembly in order to defend his actions at Troy.[53] This concern for reputation and *kleos* is, essentially, a concern for poetry, as it was through poetry and song that *kleos* was conferred and transmitted.

The other main function of poetry in the *Iliad* is commemorative, but rather than celebration, this aims at lamentation. Interestingly, the poetry of lamentation in Homeric epic is dominated by the voices of women.[54] It has already been shown that Helen serves as a kind of simulacrum of the Homeric

---

[51] For the social elite and their pre-eminence in battle, see too *Il.* 6.207–9.

[52] Thalmann 1988, 6. For the question of what kind of audience(s) might have accessed the *Iliad*, see Grethlein 2009, 130–31. For further discussion of the aristocratic associations of the poem, see pp.47–8 below.

[53] Scodel 2002, 192. On public challenges of authority in the *Iliad*, see Barker 2009, 40–88.

[54] Roisman 2006, 31, Blondell 2013, 67, and Schein 2016, 5–9. For women in the *Iliad*, see Farron 1979, Arthur 1981 and Nappi 2015.

poet in the sense of transferring *kleos*, creating her own material narrative on the battles between Achaeans and Trojans, while also prophesying her personal renown amongst future generations of men.[55] In addition to this, Helen – a figure repeatedly blamed for the war (see further p.64) – is, like other elite women, responsible for lamenting the fates of the fallen heroes.[56] It is this ritualized wailing of women that helps to confer glory upon the Achaean and Trojan warriors, ensuring that the memory of heroes such as Patroclus and Hector is kept for posterity.[57]

The most extended lament scene occurs in the final book of the *Iliad*, once Priam has conveyed the body of his dead son back to the city of Troy. As the poem closes, a trio of women each sing a dirge for the dead Trojan: Andromache (his wife), Hecuba (his mother), and Helen (his 'sister-in-law'). Andromache, who perceives a dire future for herself and her son, as well as for the city of Troy, delivers the first lament:

πρὶν γὰρ πόλις ἥδε κατ᾽ ἄκρης
πέρσεται· ἦ γὰρ ὄλωλας ἐπίσκοπος, ὅς τέ μιν αὐτὴν
ῥύσκευ, ἔχες δ᾽ ἀλόχους κεδνὰς καὶ νήπια τέκνα·
αἳ δή τοι τάχα νηυσὶν ὀχήσονται γλαφυρῇσι,
καὶ μὲν ἐγὼ μετὰ τῇσι·

Before that [the death of Astyanax] this city will be wasted
utterly; for you who watched over it have perished, you who guarded
it, keeping safe its noble wives and little children.
They will soon be taken away on the hollow ships,
and I with them.

Iliad 24.728–32

Hector's mother Hecuba follows Andromache. She sings of Hector as her most beloved son, whilst emphasizing that Achilles had taken the lives of some of her other children. Hecuba's speech reinforces Hector's bravery, even suggesting that he now lies in her halls as though he were the victim of Apollo

---

[55] For a subtle analysis of Helen's uniquely powerful role in the *Iliad*, see Blondell 2013, 53–72, cf. Arthur 1981, 26 (with some caveats) Roisman 2006.

[56] For a full list of passages in which women lament, see Nappi 2015, 49, n.2. For women's laments in the *Iliad*, see further Derderian 2001, 31–61, whose view that female lament (the γόος) is presented as inferior to the epic medium can be usefully countered by Dué 2002 and Bachvarova 2016a, 68–70.

[57] Nappi 2015, 37.

(24.758–9). It is the third and final lament of Helen, however, that is the most striking.[58] Her speech offers a moving and deeply personal account of Hector, while also underlining her own ambivalent status in the poem.[59] Helen sings:

Ἕκτορ, ἐμῷ θυμῷ δαέρων πολὺ φίλτατε πάντων,
ἦ μέν μοι πόσις ἐστὶν Ἀλέξανδρος θεοειδής,
ὅς μ᾽ ἄγαγε Τροίηνδ᾽· ὡς πρὶν ὤφελλον ὀλέσθαι.
ἤδη γὰρ νῦν μοι τόδ᾽ ἐεικοστὸν ἔτος ἐστὶν
ἐξ οὗ κεῖθεν ἔβην καὶ ἐμῆς ἀπελήλυθα πάτρης·
ἀλλ᾽ οὔ πω σεῦ ἄκουσα κακὸν ἔπος οὐδ᾽ ἀσύφηλον·
ἀλλ᾽ εἴ τίς με καὶ ἄλλος ἐνὶ μεγάροισιν ἐνίπτοι
δαέρων ἢ γαλόων ἢ εἰνατέρων εὐπέπλων,
ἢ ἑκυρή – ἑκυρὸς δὲ πατὴρ ὣς ἤπιος αἰεί – ,
ἀλλὰ σὺ τὸν ἐπέεσσι παραιφάμενος κατέρυκες,
σῇ τ᾽ ἀγανοφροσύνῃ καὶ σοῖς ἀγανοῖς ἐπέεσσι.
τῶ σέ θ᾽ ἅμα κλαίω καὶ ἔμ᾽ ἄμμορον ἀχνυμένη κῆρ·
οὐ γάρ τίς μοι ἔτ᾽ ἄλλος ἐνὶ Τροίη εὐρείη
ἤπιος οὐδὲ φίλος, πάντες δέ με πεφρίκασιν.

Hector, most dear to my heart of all my husband's brothers;
my husband is godlike Alexander,
who led me to Troy. Oh how I wish I had perished before then!
For this is now my twentieth year away,[60]
since I came from there and departed my native land.
But I have never yet heard an evil or spiteful word from you.
But if someone spoke harshly to me in the hall –
one of your brothers or sisters or you brother's well-dressed wives,
or your mother – though your father was always kind to me like a father,
then you would speak with gentle words to them and deter them
with your gentle spirit and your gentle words.
Thus I weep both for you and for unlucky me with grief at heart.
For I have no other in the broad land of Troy
who is gentle or a friend; they all shudder at me.

Iliad 24.762–75

---

[58] See especially Taplin 1992, 119–20 and Farron 1979, 21–22. Pantelia 2002 argues that Helen is purposefully positioned as the last woman to speak, since it is she who best understands 'the importance of heroic *kleos* and poetry as the means for conferring it' (p.21).

[59] Taplin 1992, 118.

[60] For Helen's problematic reference to her twentieth year at Troy, see further discussion in Richardson 1993, ad. 24.765-67.

Helen's speech expresses powerfully the tensions that undergird her story. She acknowledges that it is her elopement with Alexander that has caused such evil and she is careful to commemorate kindly Hector, who (along with Priam) refused to castigate her. But her speech is also remarkably self-serving: in front of a Trojan audience,[61] she lists the different individuals that treated her balefully and she closes her lament both for Hector and for herself, as there will be no other left in Troy to be her friend. It has been suggested that Helen here intimates that it was Hector's kindness to her that ultimately helped to ensure his death.[62] Yet, the very individual that precipitated Hector's death is also the same individual that preserves his memory, enriching her internal and external audience's understanding of the warrior Hector, who emerges as an admirable figure on *and* off the battlefield. In this speech, then, Helen transcends her status as the cause of the war or a possession to be fought over; in delivering her speech in front of a public audience, flanked by two royal Trojan women, Helen more firmly establishes her position in the Trojan community and its leading female victims.[63]

It is by no means the case, of course, that women are exclusively responsible for lamentation in the *Iliad*. The poet refers to male 'singers, leaders of the *threnoi* (lyrical lamentations) [for Hector]' (ἀοιδοὺς | θρήνων ἐξάρχους, 24.720–21), and, after the death of Patroclus, Achilles leads the Achaean dirge for the fallen hero, singing of the ill fate that has destined them both to die in the land of Troy (18.324–42; cf. 19.315–37). But it is the laments of captive women, widowed wives, bereaving mothers as well as the enigmatic figure of Helen that are prioritized by the poet.[64] Lamentation is one of the crucial ways in which women speak in the poem, and as the example of Helen mourning for both Hector and herself reveals, women's laments are sometimes surprisingly personal accounts that afford further character depth and, like the *Iliad* itself, help to confer memory on fallen heroes.

[61] Roisman 2006, 30 focuses on how the speech 'brings her into the commonality she so longs for'.
[62] Taplin 1992, 282.
[63] Roisman 2006, 30–32 explores the difference between this and Helen's other Iliadic scenes. As she points out, this is the first time that Helen speaks in front of a public audience, and it is striking that in her first public speech, Helen explicitly reproaches the vast majority of the Trojans for the way that they have treated her so cruelly.
[64] Taplin 1992, 213: 'The two leading casualties of the poem [Patroclus and Hector] are each lamented by a woman'.

Before leaving this section, it is worth saying a little more about another of the *Iliad*'s more enigmatic figures: Briseis.[65] Having been seized by Agamemnon, Briseis becomes a kind of second Helen, prefiguring another dispute between heroes and further calling into question the notion of woman as *causa belli*.[66] Silent for much of the narrative, and objectified by her Achaean captors, Briseis will eventually deliver a devastating lament for Patroclus in Book 19, which complicates her initial status in the poem as little more than a passive object. Briseis clings to the body of Patroclus and speaks of his gentle nature and his promise to make her Achilles' wife (19.297–98), a not entirely implausible scenario, given Achilles' professed love for her (9.342–43).[67] Yet she sings too of her husband Mynes' and her three brothers' slaughter at the hands of Achilles, who sacked her hometown Lyrnessus. Given this bleak past, it is hardly a surprise to see her cry 'thus for me evil always follows on from evil' (ὥς μοι δέχεται κακὸν ἐκ κακοῦ αἰεί, 19.290). Widow, refugee, plunder – like Andromache and her ancestors, the victim of warlike Achilles (6.414-28) – Briseis will not be silenced. For it is a very bold and notable feature of the poem that its two leading casualties should both be lamented by women on the margins of society.

The Poet(s) of the *Iliad*

This section has examined some of the metapoetic qualities of the *Iliad* – a text that is consciously engaged with its status as a literary artefact. The Homeric poet, along with some of the *Iliad*'s chief human protagonists, such as Helen and Achilles, is keenly aware of the role of poetry in the commemoration of past events; specifically in the transmission of *kleos* and in the commemorative mourning of sorrows. The poem makes no explicit reference to its sources, its predecessors, or contemporary narrative traditions, with the poet instead claiming at various points to serve as a conduit for the omniscient Muses. Nevertheless, the Homeric epics still display a profound awareness of a much broader tradition of stories and depict a world where a range of different

---

[65] See especially Taplin 1992, 212–18 and Dué 2002.
[66] Suzuki 1989, 21–29.
[67] Note too that Achilles is reunited with Briseis at the end of the poem (24.676) – a foil, perhaps, for Helen and Menelaus, whose separation overhangs the Achilles–Briseis relationship.

people can engage in poetic activity – bards and non-bards, men and women, victors and vanquished. As this demonstrates, the world of the *Iliad* was a world where poetry was everywhere, where it enjoyed a high status, and where it served a range of important social functions.

But were these metapoetic qualities of the Homeric poems unusual? Can similar concerns be found in the interconnecting epic traditions from which the Homeric poems emerged? In this next section of the chapter, Naoíse will seek to address these questions.

Naoíse: The *Erra's* poems

The metapoetics of the *Iliad* can be compared with those in the poem of *Erra and Ishum*, an 'epic'[68] poem composed over a period of time between 1150 and 750 BCE, roughly around the same time as the *Iliad*.[69] The *Erra* also has some thematic similarities with myths of the Trojan War – it describes the destruction of cities and the devastation of population through the will of the gods, specifically through the anger of the god Erra. Like the *Iliad*, its key theme is the wrath of its central character and the havoc caused by this wrath.[70] More significantly for the topic of this chapter however, the *Erra* is also like the *Iliad* in that it is deeply concerned with poetry and the poetic process.

In this section, I shall first consider the complex narrative strategies adopted in the *Erra* to highlight issues of storytelling and memorialization through song. This will be followed by an examination of the poem's representation of both itself and its author. I will then expand the analysis to include other examples from Mesopotamian literature, reflecting first on how poems are represented, and then on the treatment of poets and authors. This comparison of Homeric and Mesopotamian poetics should prompt reflections on what

---

[68] By 'epic', I mean longer narrative poems telling of the deeds of gods and humans. For the difficulty in defining 'epic' as a distinct genre in Mesopotamian literature, see n.14 above.

[69] For discussion of the date of the poem, see George 2013, 47 with references. For the Akkadian text and critical edition, see Cagni 1969. For translations, see Cagni 1974, Lambert (1962b), Dalley 2000, 282–316, Foster 2005, 880–911. The translation used in this chapter is that of Foster 2005, and the text is that of Cagni 1969.

[70] For the depiction of wrath and violence in this poem, see George 2013. As Foster says, 'The text is a portrayal of violence' 2005, 880.

is unique in both traditions, whilst highlighting in both cases the shared significance of tradition itself.

The Narrators of the *Erra*

The poem of *Erra and Ishum* is noted for its unusual interest in the process of narration and the voice of the narrator. Unusually for Akkadian poetry, much of the action of the story is told in direct speech, voiced by several different characters and using various different narrative strategies.[71] This marks the poem out from other Akkadian compositions.

The poem is focused on the deeds of the god Erra, and specifically on his destruction of cities and populations in a fit of heroic wrath. The initial scenes of the poem deal with the prelude to this violence, and the reasons for Erra's anger. The final scenes describe how Erra was eventually calmed by his counsellor Ishum, and the aftermath of Erra's rage. At the core of the poem, however, is the narration of Erra's destructive rampage. The poem offers no fewer than three separate accounts of these events, presented by three different narrators, with the tale told at increasing length each time.

In the first tablet, Erra is encouraged to violence by seven magical warriors called the Sibitti, who, in a brief speech (Tablet 1, lines 45–91), wish for the destructive events that will happen later in the poem. The Sibitti foretell the events of the epic in the future tense, raising audience expectations and anticipation of the events themselves. Later in the poem, Erra's dismissal from his guard post leads to him to embark on precisely this foretold rampage, the details of which are described at greater length and in the present tense in another, more extended speech (Tablet 2, Pericope C2, line 40′ – Tablet 3, Pericope A). Remarkably, it is Erra himself who is the narrator of this section. In the speech, Erra gives a running commentary in the first person on the death and destruction he is currently causing, describing each new violent action apparently as he undertakes it. This speech is unique in Akkadian literature

---

[71] For the unusual nature of the *Erra* in this respect, see Lambert 1962b, 119, and Foster 2005, 880–81. As George puts it: 'its form is much less the customary narrative and much more extended rhetorical monologue' (2013, 47). For the strategies of introducing direct speech in Akkadian poetry in general, see Vogelzang 1990; the *Erra* usually conforms to standard formulae for introducing direct speech, save in Tablet 1 where there are some innovative ways of introducing speech (Vogelzang 1990, 65–7).

and has prompted much discussion due to the strangeness of recounting events in the first person present tense.[72] Yet later, when Erra is calmed by Ishum, Ishum then delivers one of the longest speeches in Akkadian literature (Tablet 3, Pericope D, line 2 – Tablet 5, line 127).[73] This speech recounts for a third time the same terrible events, now at even greater length and in the past tense. It seems that Ishum is eventually able to placate Erra through this speech – by describing to him his own recently completed deeds in poetry. The poem then concludes with Erra ordering that the story of his deeds (i.e. the poem itself) be preserved and honoured – a topic that we will return to later.

The main action of the poem – Erra's wreaking of war and destruction over the lands – is therefore recounted in direct speech no less than three times, by three different voices, in three different tenses. It is obvious that the *Erra*, no less than the *Iliad*, is crucially interested in the *praxis* of poetry. The experimentation we see here with the narrative voice is complex – first, the use of direct speech to recount the key events of the story; secondly, the use of different persons and tenses; finally, the use of narrative repetition, with the cumulative effect of each new layer expanding and building on the last. The poet of the *Erra* is playing games with the idea of storytelling and pushing at the conventions of how a tale should be told.

These 'songs within a song' in the *Erra* are markedly different to comparable episodes in the Homeric epics. As Jan described above, when characters in the Homeric poems engage in song, they are usually self-consciously aware of their own poetic practice. In contrast, internal narrators in the *Erra* offer no explicit clue that they acknowledge their actions involve poetry. Instead, each of the three 'songs' begin, not with a statement of poetic intent, but in tradition hymnic form with an invocation to a god (in these three cases, Erra). The Sibitti begin their speech with an appeal to Erra: 'Up, do your duty!' (*tebi izīzma*; Tablet 1, line 46; trans. Foster 2005); the main body of which is a string of subjunctive phrases, such as: 'Let sovereigns hear and fall prostrate before you' (*mālki lišmuma likmisu šápalka*: Tablet 1, line 65; trans. Foster 2005). Erra's own speech opens with the god struggling to control his feelings of outrage.

---

[72] Foster 2005, 894.
[73] Foster 2005, 901.

His heart had been 'stung' (Tablet 2, Pericope C2, line 38'), and he addresses it directly, asking it to: 'Lead the way, and let me begin the campaign!' (*ṭuda pitema lūṣbat ḫarannu*: Tablet 2, Pericope C2, Line 12; trans. Foster 2005). The speech from this point is comprised of present tense first person narrative statements. At no point does Erra make reference to the fact he is narrating his actions, or engaging in any kind of speech act. Ishum's speech is similarly structured to that of Erra, also beginning with an invocation: 'O warrior Erra!' (*quradu¹ ᵈÈrra*: Tablet 3, Pericope D, line 1; trans. Foster 2005). After this follow several lines of praise, before the main body of the speech comprising narrative statements in the present tense and second person. At its conclusion, Ishum speaks in Erra's voice, reporting in the future tense what Erra has said he would do (Tablet 5, lines 115–28). This final narrative shift – with one internal narrator adopting the voice of another – is further testament of the poem's metapoetic interest. But once more, there is no explicit acknowledgement in the speech that Ishum is creating or performing a song. It seems that neither Ishum and Erra nor the Sibitti narrate tales in the self-consciously poetic manner of Homeric storytellers.

Poet and Poem in the *Erra*

If the poets within the poem do not explicitly refer to their own poetic *praxis*, the same cannot be said for the poet of the *Erra* itself, who is a significant presence within the poem. The three speeches discussed above and other sections of direct speech are all connected by the poet as external narrator; but the poet's voice is most evident at the start and the end of the poem. He opens the epic in traditional fashion by invoking a deity (interestingly, while the three songs within the poem begin by invoking Erra, the poem itself invokes Ishum). In this case, he addresses Ishum in a pair of honorific couplets (Tablet 1, lines 1–4) before turning to describe Erra in a state of restlessness. During the description of Erra, the poet establishes himself within the frame of the poem by addressing Ishum directly twice in the second person: 'he even says to *you*' (*iqabbima¹ ana kašā²*: Tablet 1, line 9; trans. Foster 2005, emphasis added); and 'until *you* rouse him, he will sleep in his bedroom' (*adi atta tadēkkušú ṣalil uršūššú*: Tablet 1, line 19; trans. Foster 2005, emphasis added).[74] It is worth noting that in a performance context, this direct address of a character would have blurred into the direct address of the audience, resulting in an identification of the audience with Ishum (I shall return to this point below).[75]

The poet then comes into focus fully in the final section of the poem. Strangely, given the prevalence of direct speech elsewhere in the poem, we do not hear the poet's voice in this passage. Instead, he is named in the third person, with the rather odd effect of making him a character within his own story.

šá [d]Èr-ra i-gu-gu-ma ana sa-pan matāti[meš]

ú ḫul-lu-uq ni-ši-šin iš-ku-nu pa-ni-šú   (40)

[d]I-šum ma-lik-šú ú-ni-ḫu-šu-ma i-zi-bu ri-ḫa-ni-iš

ka-ṣir kam-mi-šú [m]Kab-ti-ilani[meš d]Mar-duk mār [m]Da-bi-bi

*ina šat mu-ši ú-šab-ri-šú-ma ki-i šá ina mu-na-a-ti id-bu-bu a-a-am-ma ul
     iḫ-ṭi*

e-da šu-ma ul ú-rad-di a-na muḫ-ḫi

iš-me-šu-ma ul [d]Èr-ra im-da-ḫar pa-ni-šú   (45)

šá [d]I-šum a-lik maḫ-ri-šú i-ṭib elī-šú

ilāni [meš] nap-ḫar-šú-nu i-na-ad-du it-it-šú

How it came to pass that Erra grew angry

and set out to lay waste   (40)

the lands and destroy their peoples:

But Ishum his counsellor calmed him and he left a remnant:

The composer of its text was Kabti ilani Marduk, of the family Dabibi.

He revealed it at night, and, just as he (the god) had discoursed it while he

    (K.) was coming awake, he (K.) omitted nothing at all.

[74] This passage in which Erra is described in his restless state also employs complex narrative strategies. First, there is some debate over whether Erra or Ishum is being addressed (see Foster 2005, 881 n.4 with references). In reading this passage as the external narrator addressing Ishum, I am following the interpretation of Vogelzang 1990, 66 and George 2013, 49–51 with notes. Second, we hear not only the narrator's own voice, but also that of Erra speaking to his own heart (lines 15–6) and to the Sibitti (17–8); Erra's heart speaking to the Sibitti (lines 7–8), as well as to Ishum (9–12) and Erra himself (13–4). In this passage, as well as in the poem as a whole, the audience is treated to a cacophony of different voices addressing different hearers in direct speech.

[75] This slippage between an internal and an external audience, and a doubling of perspectives when the poet addresses both the external audience and an internal character at the same time, has been identified as a key feature of performance in traditions of oral poetry in modern Egypt. This is sometimes coupled with ambiguity of tenses, so that statements can be interpreted as applying equally to the past of the poem's events and to the present of the poetic performance. See Reynolds 1995, 77–78 for a particularly apt example of a poet addressing both an internal character and their external audience at the same time; and p.208 for the 'duplication of the epic performance within the epic'. I am grateful for Gregory Nagy for pointing me in the direction of this work.

Nor one line did he add to it.

When Erra heard it he approved.   (45)

What pertained to Ishum his vanguard satisfied him.

All the gods praised his sign.

Erra and Ishum, Tablet 5, lines 39–47 (trans. Foster 2005)

This passage explicitly names the author as Kabti-ilani-Marduk, and his relationship to the poem is described in some detail.[76] The key formula used to refer to him is: 'the composer of the text' (*kāṣir kammišu*; line 42). The word used for composing, *kaṣāru*, which has the literal meaning of someone who 'binds something together', can also be used of weaving cloth. The use of this image for authors – those who bind or weave words together – is familiar from elsewhere in the Mesopotamian literary corpus,[77] and the Homeric resonances of weaving of stories or words have already been explored above. What Kabti-ilani-Marduk is weaving in this phrase however, is not words but rather a 'text'. The word used here for 'text', *kammû*, is a rare one, and implies written documents of venerable antiquity.[78] It seems, then, that Kabti-ilani-Marduk was not responsible for an act of poetic creation, or the composition of a poem in the way that we would usually envisage it. Instead, he is described as undertaking the writing of a pre-existing account.[79]

This is made more explicit by what we are told of the process of composition. It is said that the poem was revealed to Kabti-ilani-Marduk by Ishum – that Ishum literally 'caused him to see' it (*ušabrišuma*: line 43). It is unclear whether the implication is that Kabti-ilani-Marduk 'saw' the events of the poem unfold before his eyes in some kind of cinematic vision, or whether he 'saw' the poem in its physical written form as words on a divine tablet (i.e. that he read the poem). In either case, the central action involves the perception of something pre-existing, rather than the wholesale creation of something new. Following

---

[76] For a discussion of poetic composition in Akkadian poetry, see Foster 1991.

[77] Indeed, it can be traced back as early the third millennium BCE. It appears in the hymns of Enheduanna, although these poems were written in Sumerian rather than Akkadian, and so the specific vocabulary if not the imagery would have been different: De Shong Meador 2000, 2009.

[78] Indeed, the rarity of this word is such that translators could only infer its meaning because it was used in parallel with the more common term *zamāru* (poem/song) by the Neo-Assyrian king Ashurbanipal in the seventh century BCE. In this context, it was used of ancient Sumerian texts, which would have been over a millennium old by the time of Ashurbanipal's reign. See Bodi 1991, 56 n.25.

[79] As Röllig 2009, 45 puts it, Kabti-ilani-Marduk is perhaps 'weaving together' different mythic and poetic strands.

this, we are told that Kabti-ilani-Marduk 'spoke' the poem (*idbubu*: line 43) exactly as it had been revealed to him. This is not an act of invention but one of repetition, once more predicated on the pre-existence of the thing being repeated. At the end of a long poem that plays throughout with expectations of speech and narration, this final image of Kabti-ilani-Marduk 'speaking' the entire poem is especially loaded. The external narrator now presents himself as an internal narrator, and makes the recounting of the tale into part of the tale itself. Furthermore, the sound of the verb used for speaking – *idbubu* – puns on the sound of Kabti-ilani-Marduk's family name of Dabibi.[80]

Kabti-ilani-Marduk was not, therefore, credited with the creation of the *Erra*. His poem, like those of the Homeric poet(s), was ultimately attributed to a divine source. Kabti-ilani-Marduk's role is to repeat and disseminate what he has been shown by Ishum. But Ishum is no Muse – his role in the poetic process is more direct.[81] It is Ishum who first narrates the deeds of Erra in full detail after they have occurred (Tablet 3, Pericope D, line 2 – Tablet 5, line 127), thereby bringing into existence the first account of the epic events. Indeed, in the passage from Table 5 quoted above, the poem itself is explicitly said to belong to Ishum: 'What pertained to Ishum his vanguard satisfied him [Erra]' (*šá ᵈIšum alik maḫrišú¹ iṭib elíšú²*: line 46; trans. Foster 2005). This attribution of the poem to Ishum is particularly interesting, given the slippage between Ishum and the audience at the start of the poem. Here we are presented with the poet, describing himself narrating a poem to an audience which has itself been cast as the poem's initial creator. The lines of responsibility for this poem, then, implicate not only the authors, both human and divine, but also the audience. One more figure is also implicated in the creation of this poem however: Erra. Crucially, the poem is described as partaking of Erra's essence: we are told that Erra was pleased with the poem and that the other gods praised Erra's 'sign' (*ittu*: line 47). In this context, the poem is evidently being referred to as the 'sign' of the god.

If Kabti-ilani-Marduk was the writer of the poem, and Ishum (or the audience?) was its creator, then why are we eventually confronted with a description of the poem as a 'sign' of the god Erra? At several points during the

---

[80] Noegel 2011, 180. This passage as a whole is heavily laden with puns and wordplay Noegel 2011, 180–82.

[81] Indeed, the difference in relationship between the Muses and Homeric bards is evident when we consider Kabti-ilani-Marduk could never hope to usurp the role of Ishum, as Thamyris did the Muses (although as Jan points out above, this was to cause Thamyris' downfall: *Il.* 2.595–600).

poem, we are told that Erra's anger flared up because, as he saw it: the people of the earth 'hold me in contempt' (*leqû šīṭūṭī*: Tablet 1, line 120: Tablet 3, Pericope D, line 15; Tablet 4, line 113). With the creation and praise of the poem – his sign – he was appeased. His was a quest for recognition, or perhaps for the *kleos* that can be bestowed by poetry.[82] As we have already seen, there is relatively little *kleos* here for Kabti-ilani-Marduk, in contrast to the poetic professionals within the Homeric epics (e.g. Demodocus and Phemius in the *Odyssey* 8.479–81 and 9.3.11, respectively; see above for discussion). There is limited *kleos* even for Ishum, although he is celebrated at the start of the poem (Tablet 1, lines 1–4), and Erra acknowledges that he has benefitted from Ishum's calming influence towards the end (Tablet 5, line 14). Instead, most of the *kleos* generated by the poem seems to have been directed to Erra. For it is Erra who literally has the final say, the poem closing with him engaging in direct speech, setting out the divine benefits that will be bestowed on all those who honour the poem.

> *u ki-a-am iq-ta-bi qu-ra-du ᵈÈr-ra*
> *ilu šá za-ma-ru šá-a-šú i-na-du ina a-šìr-ti-šú lik-tam-mer-ta hé-gál-lum*
> *ù šá ú-šam-sa-ku a-a iṣ-ṣi-na qut rin-na* (50)
> *šarru šá šu-mi ú-šar-bu-ú li-be-el kib-ra-a-ti*
> *rubú šá ta-nit-ti qar-ra-du-ti-ia i-dab-bu-bu ma-ḫi ra a-a ir-ši*
> *ˡᵘnāru šá i-ṣar-ra ḫu ul i-mat ina šip-ṭi*
> *eli šarri u rubê da-mì-iq at-mu-šú*
> *ˡᵘṭupšarru šá iḫ-ḫa-zu i-šet ina māt ˡᵘnakri i-kab-bit ina mātī-šú* (55)
> *ina a-šìr-ti um-ma-a-ni a-šar ka-a-an šu-mì i-zak ka-ru ú-zu-un-šú-nu*
>   *a-pet-ti*
> *ina bīti a-šar ṭup-pu šá-šú šak-nu ᵈÈr-ra li-gug-ma liš-gi-šú ᵈSi-bi-it-[ti]*
> *pa-tar šip-ṭi ul i-ṭe-ḫi-šu-ma šá lim-tu šak-na-as su*
> *za-mar-ru šá-a-šú a-na ma-ti-ma liš-šá-kin-ma li-kun ga-du ul-la*
> *ma-ta-a-ti nap-ḫar-ši-na liš-ma-ma li na-da qur di-da* (60)
> *nišiᵐᵉˢ da-ád-me li-mu-ra-ma li-šar-ba-a šu-mì*

Then the warrior Erra spoke thus:
In the sanctuary of the god who honours this poem, may abundance heap up.
But let the one who neglects it never smell incense.   (50)
Let the king who extols my name rule the world.

---

[82] Although wordplay suggests ambiguity over whether song ultimately praises Erra or Marduk as its subject, as it was Marduk's assent which allowed for the events to occur: Noegel 2011, 188.

Let the prince who discourses this praise of my valour have no rival.
The singer who chants it shall not die in pestilence,
But his performance shall be pleasing to king and prince.
The scribe who masters it shall be spared in an enemy land and honoured
    in his own.   (55)
In such sanctum where the learned make frequent mention of my name, I
    shall grant them understanding.
The house in which this tablet is placed, though Erra be angry and the
    Seven [the Sibitti] be slaughtering,
The sword of pestilence shall not approach it: safety abides upon it.
Let this song abide forever, let it endure till eternity.
Let all lands hear it and praise my valour.   (60)
Let all inhabitants witness and extol my name.

Erra and Ishum, Tablet 5, lines 48–61 (trans. Foster 2005)

In this closing passage, we are presented with a final recipient of *kleos* – this time, it is the poem itself. It is the poem that is honoured (line 49), extolled (line 51), discussed (line 52), chanted (line 53), performed (line 54), written out (line 55), mentioned frequently (line 56), stored safely (ling 57), and preserved for eternity (lint 59). This implies a different conception of poetic practice from that seen in the Homeric epics: this poem is not only a means of acquiring, transferring, and communicating *kleos* for both poetic subject and poetic practitioner – it also commands *kleos* for itself.

Part of the explanation for this may lie in the way the poem describes itself. In this passage, it appears to have a number of different manifestations. It is described as a 'song' (*zamaru*; lines 49 and 59), as Erra's 'name' (*šumi*; lines 51 and 61), and as a 'tablet' (*ṭuppu*; line 57). As we have already seen, in the preceding passage it was referred to as a 'sign' (*ittu*: line 47) of the god. Common across these various manifestations, however, is the idea of the poem as a *thing* – an entity in its own right with a range of attributes or powers. As a thing, the poem can be the recipient of praise; and in this passage it also appears as a repository for magical and protective powers.[83] Although the poem might take many different forms, the way it is described here is anything but ephemeral.

---

[83] These final lines stress the role of the poem as a physical sign of the god and suggest that the poem was imbued with apotropaic power. This goes some way to explaining the poem's widespread popularity, and it has been found carved in miniature on several talismans and amulets (Reiner 1960).

Songs as *things*

The sense of a text as an entity – a *thing* – can be found more widely in Mesopotamian writing. This must stem in part from the practical existence of most Akkadian texts as artefacts, comprising both the inscribed material and the written script. This textual physicality is vividly described in the prologue of the *Gilgamesh*,[84] the standard form of which seems to have emerged in the late second millennium.[85]

[a-mur?] ^{giš}tup-šen-na šá ^{giš}erēni(erin)
[pu-uṭ-ṭe]r ḫar-gal-li-šu šá siparri (zabar)
[pi-te-m]a? bāba(ká) šá ni-ṣir-ti-šú
[i-š]i?-ma ṭup-pi ^{na4}uqnî(za.gìn) ši-tas-si
[mim-m]u-ú ^{d}GIŠ-gím-maš ittallaku(DU.DU)^{ku} ka-lu mar-ṣa-a-ti

See the tablet-box of cedar.
release its clasp of bronze!
Lift the lid of its secret,
pick up the tablet of lapis lazuli and read out
The travails of Gilgamesh, all that he went through.
    The Epic of Gilgamesh, Tablet 1, lines 24–8 (text and trans. George 2003)

The prologue invites its audience to engage with the text as an inscribed artefact as well as a literary composition.[86] In addition, the previous lines suggest that the tablet box is to be discovered by examining the walls of Uruk, Gilgamesh's great city.[87] The poem, then, describes itself as a physical artefact with an almost archaeological provenance.

---

[84] See Haubold 2013, 32–35 on the emphasis on the visual in this passage. In an earlier version of this prologue found at the Levantine port city of Ugarit, this is phrased, not as an invitation to the reader but as a description of Gilgamesh's actions (George 2007, 245). It is unclear whether the invitation to the reader was a later innovation or whether the difference here in the Ugarit text was produced by changes during the process of textual transmission.

[85] The development of standard versions did not necessarily mean that alternative written (and perhaps also oral) versions of the poem did not continue to exist. The development of these standard versions involved not only the compilation and editing of older poems, but also the composition of completely new lines and passages. In the case of *Gilgamesh*, Babylonian tradition suggests that this work was attributed to a scholar known as Sîn-lēqi-unninni. For the development of the standard version of *Gilgamesh*, see: George 2003, 28–33 and Michalowski 1996, 187.

[86] The prologue of *Gilgamesh* raises questions of reading and writing, story and experience, through its description of the storage and rediscovery of the text: Gilbert 2012, 147–48. I am grateful to Martin Worthington for pointing me in this direction.

[87] George 2003, 446. I am grateful to Nicholas Postgate for highlighting this point.

This same emphasis on the physicality of texts can be found more widely across the writing cultures of Mesopotamia, including prose texts and documents that we may not immediately consider to be 'literary'. For example, in 670 BCE the Neo-Assyrian king Esarhaddon erected an inscription to celebrate his victory over the pharaoh Taharqa.[88] The inscription ends with a description of itself as a 'stele/inscription' (*narû*; lines 50, 53, and 56), and a warning for those who would damage either the physical stone of the stele (lines 53–6) or the written words of the text (lines 56–7). Many similar formulae can be found on inscriptions of this and earlier periods.[89] In official proclamations as well as poetry, then, texts were conceived of as physical as well as literary objects.

This idea finds particular expression in a genre sometimes known as *narû* literature. The precise definition of the genre is debated,[90] but in general these are prose texts claiming to be an official inscription (hence *narû*) of a great or legendary king. Royal inscriptions, as we have seen above, often recount the achievements of the king, and *narû* literature has the same narrative focus. The genre is also sometimes referred to as 'fictional autobiography', as these texts were written in the first person despite their subjects being mythical or long-dead by the time of composition. While the genre must have developed out of actual *narû* inscriptions, by the early first millennium these texts may not always have been inscribed on stone. The claim of being a *narû* is therefore a symbolic one, with the physical durability of the form standing for the endurance of the text and the preservation of memory.[91]

---

[88] The inscription can be found in Leichty 2011, no.98 (*RINAP* 4, 98). For a discussion of the iconography of the stele, see Porter 2003, 75–77; for the stele in the context of Assyrian-Egyptian conflict, see Eph'al 2005.

[89] To cite another Neo-Assyrian example, in the Annals of Sennacherib as preserved in the Taylor Prism, the king places a curse on the 'one who alters this inscription or my name' (Taylor Prism, Side 6, lines 80–1: see Grayson and Novotny 2012, no.22).

[90] Longman 1991, 48, 199–203, Jonker 1995, 92–95 and Westenholz 1997, 16–20.

[91] Jonker 1995, 98–102. One well-known example of the genre is *The Cuthean Legend of Naram-Sin*. Although this poem existed in various earlier forms, at the start of the first millennium the standard version began: 'Open the tablet-box and read out the stela, | Which I, Naram-Sin, son of Sargon, | Have inscribed and left for future days' (lines 1–3, trans. Westenholz 1997, 301). This closely parallels the passage from the prologue of *Gilgamesh* quoted in the main text above. Where the *Gilgamesh* prologue deviates from the *narû* literature format, however, is that while it makes reference to the setting up of a *narû* inscription recounting Gilgamesh' adventures (line 10), it does not openly claim that the text of the inscription is the same as that of the poem. This claim is made, in contrast, in the explicitly in the final section of the *Cuthean Legend*: 'Read this stela! | Heed the wording of this stela!' (lines 152–3; trans. Longman 1991, 231). Indeed, the very final lines of the *Cuthean Legend* return once more to the idea that the text that is being read is an inscription: 'You who have seen the things on my stela and set out your record, (just as) you have blessed me, may a future (ruler) bless you' (lines 174–5; trans. Longmann 1991, 231).

The physicality of Mesopotamian texts stands in marked contrast to the self-conscious orality of song in the Homeric epics. The *Iliad* and the *Odyssey* were not composed in a pre-literate age – indeed, they came into existence around the very time when the Greek alphabet was in development, and the *Iliad* itself acknowledges the existence of writing. When Glaucus tells the story of his ancestor Bellerophon in Book 6, he mentions that the hero had been sent to Lycia bearing 'ominous signs, written on a folded tablet, life-destroying and many' (σήματα λυγρά, | γράψας ἐν πίνακι πτυκτῷ θυμοφθόρα πολλά, *Iliad* 6.168–69).[92] Glaucus is engaging here in his own poetic practice – his 'tale within a tale' is a poetic account of the deeds of (what is from his perspective) the heroic past. He delivers his story, as most other storytellers and poets in the Homeric poems, orally. And yet, the story hinges on the new technology of writing. The orality of poetry in the Homeric epics is therefore a choice – while Homeric epics are aware of the existence of written traditions, they seem to position themselves as oral.

A slightly different juxtaposition of the oral and the written can be found in Tablet 11 of *Gilgamesh*. In this tablet, Gilgamesh is told the story of the great flood by Utnapištim, who survived its waters by following the instructions of the god Ea. Utnapištim's story is therefore yet another song embedded within a song, but explicitly marked out from the main narrative as an oral rather than a written tale. Utnapištim prefaces his story by saying: 'I will disclose to you, Gilgamesh | and I will tell you a mystery of the gods' (*lupteka gilgameš amāt niṣirti | u piništi ša ilāni kâša luqbika*: Tablet 11, lines 9–10; trans. George 2003). There is no suggestion of a written version of the story, despite the fact that a Mesopotamian audience would almost certainly have been aware of the *Atraḫasis*, a well-known poem that focused specifically on the legend of the flood.[93] Indeed Utnapištim does not describe his composition as a poem or a tablet, but as a 'secret/treasure' (*niṣirti*; line 9), and a 'mystery' (*piništi*; line 10). There are structural parallels between this episode and Book 9 of the *Odyssey*, in which Odysseus begins to tell the story of his adventures to the Phaeacians.

---

[92] See Powell 1997, 27–28 for a discussion of this passage, coming to the conclusion that the Homeric poet did not fully understand the technology of writing.

[93] The story of the flood presented in Tablet 11 of *Gilgamesh* differs in several respects from the fuller version of the tale in the *Atraḫasis*. The standard version of the *Atraḫasis* dates back to the Middle Bronze Age, *c.* 1700 BCE, although it continued to be copied well into the first millennium: Lambert and Millard 1969.

Both characters appear as masters of oral poetry, constructing their identities by composing epic autobiographies.[94] But while Odysseus acts as a mirror or stand-in for the poet of the *Odyssey*, Utnapištim's storytelling is qualitatively distinct from that of the *Gilgamesh* epic as a whole – as an oral rather than a written tale, it involved a subtly different type of activity.

And yet, despite its orality, Utnapištim's story is closer to Mesopotamian written texts than the Homeric oral epics in one important respect. In this episode, the tale itself is a *thing*, just as the text of *Erra*, the Neo-Assyrian royal inscriptions, and the overall poem of *Gilgamesh* are also *things*. Utnapištim's story is described as if it were an entity in its own right, which has an existence beyond the ephemeral moment of its performance. In telling his story, Utnapištim is not creating something – he is merely uncovering something that was already there so that Gilgamesh might behold it. The verbs Utnapištim uses for the telling of his tale are significant in this respect. He claims that he wishes to 'reveal' or 'open up' (*lupteka*) the secret for Gilgamesh, and to 'speak out' (*luqbika*) the mystery. In this way, Utnapištim's story resembles the *Erra* poem. Both has its own independent existence – they are 'story-entities' even before they are crystallized into their poetic form. This is true, irrespective of whether the tale was a written poem (as in the case of the *Erra*) or an oral account (as in the case of Utnapištim's story). It seems that the 'thingyness' of Mesopotamian heroic tales did not depend on their final form.

This differs from the poetic practice represented within the Homeric epics. The *Iliad* begins with an invocation to the Muse to sing, not the song of Achilles' wrath, but to sing that very wrath itself (μῆνιν ἄειδε; *Iliad* 1.1). In the equivalent line of the *Odyssey*, the Muse is called upon to speak the man, rather than speak a tale *about* the man (ἄνδρα μοι ἔννεπε; *Odyssey* 1.1). Similarly, when Odysseus sings his own *Odyssey*, he says: 'come now, I will recount to you my stressful homecoming' (εἰ δ' ἄγε τοι καὶ νόστον ἐμὸν πολυκηδέ' ἐνίσπω, *Odyssey*, 9.37). Crucially, the object of the verb 'recount' (ἐνίσπω) is the 'homecoming' (νόστον) – not a song, a story, or a secret about that homecoming, but the homecoming itself. For Odysseus, as for the poet

---

[94] Utnapištim's tale, like that of Odysseus, makes use of linguistic games and literary deceptions, in a self-aware and self-referential way. In both poems, the extended sections given over to these embedded poet-narrators are a means of exploring the control of discourse. See Michalowski 1996, 188–90.

of the Homeric poems, there is no *thing* that mediates between the events and their telling. In contrast, in the *Erra* poem, Kabti-ilani-Marduk does not write the events, but rather the text (*kaṣir*) of them. Similarly, the gods do not praise Erra or his exploits, but rather his sign (*ittu*). And in *Gilgamesh*, Utnapištim does not recount his own exploits, but rather the secret (*niṣirti*) that enfolds them. The difference between the Homeric tradition and these Mesopotamian examples is, in part, one of grammar. Nonetheless, the poetic and social implications of this are significant.

Stories and storytellers

One of the results of this subtle linguistic difference is a much more significant disparity in the status of the poet. It is significant that compared with the later Greek literary tradition, we know the names of very few Mesopotamian poets.[95] The *Erra's* Kabti-ilani-Marduk is a notable exception – a poet who names himself in his work. There are some genres of Mesopotamian literature in which the names of supposed authors appear more often, including hymns,[96] royal annals, and inscriptions, and the aforementioned *narû* literature.[97] Beyond these classes of text however, it was rare for Mesopotamian texts to name or make reference to their authors. The *Enuma Eliš* (the Epic of Creation), for example, claims that its text was initially set out by the god Marduk, and then written down by an unnamed 'first one' (*maḫrû*; Tablet 7, line 157). The *Gilgamesh* in contrast offers us no explicit reference to its composition or a poet at all.[98]

Not only was there relatively little interest in the identity of the poet, but there was also comparatively little celebration of human agency in poetic composition. As we have seen for the *Erra*, creativity was attributed to the divine agents or heroic subjects of poetry, rather than to its scribes; and praise was directed more towards the poem/song/tale itself than to any of the

---

[95] On authorship and anonymity in Mesopotamian literature, see Foster 1991, Michalowski 1996, and Röllig 2009, 44–45.

[96] Indeed, the earliest named Mesopotamian author is known 85 for her hymns – Enheduanna, a Sumerian priestess in the third millennium. See n.77 above.

[97] Although of course the autobiographical names offered in *narû* literature cannot be the true authors of these works. See p.90 above.

[98] Indeed, it is only through a relatively late tradition which links the composition of the standard form of *Gilgamesh* to a scholar known as Sîn-lēqi-unninni. See n.85 above.

individuals involved in its composition. While there is of course some prestige in Kabti-ilani-Marduk's claim to be the person to whom the song was revealed, and the first to commit it to writing, this prestige is qualitatively different from the explicit praise that is given to the poem itself. This is a metapoetic vision subtly different from that of the Homeric world, where the praxis of poetry commanded *kleos*; where praise was offered to the singers of songs; and where the performance of poetry was considered to be an heroic activity. In the *Erra*, it was not the poet who stood centre stage, or even the action of 'doing' poetry – it was the poem itself that was the *thing*.

And yet, beyond this difference in metapoetics, the *Erra* and the Homeric poems have something important in common – that they *had* a strong sense of the metapoetic at all. Both are crucially concerned with the practice of telling stories, and both play innovative games with the idea of storytelling, speech, and the voice of the narrator. Although the *Erra* and the *Iliad* developed their metapoetic interest in different directions, it is significant that they shared this interest at all.

It is perhaps possible that the *Erra* reflected a broader shift in Mesopotamian literature. Only two Akkadian poems are known from the entire span of antiquity that claimed for themselves non-royal authors, and both date from around this time – *Erra* and the *Babylonian Theodicy*.[99] A broader interest in authors may also lie behind the writing a tablet from Ashurbanipal's library at Nineveh, dated to the mid-seventh century BCE, which lists texts in the library categorized by author.[100] The first author in the list is the god Ea (Tablet 1, line 4), followed by Adapa, one of the mythical seven sages (Tablet 1, lines 6–7). Although the intervening text is fragmentary, a tablet and a half later we are met by a familiar name – Kabti-ilani-Marduk (Tablet 3, line 2). Several other human authors are listed, including the supposed compiler of *Gilgamesh*, Sîn-lēqi-unninni.[101] By bringing together divine, mythical, and human authors, this catalogue tablet may suggest perhaps a subtle shift in the representation of

---

[99] The *Babylonian Theodicy* preserved the name of its author, Esaggil–kinam–ubbib, as an acrostic (Oshima 2014, 121–25). Several hymns use the same format for naming their authors (Foster 1991, 17 nn.3–4).

[100] Lambert 1957, 1962a.

[101] Although the catalogue initially seems to follow a hierarchical structure, legendary figures are found alongside 'historical' human authors in the latter tablets of the text. Some of the 'historical' human authors are given ancestral surnames, while others are known only by their own given names. Lambert 1957, 1962a argues that this is evidence for the emergence of scribal dynasties and schools.

poetic composition. If so, it is perhaps significant that this would be occurring in the early centuries of the first millennium, at around the time that the material of the *Iliad* and the *Odyssey* were coming together.

It may not be possible to determine precisely how the metapoetic consciousness of the *Erra* relates to that of Homeric poetry – in particular, I suspect it may be unhelpful to debate whether Homeric epic derived its metapoetic interest from the *Erra* or vice versa. Instead, it is probably more fruitful to think of these developments as emerging out of the same broader historical context – the same interconnected world, inhabited by overlapping and interacting literary traditions. This may not be evidence for the *Iliad* and the *Erra* speaking directly to each other in a dialogue, but I would argue that both texts were saying the same kinds of things, each engaged in dialogue with a broader set of traditions which we can only begin to piece together.

The *Iliad* and the *Erra* both emerged out of a world full of poetry. They may have occupied different positions within this poetic world, and clearly they both had different immediate literary and cultural contexts, but nonetheless they were both embedded in the same wider world of interconnected poetic traditions. While these poems drew from this broader field of traditions, they also innovated on them – crucially, as we have seen in this chapter, in their conception of poetry itself. The poems were therefore works of reception, not just in terms of stories, themes, and motifs but also by virtue of their metapoetic consciousness. The *Iliad* and the *Erra* both reflect deeply on the nature of poetry – something that would not have been possible if there had not already existed a variety of poetic practices to reflect on.

But the *Erra* and the *Iliad* emerged *into* a world full of poetry as well as out of one. Their impact on later tradition was not just one of stories, themes, and motifs, but also one of metapoetic consciousness. As we shall see in the rest of this book, this self-conscious sense of *poesis* also features in many later contributions to the Trojan War tradition.

2

Visualizing Society

One of the themes that recurs in the *Iliad* is the construction and correct functioning of society. Throughout the poem, social bonds are forged and broken, and social roles are transgressed and renewed. It is a theme that also recurs in the wider Trojan War tradition, not least in the two case studies discussed in this chapter, both of which primarily discuss visual images.

In the first half of the chapter, Naoíse considers Trojan War imagery on the red figure vases of the Pioneer Group of painters in late archaic Athens, focusing in particular on an amphora by Euthymides and its playful questioning of traditional male roles. In Cleisthenic Athens, against a backdrop of social reform and political transformation, these images were politically sensitive, touching on issues of status as well as of masculinity. Subversive in many ways, the Pioneer Group intriguingly avoided playing politics in their Trojan War scenes, eschewing straightforwardly Iliadic images entirely. The Euthymides amphora is a notable exception – a vase that does engage in political games, at the same time making subtle Iliadic references. In the second half of the chapter, Jan examines *Helen of Troy*, an oil painting by the Pre-Raphaelite artist Dante Gabriel Rossetti. This and other contemporary images use Helen as a means of exploring traditional female roles, focusing especially on her dangerous sexuality. Painted during a period of rapid social change and emergent women's movements, Rossetti's painting is unusual in attributing agency to Helen beyond that afforded to her by her physical desirability.

In their own ways, both images make use of visual ambiguities in order to question the social and, in particular, the gendered roles of their day. In the case of the Euthymides amphora, two contrasting yet 'typical' areas of elite male activity are depicted together, resulting in a destabilization both of received male roles and of ideas about class and status. In the case of Rossetti's *Helen of Troy*, accepted notions about female sexuality and agency are raised, particularly in relation to the wider discourse in nineteenth-century British art on subversive women. Both images therefore challenged the social norms of their respective historical contexts. And significantly, both images made use of Iliadic ideas in order to do this.

The two examples chosen include one from an historical period when the *Iliad* was becoming increasingly important within the Trojan War tradition and one where it already occupied a central position. In late sixth-century Athens, the Homeric poems had recently been incorporated into civic ritual, but were not yet as culturally dominant as they came to be a few decades later in the early fifth century. In contrast, in late nineteenth-century Britain, several decades of cultural and political philhellenism had ensured widespread knowledge of and respect for ancient Greek literature, and the place of the Homeric poems was especially well established.

Naoíse: Euthymides' pioneer politics

This amphora presents us with a striking visual image of the Trojan War (Figure 2.1).[1] It depicts Hector arming in the presence of his aged parents,

Figure 2.1 Red-figure amphora signed by Euthymides (Munich, Staatliche Antikens-samlungen Inv. 2307). Side A: Hector arming, flanked by Priam and Hecuba.

---

[1] Munich, Staatliche Antikenssamlungen Inv. 2307; Beazley no. 200160; CAVI no.5258.

Priam and Hecuba. Each of the figures is labelled, ensuring that the (literate) viewer will make no mistake as to their identities. The pathos of the scene lies in the viewer's knowledge of the tragic fate that will soon befall its characters – Hector's death at the hands of Achilles (*Il.* 22.247–366), the murder of Priam (which Priam himself foretells in *Il.* 22.66–8), and the enslavement of Hecuba and the other women of Troy (again foretold by Priam in *Il.* 22.59–65).[2]

The scene itself does not appear in the *Iliad*. The image on the pot is therefore not an 'illustration' of the poem[3] – instead in its basic form it replicates a fairly standard type-scene of the arming warrior.[4] And yet, this scene has some obviously Iliadic resonances. The location appears to be indoors, as suggested by its enclosure within a patterned border,[5] and the scene is therefore reminiscent of Book 6 of the *Iliad*, especially Hector's encounter with Hecuba (*Il.* 6.251–295). Even more directly, by bringing Hector together with both of his parents, the scene recalls the start of Book 22 of the *Iliad*, where both Priam and Hecuba encounter their son outside at the gates of the city and appeal to him to turn away from combat (*Il.* 22.1–89). But perhaps the most glaring visual reference to the *Iliad* is the treatment of Hector's helmet. This is depicted at the top centre of the image, conspicuously breaking through the borders of the scene. The viewer is meant to notice this helmet – and perhaps to be reminded of the association between Hector and his helmet in the *Iliad*. In the poem, Hector's most common epithet is κορυθαίολος ('of the shining helmet'),[6] and the helmet also features centrally in one of the poem's most emotionally charged scenes – Hector's final farewell to his wife and son, where the baby Astyanax is frightened by the bristling helm (*Il.* 6.467–496).

This picture is therefore, although not actually Iliadic, certainly reminiscent of the *Iliad* in a way we might call 'peri-Iliadic'. For a contemporary Athenian audience at the end of the sixth century, it would have been impossible to look at this image and not to think of the Homeric Hector – a man who was central to his community, just as he is central to this scene; and a man whose heroic

---

2   Jan will discuss the treatment of the Trojan women in Athenian drama in Chapter 3 of this book.
3   For Attic vase painting and the 'illustration' of epic, see Lowenstam 2008, 80–83.
4   As Friis Johansen puts it, this is a 'heroised genre picture' (1967, 211).
5   For a discussion of Euthymides' innovative use of borders on this vase, see Squire and Platt 2017, 60–61.
6   For the relative frequency of different epithets, see Parry 1971, 142. It is notable too that Hector's helmet was a divinely charged item, given to him by Apollo (*Il.* 11.352-53).

demise was to bring about the final downfall of his city. While the scene does not depict an episode from the *Iliad*, it nonetheless recalls the poem and raises Iliadic expectations.

Given that this amphora's likely primary context of use was the symposium, the Iliadic expectations it raised would have been made some comment on the ideology of the elite citizen man in late archaic Athens.[7] Although there is some debate over the exclusivity of the symposium, in the archaic period it was usually associated with aristocratic (or at least wealthy) citizen men.[8] Viewed in such a context, images like this picture of Hector would have been a reminder of civic duty, gender roles, and class expectations. At first glance therefore, Hector seems to be presented here as a moral exemplum – the ideal type of the citizen man.

The Euthymides amphora

In terms of composition, the arrangement of three standing figures in a frame seems to have been characteristic of Euthymides' individual style. A particularly close comparison can be found in another amphora: a man labelled as 'ΘΟΡΥΚΙΟΝ' (*Thorykion*, or 'wearer-of-a-breastplate') dons a cuirass, and is flanked on either side by Scythian warriors.[9] In both the Hector and the Thorykion scenes, the eye of the viewer is drawn directly to the centre of the scene, because of both the inward-turning flanking figures and the directional movement of the central figure's arms. In addition, the central figures in both scenes have a forward-turned foot, facing out of the vase towards the viewer. This was one of Euthymides' significant stylistic innovations – it is not until nearly a century later that we find the technique used again in Athenian vase painting.[10] This detail serves to bring the central figure forwards, stepping out of the two-dimensional frame towards the viewer.

---

[7]   There is a rich body of scholarship on the symposium, some of the more recent offerings including: Topper 2012, Hobden 2013, and Wecowski 2014.

[8]   For this debate over the elite nature of the symposium, see: Topper 2012, 9 n.29 and Hobden 2013, 11–15. Archaeological evidence suggests that a wider range of people may have engaged in sympotic behaviour than previously thought, especially from the fifth century BCE onwards. However, the prevailing *cultural* image of the symposium linked it to the aristocracy (as well as privileging drinking over dining). In the representational repertoire at least, the symposium remained associated with aristocratic men (Hobden 2013, 12, 150).

[9]   Beazley no. 200161; CAVI no. 5259. Another example depicts Theseus abducting Helen (Beazley no. 200157; CAVI no. 5260).

[10] Williams 1991, 288.

Another significant aspect of the composition is its verticality. The upright lines of the figures are heightened by the vertical folds of drapery and the line of Priam's staff, creating an impression of stiffness and formality. This is somewhat disrupted by the diagonal slant of the shield, Hecuba's staff and her outstretched arm, reaching across to place a helmet on her son's head. As already mentioned, the helmet itself breaks through the frame, rupturing the otherwise carefully ordered scene. The gaze of both Hector and Priam is directed downwards, perhaps indicating stillness and reflection; Hecuba alone looks straight across the scene. The composition is as awkward as it is striking, with a tension created between stillness and movement, formality and intimacy.

This impression is further heightened when we consider the scene on the other side of the amphora (Figure 2.2). This depicts a topsy-turvy inversion of the Hector scene, the opposite side of the pot giving us a contrasting perspective on the elite citizen man. It features three standing figures once more, but unlike the upright characters of the Hector scene we are presented with three twisted individuals – their bodies physically contorted and their limbs splayed at various clashing angles. The men appear to be dancing, not in any ordered or formal fashion, but in a chaotic and individualistic manner.

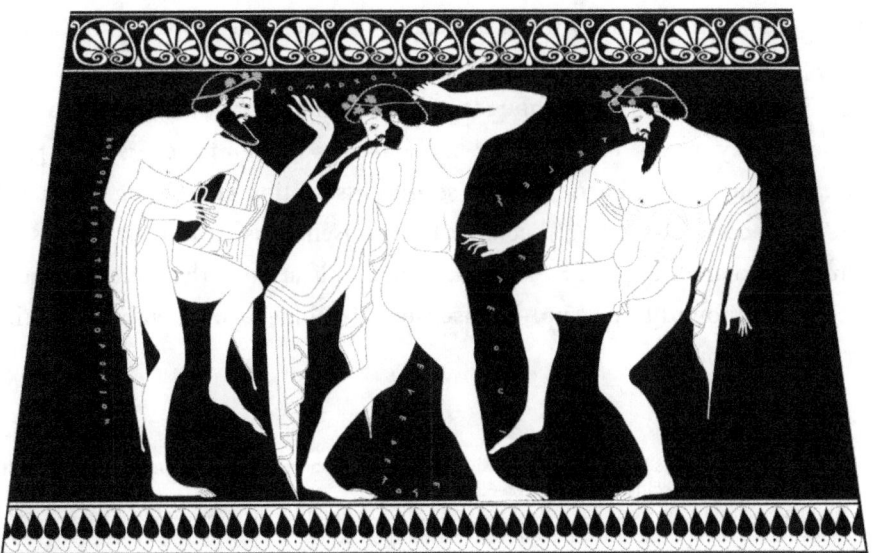

Figure 2.2 Red-figure amphora signed by Euthymides (Munich, Staatliche Antikens-samlungen Inv. 2307). Side B: Three drunken revellers.

With the movement, their cloaks are slipping off their bodies, revealing the naked flesh underneath. Thiers is not an heroic nudity however – the flesh uncovered is saggy, and while they still retain some muscle, these bodies are far from the ideal manly physique.[11] The men have clearly been drinking – they wear wreaths of vine leaves, and instead of Hecuba holding out her son's helmet, the man on the left of the scene clutches a *kantharos*, presumably full of wine. In contrast to the sober verticality of Priam's staff, the central figure in this scene wields his staff at head level, breaking through the top frame in a direct mirroring of the helmet in the Hector scene. Once more, two of the three figures are looking downwards, while the man on the left directs his gaze straight across the frame. In terms of composition, we are presented with a distorted mirror image of the Hector scene.

This figures on this side of the amphora are, like those in the Hector scene, tagged with labels. Above the raised hand of the figure on the left is the word 'ΚΟΜΑΡΧΟΣ'; between the legs of the central figure is written 'ΕΥΕΔΕΜΟΣ'; over the arm of the figure on the right is 'ΤΕΛΕΣ', while between his legs is 'ΕΛΕΟΠΙ'. The labels attached to each of the three drunken revellers are vital for their interpretation. The man on the left seems to be directing the party, as his name literally suggests – he is the leader (*archos*) of the revels (*komos*). The name of the central figure may be more tongue-in-cheek, as the behaviour portrayed is certainly not what is associated with good or proper (as indicated by the prefix *eu-*) members of the citizen body (the *demos*).[12] The man on the right is clearly meant to be thought of as the final figure of the scene, as his name literally means 'last one'. The name itself is written in reverse and runs along his outstretched arm, while a second inscription runs along his raised leg. This second label (*eleopi*) seems to be a nonsense inscription, as it bears no similarity to any known Greek word.[13] The implication is that Teles is where the party is bound to end up – nonsense and gobbledegook, with things the wrong way around.

---

[11] On concepts and ideas of the body in classical Greece, see Osborne 2011. On bodily distinctions in red-figure pottery specifically, see pp.57–65.

[12] Although it is also possible that this was shortened form of Eu[thy]demos, or even a metathesis of Euthymides. I am grateful to Robin Osborne for this point.

[13] Although it has been suggested that this word might represent a celebratory cry, such as the modern 'whohoo!', or the modern Greek 'opa!'. This would be appropriate given the symposiastic and komastic context; see Pappas 2012, 78.

The two scenes – that of Hector and that of the revellers – are designed to be viewed in tandem. In content as well as in composition, one is clearly meant to be the opposite of the other: the ideal of Iliadic manhood is subverted by the self-consciously naughty behaviour of the three komasts. The contrast of the scenes results in a questioning of received social roles, and in particular undermines a clear notion of elite masculinity. Although it might initially seem that the pot presents the viewer with 'good' and 'bad' role models,[14] it is unclear, given the symposiastic context in which the amphora would have been viewed, who the viewer might have identified with. Is this a case of ideal versus reality – the exemplar of the elite citizen man contrasted with his real-life counterpart? Or is this a case of conflicting personal choices; would you chose to end up like Hector (glorious but dead), or like Teles (misbehaving but having fun)? Or perhaps these are two sides of the same coin – the elite man both getting dressed for battle and falling out of his clothes at a party? With this amphora, Euthymides is not instructing the viewer or dictating what the response to the images ought to be. Rather, the contrast of the two scenes poses questions which only the viewer can answer for himself (and the primary viewer would most likely have been a *him*). The juxtaposed scenes create an ideological instability around the traditional role of the elite man.

The politics of the pot

Euthymides painted these scenes in the late archaic period, between around 510 and 500 BCE. His artistic choices must be seen in the context of wider developments in Athens at this time. A generation later, the Trojan War would come to be seen as a parallel for the Persian Wars, and images of Troy would acquire an ethnic significance.[15] At this moment, however, the Trojan War and the poem of the *Iliad* in particular were more closely associated with the politics of class.

[14] See Hobden 2013, 117–56 for the limits of acceptable behaviour and the politics of how one was meant to comport oneself at a symposium. In this context, the behaviour of the three revellers on Euthymides' amphora seems like it would have been at least pushing at the boundaries of acceptability.

[15] For references and a discussion of this, see below p.113 and especially n.24. Visual images of the Trojan War multiplied in the fifth century, from the Parthenon metopes and the paintings in the Stoa Poikile (Anderson 1997, 249–55; Castriota 2005) to vase imagery (for which, see p.53 and especially n.37 below).

The *Iliad* offers a vision of aristocratic ideals, and while it explores tensions within the aristocracy and presents negative instances of leadership, it ultimately upholds these ideals.[16] Its contents aside, the poem would also have had aristocratic associations in late archaic Athens by virtue of its cultural status. It would have been performed at a range of different public events including religious festivals and musical contests, and it would also have featured at occasions that highlighted aristocratic identity, such as at the symposium or feasts.[17] In addition, it seems that the Homeric poems were promoted by leading aristocrats over the course of the sixth century. The Peisistratid dynasty is closely associated with the popularization of the epics: with Peisistratus himself sometimes said to have produced an edition of the poems;[18] and his oldest son, Hipparchus, credited for bringing the Homeric epics to Attica.[19] The institution of full recitals of the poems at the Panathenaea, with rhapsodes picking up from each other in relay, is attributed to either Hipparchus or Solon.[20] More widely, several Athenian aristocratic families claimed descent from the heroes of the *Iliad* – the Alcmeonidae and the Peisistratids both traced their ancestry to Nestor, while the Philaedae claimed the Telamonian Ajax amongst their forefathers.[21] In late

[16] The extent to which the *Iliad* can be considered a poem for the elite or aristocracy has been widely discussed, with much analysis focusing on the passage where Thersites questions the social order, and is struck down by Odysseus to the general amusement of the Achaean host (*Il.* 2.212-77: for various readings of the Thersites episode, see Rose 2013, 118–19 and especially n.65 with references). For the failure of leaders leading to the sufferings of the *laos* in Homeric poetry, see Haubold 2000. See also Rose 2013, 104–06, 132–33 with references for the potentially 'conflicting ideology' of the *Iliad*. It has been pointed out that the presentation of Trojan political assemblies is subtly different from that of the Achaean structures – while the latter are aristocratic and oligarchic, the former are more monarchical (Christensen 2015).

[17] For an introduction to poetic performance in the archaic period, see Power 2016. For Panhellenic festivals as a crucial venue for the performance of Homeric epic, contributing to the presentation of collective decision-making in the *Iliad*, see Elmer 2013.

[18] For a discussion, see Nagy 1996, 104–05. The tradition appears only in relatively late texts: Cicero, *De Oratore* 3.37.137; Anthologia Palatina 11.442.3-4; Aelian, *Varia Historia* 13.14; Pausanias 7.26.13; Schol. T on *Iliad* 10.1.

[19] Ps-Plato, *Hipparchus* 228b-c: 'Hipparchus, who was the oldest and wisest of Peisistratus' children, who among showed many good proofs of his wisdom, including first bringing the epics of Homer to this country, and forcing the rhapsodes to recite them one after the other, as they do today' (Ἱππάρχῳ, ὃς τῶν Πεισιστράτου παίδων ἦν πρεσβύτατος καὶ σοφώτατος, ὃς ἄλλα τε πολλὰ καὶ καλὰ ἔργα σοφίας ἀπεδείξατο, καὶ τὰ Ὁμήρου ἔπη πρῶτος ἐκόμισεν εἰς τὴν γῆν ταυτηνί, καὶ ἠνάγκασε τοὺς ῥαψῳδοὺς Παναθηναίοις ἐξ ὑπολήψεως ἐφεξῆς αὐτὰ διιέναι, ὥσπερ νῦν ἔτι οἵδε ποιοῦσιν...).

[20] Diogenes Laertius 1.57: 'And he established that the reciting of Homer should be from prompt, so that where the first rhapsode stopped, the next would begin from there. In this way Solon did more for Homer than Peisistratus' (Τά τε Ὁμήρου ἐξ ὑποβολῆς γέγραφε ῥαψῳδεῖσθαι, οἷον ὅπου ὁ πρῶτος ἔληξεν, ἐκεῖθεν ἄρχεσθαι τὸν ἐχόμενον. μᾶλλον οὖν Σόλων Ὅμηρον ἐφώτισεν ἢ Πεισίστρατος ...).

[21] Alcmeonidae: Pausanias 2.18.7; Peisistratids: Herodotus 5.65; Philaedae: Herodotus 6.35.

sixth-century Athens therefore, the *Iliad* would had had inescapably aristocratic associations.[22]

This would have meant that the *Iliad* occupied a problematic cultural space in the closing years of the century. This period saw the power struggles between leading aristocratic families take on a new popularist flavour. In 510 BCE, the Peisistratid tyrant Hippias was expelled, and the Alcmaeonid statesman Cleisthenes eventually emerged in 507/8 BCE as the leading politician in the city. Cleisthenes relied on a broad base of popular support in order to maintain his position, and undertook a series of reforms which are often credited as marking the revolutionary start of Athenian democracy.[23] While the extent to which the new system might be considered 'democracy' is open for debate, it is evident that the fast-moving politics of the day were characterized by a new emphasis on popularism and the *demos* of Athens.[24]

The new politics had an impact on the physical environment of the acropolis, at the very heart of the city. Particularly prominent was the dedication of a monumental bronze statue group of Harmodius and Aristogeiton, the 'tyrant-slayers', on the acropolis. The commissioning of this statue group at state expense would have been an overtly political statement, not least because it was a public portrait of individuals from recent history (the first of its kind according to Pliny, *NH* 34.17).[25] Around the same time, non-aristocratic Athenians became increasingly visible on the acropolis through private dedications.[26] Amongst these new dedicators, several explicitly identified themselves as potters, while others can be linked to pot painters known from vase inscriptions. While many of these non-aristocratic

[22] This is not to say that a cultural product with elite associations was restricted *only* to the elite, and either inaccessible or unfamiliar to wider society. For example, the aria 'Nessun dorma' from Puccini's opera *Turandot* was used as the theme song for the 1990 football (soccer) world cup – an instance of a cultural product with elite associations (opera) being widely recognized and appreciated in a social context that is not considered to be restricted to elites.

[23] According to the Aristotelian *Athenian Constitution*, Cleisthenes 'won over the people (*demos*), giving over the government to the multitude' (προσηγάγετο τὸν δῆμον, ἀποδιδοὺς τῷ πλήθει τὴν πολιτείαν. *Athenian Constitution* 20.1). For Cleisthenes and Athens' democratic 'revolution', see: Ober 1996, 32–52, Osborne 2010, and Rose 2013, 350–65.

[24] Although we tend to attribute the reforms to Cleisthenes, it may be more accurate to say that the reforms were a response to popular demands, and what Ober has called 'a revolutionary situation' where 'the *demos* stepped onto the historical stage as a collective agent, a historical actor in its own right and under its own name' (Ober 2007, 86).

[25] Azoulay 2014. For other ancient descriptions of the tyrannicides statue group, see: Pausanias 1.8.5; and Lucian, *Philospeudes* 18.

[26] For this phenomenon, see: Raubitschek 1949, 465, Holloway 1992, 272–73, Hurwit 1999, 126–29, and Keesling 2005.

dedicators chose traditional votive forms such as *kouroi* and *korai*, others such as the dedicator of the 'Potter Relief' used their votives to portray their professional activities.[27] Items may even have been dedicated by Euthymides' immediate circle – a group of potters and pot painters known as the 'Pioneer Group' (for more on which see below). One such individual, Euphronios, left a marble pillar with a fragmentary inscription recording his dedication of a tithe, explicitly referring to his profession: 'Euphronios dedicated this … the potter: to Athena a tithe' ([E]ὐφρόνιος [⋮ ἀνέθηκε]ν [⋮ —c. 7—] | κεραμεὺς ⋮ [τάθεναί]αι δε[κάτεν]).[28]

When Euthymides sat down to paint this particular amphora, therefore, he did so in an Athens that was gripped by political transformation and a new popularist fervour. His choice of subject matter must be seen in this context, as must the likely responses of contemporary Athenian viewers. Both scenes on this amphora would have had aristocratic associations. The image of Hector arming recalled the Iliadic model of the elite male warrior and the aristocratic world of Homeric poetry; while the scene of drunken revellers located it at the symposium, the prevailing cultural image of which was still aristocratic. The pot was clearly political. It remains unclear precisely how we should interpret the politics of the pot however. Is Euthymides lampooning the aristocracy (you might think you are like *this,* a heroic Hector; but actually you are really like *this,* a bunch of flabby drunks)? Or is he condoning aristocratic license (of course, sometimes you behave like *this,* in drunken fun; but that's okay because when necessary you also act like *this,* staunch in the face of duty)? Euthymides' amphora provokes questions, rather than offering answers; the pot presents its viewer with a playful reflection on the role models, ideals, and behaviour of elite men in late archaic Athens. That Euthymides does this on a vessel designed for use in the symposium, and during a time of marked political change, adds an immediacy and timeliness to the visual play.

The Pioneer Group

Euthymides was not the only Athenian pot painter using his work to engage in political commentary at this time. The 'Pioneer Group' has already been

---

[27] Hurwit 1999, 60–61, fig.46. For other potter dedications, see Suk Fong Jim 2014, 133–38.
[28] *IG* I³ 824. See Suk Fong Jim 2014, 135.

mentioned in this chapter; this is the name given to a set of painters active at around the same time in late archaic Athens, who may have worked within a single workshop but who were certainly aware of and influenced by each others' work.[29] These painters were not only innovators in their early use of the red-figure technique of decoration, but also in their developing new methods of representing the human body, to include complex physical poses and movement.[30]

As well as their technical originality, the Pioneer Group are also characterized by their engagement with the playfulness and the politics of the symposium, and with their interest in the public persona of the artist. This latter characteristic manifests itself most clearly in the signing of vases, in which pot painters explicitly claimed their work as their own. For example, this particular amphora was signed by Euthymides between the figures of Priam and Hector: ΕΥΘΥΜΙΔΕΣ ΕΓΡΑΦΣΕΝ ΗΟ ΠΟΛΙΟ ('Euthymides the son of Pollio painted this'). While some used their own names in these signatures, in other cases pseudonyms may have been used, creating fictive artistic personae not unlike the modern graffiti artist 'Banksy'.[31] Bringing together image and text, in some scenes figures were also labelled with the names of known potters from the Group, resulting in a set of scenes known as the 'potter portraits'.[32] Overall, these were pot painters who were crucially interested in their own identities as the painters of pots.[33]

This interest is evident on Euthymides' amphora. As well as the signature on the Hector scene, on the opposite side of the pot another inscription runs along the left-hand frame, claiming: ΗΟΣ ΟΥΔΕΠΟΤΕ ΕΥΦΡΟΝΙΟΣ ('as never Euphronios' or 'Euphronios never did *this*'). The two authorial inscriptions on this pot are often understood as a proud boast about technical prowess – Euthymides is taunting a rival, claiming that Euphronios never painted anything as accomplished as the scenes on this amphora.[34] This is certainly one possibility, and it would indicate that a traditionally humble (and definitely

[29] For the Pioneers, see Boardman 1975, 29–36, Robertson 1992, 136, and Neer 2002, 51–134.
[30] This is often discussed in terms of emerging 'naturalism'. For critical discussion, see Elsner 2010 and Neer 2002, 27–86. For 'naturalism' in Euthymides, see Stewart 2008, 606.
[31] For example, Smikros may have been an alter-ego of Euphronios (Hedreen 2016, 22–58).
[32] For these 'potter portraits', see: Neer 2002, 87–134, Topper 2012, 147–53, and Hedreen 2016, 233–79.
[33] To paraphrase Hedreen 2016, 179.
[34] Hedreen 2016, 40 outlines this argument, with especially n.56–7 with references.

non-aristocratic) profession had become an arena for status competition. This would also suggest that the agonistic ethic, previously focused on elite activities such as athletics, had spread to craftsmanship; and that art had become a valid way to make both fortunes and reputations. Such a reading would sit comfortably with the new political rhetoric of social mobility and with other evidence for the status of craftspeople, especially potters at this time.

Another interpretation sees the Euphronios inscription as linked directly to the particular scene in which it features – the revellers scene, especially the figure of the komarch next to which it appears. This would imply that Euthymides was teasing his colleague, suggesting that Euphronios never got drunk like these men, and never led komastic revels like the figure on the right. This would not, as we might assume, have been a comment on Euphronios' sobriety, but rather on his social status. It is relevant here that the 'potter portraits' mentioned above often occur in the context of symposium scenes. The explicit depiction of craftspeople taking part in activities that were traditionally associated with aristocratic men is remarkable. If the scenes reflect social reality, then the implications are significant. In this case, the 'Euphronios never did *this*' inscription would be a sneer that Euphronios' wealth and status was not yet sufficient for him to be a successful komarch. If the scenes do not reflect social reality, then they might potentially have been risqué – challenging traditional social structures and hierarchies.

A third and perhaps more likely approach argues that the scenes are designed to be satirical and humorous, and that the depictions of artists on sympotic pottery are a means of constructing comedic public personae, in much the same way as iambic poets did through sympotic poetry.[35] Perhaps it was never in question whether Euphronios would have led the revels at a traditional aristocratic symposium – the idea would have been ridiculous to the point of being humorous.[36] Yet this interpretation also implies a heightened social standing for potters. It assumes that potters were well known enough amongst the aristocratic guests of a symposium for them to have a recognized public persona in the first place. This would raise the

[35] Hedreen 2009.
[36] Topper 2012, 147–53. This interpretation, however, depends on the acknowledgement that the symposium did indeed have aristocratic associations; see p.44 n.8 above.

status of pot painters on par with those of poets, implying that their artistic endeavours were comparable.

Whichever way we interpret the inscriptions on the amphora, they complement the figural scenes. Like the images, these texts play into a wider and ongoing joke about artists and aristocrats, status and social change. Although Euthymides' amphora is not an artefact forged out of a firebrand social radicalism, it did engage with the political discourse of the day.

Troy, the *Iliad*, and the Pioneer Group

Euthymides' choice of a Trojan, but not specifically an Iliadic, image also plays into this dynamic. While Trojan themes can be found in Attic pottery from across the archaic period, in the final years of the sixth century there is a notable increase in the number of specifically Iliadic scenes.[37] The shift can be seen especially clearly in the work of the pot painter Oltos. Oltos was a slightly older contemporary of the Pioneer Group, who is best known for his 'bilingual' pots, which brought together black-and-red figure techniques.[38] Despite painting a broad range of Trojan scenes in his earlier works, Oltos begins to show a preference for recognizably Iliadic images in the closing years of the century: for example, explicitly pairing Achilles with Briseis; or depicting Priam's supplication of Achilles for the ransom of Hector's body.[39] A slightly younger contemporary of the Pioneer Group, the Kleophrades Painter is also known for his interest in Iliadic imagery,[40] including, for example, his portrayal of the exchange of armour between Diomedes and Glaucus.[41]

Overlapping with both Oltos and the Kleophrades Painter, the Pioneer Group seem to have shared little of either's enthusiasm for either the story of the Trojan War or the text of the *Iliad*. Of the 227 vases attributed to the Pioneer

---

[37] In contrast, specifically Iliadic scenes appear earlier in the sixth century in Corinthian pottery: Friis Johansen 1967, 224–26 and Brilliante 1983, 113–15. Boardman 1975, 230–31 identifies a 'boom' in Iliadic scenes in Attic pottery at the turn of the sixth to the fifth centuries, largely due to the Kleophrades Painter's apparent interest in the poem.

[38] Böhr 2006.

[39] Friis Johansen 1967, 226 and Schefold 1992, 217. Achilles and Briseis: London, British Museum E258; Beazley no. 200436; CAVI no.4541. Priam's supplication of Achilles: Munich, Staatliche Antikensammlungen 2618; Beazley no. 200510; CAVI no. 5318.

[40] Boardman 1976.

[41] Boardman 1976, 15–19; New York, Metropolitan Museum of Art 08.258.58; Beazley no. 201688; CAVI no. 5585.

Group by the Beazley archive,[42] only 18 depict scenes from the Trojan cycle.[43] Trojan images therefore account for only a measly 7.9 per cent of all Pioneer Group pots – surprisingly few, given the increasing popularity of Trojan themes amongst their contemporaries.[44] Furthermore, none of the scenes on these eighteen pots represent identifiable episodes from the *Iliad* (Figure 2.3). Instead, most portray events that occurred outside the temporal remit of the poem. Six show scenes from before the war including Peleus, Thetis, and the Judgement of Paris; five show scenes from after the death of Hector including Memnon, Troilus, and the death of Achilles.

Only seven vases depict either generic episodes or events that occur within Iliadic time. None of these, however, conform to a specifically Iliadic view. Two scenes combine characters that do not appear together in the poem – Diomedes and Patroclus on one; and Ajax, Achilles, Phoinix, Thetis, and Odysseus on the other. The remaining five seem to be 'peri-Iliadic', in that they suggest knowledge of the poem, while at the same time deviating from its details. We have already discussed this in the context of the Euthymides amphora, but we can see a similar play on Iliadic expectations on a krater signed by Euthymides' erstwhile rival, Euphronios.[45] The scene depicted here shows the body of Sarpedon being gently lifted by Sleep and Death, in

[42] This number includes all red-figure vases attributed in the Beazley archive to: Euthymides, Euphronios, Phintias, Sosias, Smikros, the Dikaios Painter, the Gales Painter, the Pezzino Group, the Pythokles Painter, or generically to the Pioneer Group. The membership of the Pioneer Group is debated (see n.29 above). I have conservatively followed Beazley's list for inclusion (Beazley 1963), which is broadly similar to those of Boardman (1975, 29–36) and Neer (2002). Other individuals who are sometimes included within the group include: the Andokides Painter, Oltos, Psiax, and Epiktetos, but these seem to have been slightly earlier or older contemporaries who did not engage with the Pioneer Group's sympotic or political play (Beazley 1963; Boardman 1975, 15–29, 56–62; Neer 2002, 205); as well as Douris, Kleophrades, the Kleophrades Painter, the Berlin Painter, and the Foundry Painter (Neer 2002, 56, 65, 77–85), all of whom may have overlapped with and even began their careers in the Pioneer Group workshops, but whose work is generally slightly later and therefore belongs to a different political context.

[43] The most common type of scene depicted, perhaps unsurprisingly, is that of the symposium (forty-eight pots), followed by Dionysiac scenes (forty-one pots). Generic images of warriors (thirty-three pots) and athletes (twenty-one pots) also appear, as do a range of scenes from what may be termed 'daily life' (nineteen pots). Amongst religious and mythic subjects, there are roughly equal numbers of pots depicting scenes of the gods with no identifiable mythic narrative (twenty pots), pots with scenes of the labours of Hercules (nineteen pots), and pots with scenes from the Trojan War (eighteen pots). Smaller numbers of pots have scenes of Theseus (six pots), and a range of other identifiable myths also appear (on nineteen pots). Many of the vessels, however, are fragmentary and the scenes cannot be identified (thirty pots). In these counts, I have counted pots in more than one category when they depict more than one type of scene – for example, a pot with a Heracles scene on one side and a symposium scene on the other has counted towards both categories.

[44] By the early fifth century, images of Trojan scenes were extremely popular: Boardman 1976, 3.

[45] Rome, Villa Giulia L.2006.10 (previously New York, Metropolitan Museum); Beazley no. 187; CAVI no. 5724.

Figure 2.3 Table of Pioneer Group vases depicting scenes from the Trojan War myth.

Collection	CAVI no.	Beazley no.	Attributed to	Shape	Trojan War scene	Other scene(s)
Munich, Antikensammlungen J378	5258	200160	Euthymides	Amphora	Hector arming, flanked by Priam and Hecuba	Three drunken symposiasts
Boston 1900.335	2685	200178	Euthymides	Plate	Thetis and dolphins	n/a
New York 1981.11.9	5731	9988	Euthymides	Oinochoe	The judgement of Paris	n/a
Berlin, Antikensammlung F2278	2324	200108	Euthymides or Sosias	Cup	Int: Achilles tends wounded Patroclus	Ext: Introduction of Hercules to Olympus
Rome, Villa Giulia L.2006.10	5724	187	Euphronios	Krater	The body of Sarpedon being carried away by Sleep and Death	Warriors arming
Palermo 674	n/a	3440	Euphronios	Lekythos	Achilles pursuing Troilus	n/a
Rome, Villa Giulia	3345	7043	Euphronios	Cup	The body of Sarpedon being carried away by Sleep and Death	Pyrric dance, youths and woman
Malibu, Getty Museum 77.AE.20	n/a	7045	Euphronios	Cup fragments	Ajax and Achilles, Phoinix and Thetis, Odysseus	Warriors harnessing a chariot
Rome, Villa Giulia	n/a	29570	Euphronios	Krater fragments	Ajax carrying the body of Achilles	n/a
Leipzig, Antikenmuseum T523	4155	200070	Euphronios	Stamnos fragments	Peleus and Thetis	Athletes and pipe-player
Athens, Acropolis 15214	1281	200081	Euphronios	Cup fragments	Wedding of Peleus and Thetis	n/a
St Petersburg, Hermitage 1843	7395	200122	Phintias	Krater fragments	Diomedes and Patroclus	Theseus

Figure 2.3 (*Continued*)

Thasos	4216	200123	Phintias	Krater fragments	Achilles and Memnon	n/a
Berlin, Antikensammlung F2318	2355	200212	Pythokles painter	Skyphos	Eos with body of Memnon	Hercules and Apollo struggle for the tripod
London, British Museum E438	4591	200104	Smikros	Stamnos	Athena between Ajax and Hector	Warriors fighting over fallen warrior
St Petersburg, Hermitage B1574	n/a	200105	Smikros	Pelike	Peleus and Thetis	Athletes
Paris, Louvre CP709	6430	200106	Smikros	Pelike	Peleus and Thetis	Warriors fighting
Malibu, Getty Museum 76.AE.108.10	n/a	3735	Pezzino Group	Krater	Ethiopians with the body of Memnon	n/a

a fashion that recalls the description of *Iliad* 16.676–83. Euphronios' scene deviates from the *Iliad* however: on the vase it is Hermes overseeing the scene, rather than Apollo; and on the vase Sarpedon's body is still clothed, whereas in the poem he has already been despoiled.[46] The almost-but-not-quite Iliadic nature of this scene is even more remarkable when compared with an earlier pot, also painted by Euphronios and treating the same theme. In this earlier pot, the Iliadic resonances are fewer, implying a deliberate choice to introduce allusions to the poem in the later pot whilst still retaining some overtly non-Iliadic details.[47] A similar peri-Iliadic image appears on a stamnos signed by Smikros.[48] On this stamnos, Athena is stepping in to halt the duel between Hector and Ajax – a role that is taken by the herald Idaeus in the *Iliad* (7.206–82). Our final peri-Iliadic scene comes from the tondo of a cup by Sosias.[49] In this scene, Achilles carefully tends to Patroclus' wounds, demonstrating an intimacy and tenderness that is reminiscent of the Iliadic portrait of their relationship. And yet, such a scene does not itself appear in the *Iliad*.[50]

How can we account for this apparent disinterest in depicting the Trojan War, and the more specific avoidance of Iliadic scenes? The rarity of Iliadic scenes on earlier archaic pottery has already been the subject of some scholarly discussion, with explanations ranging from ignorance of Homeric epic to deliberate disregard for it. It has recently been argued, however, that archaic pot painters did not choose to portray Homeric scenes because the Homeric epics were concerned with individual heroes and the experience of the individual, whereas archaic pot painters were more concerned with the broader condition of being human.[51] With the Pioneers working at the end of the archaic period, a similar process may be at work. A likely contributing factor is the Pioneers' thematic interests in politics, artistry, and sympotic play. The few Trojan scenes that do appear on Pioneer Group pottery are remarkable for their sobriety, paired most often with images of warriors or athletes (Figure 2.3). In contrast, their scenes of Hercules often appear alongside sympotic or Dionysiac images, and a larger number feature erotic *kalos* inscriptions.[52] Perhaps it was simply

---

[46] von Bothmer 1981, 68–69.
[47] Shapiro 1994, 22–24 highlights how the later of these two scenes is more Iliadic.
[48] British Museum E438; Beazley no. 200104; CAVI no. 4591.
[49] Berlin Antikensammlung F2278; Beazley no. 200108; CAVI no. 2324.
[50] Schefold 1992, 224–25 and Junker 2005, 1–18.
[51] Osborne forthcoming, with references for the previous debate on the topic.
[52] For *kalos* inscriptions on Pioneer Group vases, see Hoppin 1917, 171–73.

not appropriate to make ribald and erotic jokes in the context of a Trojan theme, even for the irreverent Pioneers. It may have been still less appropriate to play games with an Iliadic scene, given that the *Iliad* was associated with formal public ritual.

At this point, it is worth returning once more to the amphora of Euthymides. This vase is the sole example from the Pioneers' oeuvre that couples a Trojan War image with one that is explicitly sympotic. In this context, the peri-Iliadic nature of the scene is significant. While an overtly Iliadic image may not have lent itself to Euthymides' playful challenging of social roles, the almost-but-not-quite Iliadic resonances of the scene would have served to heighten the social commentary.

Despite their reticence to engage in explicitly Iliadic art, the Pioneers were certainly Homeric in one sense – their self-referential interest in their own artistry.[53] As we have seen in Chapter 1 of this book, one notable feature of Homeric poetry is a focus on metapoetics, the status of poetry, and the art of the poet. Euthymides and his colleagues, while they may have eschewed the Homeric in their imagery, were nonetheless Homeric in their practice, as crucially focused on meta-artistry, the status of pot painting, and the art of the pot painter.

Jan: Rossetti's vulnerable firebrand

Why should I blame her that she filled my days
With misery, or that she would of late
Have taught to ignorant men most violent ways,
Or hurled the little streets upon the great,
Had they but courage equal to desire?
What could have made her peaceful with a mind
That nobleness made simple as a fire,
With beauty like a tightened bow, a kind
That is not natural in an age like this,
Being high and solitary and most stern?

---

[53] See Squire and Platt 2017, 60–61 for Euthymides' visual games with the frame on this vessel as a meta-artistic comment on his own craft.

Why, what could she have done, being what she is?
Was there another Troy for her to burn?

W. B. Yeats, *No Second Troy* (1910)

The second section of this chapter focuses on a different image of a different Iliadic character from a different time: Dante Gabriel Rossetti's painting of Helen of Troy from 1863. Rossetti, like Euthymides, can be seen to engage in a kind of 'peri-Iliadic' aesthetics, making reference to the Homeric Helen but also adding contemporary layers of meaning. Like Euthymides, Rossetti made use of visual ambiguities to subvert received ideas about social roles, this time focusing on questions of femininity and power, rather than masculinity and status. I have opened this section with W. B. Yeats' 'No Second Troy', a poem that ponders the elusive qualities of Helen (though the poem's 'she' is never named), and uses Helen as a prism through which to explore Yeats' own feelings for the Irish republican campaigner Maud Gonne.[54] Yeats' poem is apt because it introduces some of the key issues that will emerge from Rossetti's painting: Helen's long-standing reputation as a great beauty, her role in precipitating the Trojan War, and the issue of her agency.

A deep and close engagement with the ancient Greek world can be found across a range of cultural outputs in eighteenth- and nineteenth-century Britain,[55] including of course the visual arts.[56] In this area, there appears to have been a particular interest in the figure of Helen. As will be discussed later in this section, a number of nineteenth-century painters engaged with Helen's mythology, adducing the mythical queen in order to comment variously on female sensuality, victimhood, and destructive power. From Moreau and his *Helen on the Ramparts* (*c.* 1880) to Leighton's *Helen of Troy* (1865), the Spartan queen beguiled artists working in various artistic movements. Of primary concern in the discussion that follows, however, is the *Helen of Troy* (1863) created by Dante Gabriel Rossetti, a major figure in the Pre-Raphaelite

---

[54] Maguire 2009, 136–37 explores the poem's connections with earlier Helen narratives and Yeats' own personal-political life; cf. also McKinsey 2002.
[55] Scholarship on cultural and political philhellenism in the Anglophone world in the eighteenth and nineteenth centuries is truly vast. See, for example, Turner 1981, Jenkyns 1980, Goldhill 2011, 1–23, and Richardson 2013. On the classics in nineteenth-century British education, see Stray 1998; and, for the wider cultural impact of the classics, see Stray 2007.
[56] See especially Wood 1983; cf. further discussion below.

movement,[57] which he founded in 1848, together with William Holman Hunt and John Everett Millais.[58]

In the discussion that follows, I begin with an examination of Rossetti's characterization of Helen as a passion-inducing liminal and destructive force – a figure with ambiguous responsibility for the horrors of the Trojan War. The analysis then moves on to consider wider developments in British art during the 1860s, focusing on other depictions of the Spartan queen. It will be argued that the dominant portrayal of Helen at this time related to a broader interest with dangerous and subversive women, which itself must be considered in the historical context of emerging women's movements and rapidly changing social roles. Finally, I will show that while Rossetti's Helen conforms in some respects to the dominant view of Helen at the time, it also challenges them, subverting the idea that Helen's power lay solely in her physical desirability. This, it will be argued, is where Rossetti's Helen is distinctively Iliadic. By offering Helen agency and a voice, Rossetti was questioning expectations of female social roles in contemporary society.

Dangerous desirability

The lavish depiction of Fanny Cornforth in the 1859 painting *Bocca Baciata* signifies an important turning point in the career of Dante Gabriel Rossetti.[59] As Spencer-Longhurst observes, the painting prefigures the single figure format that would dominate Rossetti's work in the 1860s – a point that Rossetti himself, albeit implicitly, privately acknowledged.[60] Alongside its study of a

---

[57] On Rossetti, see principally Prettejohn 1998, McGann 2000, Bullen 2011, and Donnelly 2015. For the different phases of the Pre-Raphaelite Brotherhood, see Wood 2000; on their *raison d'être*, see McGann 2000, 106.

[58] Surtees 1971, 92 and Bullen 2011, 158–59.

[59] Wood 1999, 146–50 offers a cogent, though somewhat misguided, overview of Rossetti's eccentric later years following the death of his wife Elizabeth Siddal in 1862 (Wood refers to, for instance, 'the vulgar and grasping Fanny Cornforth'). On the growing body of scholarship on Rossetti's work, see Prettejohn 2012, 109.

[60] Pollock 1988, 131, Paglia 1990, 491, Spencer-Longhurst 2000, 20–21, 36, Wood 1999, 105, 146–47, McGann 2000, xvi, and cf. Prettejohn 2012, 109, noting the potential rift this created with Rossetti's original intentions for the Pre-Raphaelites in the 1840s. For commentary on *Bocca Baciata* and further bibliography, see the online entry in *The Rossetti Archive* (<http://www.rossettiarchive.org/docs/s114.rap.html>). For Rossetti's implicit awareness of this artistic evolution, note the following correspondence to the poet William Bell Scott: 'I have made an effort to avoid what I know to be a besetting fault of mine – & indeed rather common to PR painting – that of stipple in the flesh', Rossetti 5 September 1859, in Fredeman 2003, 276.

single female figure,[61] another striking feature of this painting is Rossetti's inclusion of a Boccacian couplet on the reverse side: 'Bocca baciata non perda ventura, anzi rinnova come fa la luna' (The kissed mouth does not lose its freshness, but renews itself like the moon). Rossetti's intensive focus on a single eroticized figure, coupled with the inclusion of a short, yet evocative,

Figure 2.4 Dante Gabriel Rossetti, *Helen of Troy* (Hamburg, Kunsthalle Inv. 2469).

---

[61] Sonstroem 1970 explores Rossetti's recourse to different types of women throughout his career, including the *femme fatale* and victimized woman – tropes that are important for our reading of his *Helen of Troy*.

poetic fragment in effect encourages the viewer to explore the confluences between image and text.[62]

Such an approach recurs just a few years later in Rossetti's 1863 oil painting *Helen of Troy* (Figure 2.4).[63] This portrait depicts the model Annie Miller (whom Rossetti also painted in a separate watercolour in 1863, *Woman in Yellow*),[64] as Helen, looking skewwhiff towards the direction of the viewer, though failing to meet the viewer's eye. Meanwhile, a conflagration rages in the rear – a potent representation of the newly ransacked city of Troy. She is portrayed in aurulent shades, swathed in a luxurious, richly ornamented robe,[65] while clutching a beaded necklace with a central locket that depicts a flaming torch, and possessing bounteous amounts of undulating golden hair (the Homeric poems repeatedly refer to Helen's 'lovely hair'; e.g., *Il.* 3.329; 9.339; 13.766; *Od.* 15.58; 15.123).[66] It is a painting that undoubtedly attempts to encapsulate Helen's Marlowian status as 'the face that launched a thousand ships',[67] even if some commentators and critics have been less than impressed by Rossetti's Hel(l)enic beauty.[68] This golden Helen, nevertheless, was clearly imagined as being desirable.

As much as Rossetti focuses on Helen's desirability, this is no straightforwardly laudatory image. Indeed, there are various elements of the painting that point critically to the queen of Sparta as a destructive, culpable

[62] Donnelly 2015, 3–12; cf. Spencer-Longhurst 2000, 26, who notes the preponderance of Rossetti paintings that include verses etched into their frames; McGann 2000, xviii and Cruise 2012, 56.

[63] Although Rossetti is known principally for his engagement with Dante, Arthurian legend, and pre-Renaissance Italian art, it is clear that he had some literary interests in the classical world; see further Donnelly 2015, 6.

[64] As Marillier 1899, 131 notes, *Woman in Yellow* is an effective study in the varied tones of yellow, and indubitably speaks to the colour palette of *Helen of Troy*. On Annie Miller, see further Marsh 2001, 374–75; cf. Spencer-Longhurst 2000, 21–26 on Annie Miller and Rossetti's other chief models.

[65] Cf. *Od.* 15.107-08, where Helen presents Telemachus with a garment that 'was most beautiful and biggest in its patterning, | shining like a star'; cf. *Il.* 6. 294–95. In Greek mythology, Aphrodite is the most lavishly adorned, and is frequently associated with gold and luminosity; see further Blondell 2013, 7–10.

[66] Note too Rossetti's later poem 'Troy Town', which also refers to Helen's 'golden head' (96). Prettejohn 1997, 24 observes that Helen's bountiful strands of hair constitutes one of the more generic features of Rossetti's (and his followers') art.

[67] Maguire 2009, 160 comments on the cultural inescapability of this Marlowian aphorism. Indeed, Marlowe's line surely influenced Rossetti, especially given that it is followed by a reference to the burnt 'topless towers of Ilium'. On Rossetti's pointed interest in 'the spirit of the eyes', see Armstrong 2012, 24–25.

[68] Marillier 1899, 130: 'there is little to suggest that "daughter of the gods divinely tall and most divinely fair"'; Waugh 1928, 133: 'a negligible little oil painting', 136: '[the model's hair in *Venus Verticordia*], like an ill fitting and inexpensive wig, is arranged like *Helen of Troy*'s'; *contra* Swinburne 1875, 99, Rossetti 1889, 41, and Spencer-Longhurst 2000, 42: 'Rossetti's paragon of female allure'; Moyle 2009, 238: 'ravishing portrait'.

force. First, although Helen sits poised, her vacuous and indirect stare fails to meet the audience's eye; the resulting figure is a contemplative individual, ostensibly unaware of the viewer, immersed in her own interior life.[69] This self-reflexivity reinforces the notion of a singular Helen, who, unlike her adoptive Trojan kinsmen, is physically unscathed by the tragic events at Troy (as exemplified by her highly refined attire). As the analysis below demonstrates, this is in keeping with other broadly contemporary depictions of Helen, which combine to suggest univocally a selfish figure, unperturbed by the extreme repercussions of her actions. Moreover, Rossetti's depiction of her inattentiveness distances Helen from the viewer, who gazes not only on her face but also on precisely these repercussions in the form of the conflagration behind her. Indeed, while Helen stares absent-mindedly, a city scorches behind, swept up in a surge of flames (the very same Troy that burns in the Yeatsian poem that opened this section).[70] The ascription of Troy is unmistakable in this instance, not only because of Helen's long-standing connections with the city, but also because of Rossetti's own correspondence with his mother, in which he wrote:

Dear Mamma,
Would you give Baker the photograph of 'Old Cairo'[71] which hangs in your parlour; and, if there are any stereoscopic pictures, either in the instrument or elsewhere, which represent general views of cities, would you send them too, or anything of a fleet of ships? I want to use them in painting Troy at the back of my Helen, and will return them soon.

Rossetti c. February 1863, in Fredeman 2003, 39

Rossetti's letter makes it unquestionable that the city burning behind Helen is Troy, while dark-prowed ships sail away to the left and right of the queen. Her self-absorption in the face of a city's annihilation stresses her culpability (and even the outright cruelty of her actions!), but it also strengthens her status as an abstraction of beauty rather than her ontological reality. Her isolated stance

[69] Maguire 2009, 81 remarks on the plethora of paintings that depict Helen 'looking into the distance, abstractly, distantly', cf. 41–43.

[70] Cf. Rossetti's later poem 'Cassandra', which details Troy's terrible fate, and sings of how 'Troy glows'; see further McGann 2003, 188.

[71] It is interesting to note the orientalism implicit in using Cairo as a model for Troy. See Chapter 5 for a discussion of how notions of 'West' and 'East' have been projected onto the story of the Trojan War.

thus impresses upon the viewer the multiple, irreconcilable (and very Iliadic) themes of Helen's power, her passivity, her absence, and her agency.

In addition to these points, perhaps the clearest indication of Helen's culpability is Rossetti's inclusion of an Aeschylean phrase on the reverse of the painting, which labels Helen as a thoroughly destructive force. The text runs: '*Helen of Troy* ἑλέναυς, ἑλανδρος, ἑλέπτολις destroyer of ships, destroyer of men, destroyer of cities'.[72] This arresting line, which is a hybrid of ancient Greek and English, ultimately derives from the *Agamemnon*, wherein the Chorus sings of some invisible being (684) who created an utterly fitting name for Helen, since she proved indeed to be ἑλέναυς, ἑλανδρος, ἑλέπτολις – a play on the first syllable of her name, 'Hel'. Helen, the poet suggests, is a synecdoche for wholesale destruction.[73] In combination with these other ambivalences, Helen is characterized in a decidedly negative light; she is not the sympathetic, veiled Iliadic figure (*Il.* 3.419) who speaks warmly of the Trojan hero Hector at his funeral games in Book 24 of *Iliad*, but rather the individual that elsewhere in the *Iliad* describes herself as dog-faced (*Il.* 3.180; 4.145–6; cf. 6.354–55; *Od.* 4.145) and hateful (*Il.* 3.404).[74]

Contemporary critical responses to Rossetti's evocative portrait of Helen highlight this idea of dangerous desirability and subversive sexuality. Algernon Charles Swinburne, the essayist and friend of Rossetti's, wrote encomiastically:

> The picture of Helen, with Parian face and mouth of ardent blossom, a keen red flower-bud of fire, framed in broad gold of widespread locks, the sweet sharp smile of power set fast on her clear curved lips, and far behind her the dull flame of burning towers and light from reddened heaven on dark sails of lurid ships.[75]

Some of the qualities that run through the analysis above clearly resurface in Swinburne's rhapsody. He imagines Helen as a 'flower-bed of fire', but notes her 'sweet sharp smile of power' – the chiastic 'sweet sharp' neatly capturing Rossetti's double-edged portrait. And the 'dark sails of lurid ships' further

---

[72] Surtees 1971, 92. For the Aeschylean verse, see Aesch. *Ag.* 689–90.
[73] Bullen 2011, 214 comments on *Helen of Troy*, showing the queen as responsible for the 'downfall of a civilization'.
[74] On Helen and Homeric insults, see Graver 1995.
[75] Swinburne 1875, 99; cf. Spencer-Longhurst 2000, 42, who argues that the painting 'titillated the sado-masochistic fantasies of Swinburne'.

reinforce the sinister undertones of the narrative that proceeds 'far behind' the distant queen.

Rossetti's painting therefore invites us to censure Helen, blaming her for her callousness as well as her own dangerous desirability.[76] At the same time, however, the picture raises questions about how far Helen could really be held responsible for the destruction in the background. One key feature of the painting is the way that Helen points very clearly towards a pendant on her necklace bearing the image of a burning torch.[77] The ambiguities surrounding this firebrand are multiple. Perhaps most obviously, it is a reference to the numerous images of fire that recur throughout the *Iliad*. For instance, both Agamemnon's (*Il*. 1.104) and Hector's (*Il*. 12.466) eyes are compared to blazing fires; and the desire for war is compared to a boundless fire on the peak of a mountain (*Il*. 2.455–56). Even more significant is the use of fire as an ominous indicator of Troy's destruction, notably when Hector's death elicits terrible lamentations throughout the entire city of Troy, as though the city itself had fallen, 'and its towers were smouldering with fire' (πυρὶ σμύχοιτο κατ' ἄκρης, *Il*. 22.411). The firebrand pendant hanging around Helen's neck is therefore highly suggestive. She brings the seeds of Troy's destruction with her, and perhaps even embodies that destruction; Helen herself is the firebrand that sets the city alight.

But as much as Helen's signal towards the flame locket hints at the painting's connections with this kind of Homeric imagery, it nevertheless invites other reception contexts. Strikingly, as we will see in the next chapter in Euripides' *Troades* Helen describes her lover Paris as 'resembling a firebrand' (δαλοῦ πικρὸν μίμημ', *Tro*. 922) and explicitly blames him (along with various other mortal and immortal figures) for Troy's fall. The meaning of the pendant is therefore ambiguous: Is it Helen or Paris who is the firebrand, responsible for the fall of Troy? By pointing to this flame, Rossetti's Helen indicates a range of possible causes for Troy's ruin: her own status as a dangerous object of

---

[76] Bullen 2011, 159: 'the livid colour and frenetic brushwork ... combine to create simultaneously feelings of arousal and menace'.

[77] Perhaps this image was an inspiration for Yeats' later poem, quoted above, which asks: 'What could have made her peaceful with a mind | That nobleness made simple as a fire'. Another clear intertext here is the heroine (who is also named Helen!) of Anne Brontë's 1848 novel *The Tenant of Wildfell Hall*. In one memorable section, 'her fingers trembled with excitement, as she nervously entwined them in the hair-chain to which was appended her small gold watch – the only thing of value she had permitted herself to keep'. Note especially the reference to Helen's hair jewellery and her *gold* watch.

desire, the firebrand Paris, and the fire that drove key heroes on both sides of the conflict. As with her undirected gaze, Helen's flame locket establishes an ambiguity at the heart of the painting, at once suggesting her own responsibility for Troy's downfall, yet simultaneously evoking various other possibilities.

The painting's ambiguity is deepened further by Rossetti's possible decision to portray Helen as a victim of physical abuse.[78] Some critics have remarked on the sumptuous, even resplendent qualities of the painting, along with Helen's unmistakably compelling presence.[79] However, as Donnelly has observed, Rossetti also casts the right side of Helen's face in a shadow, and the viewer can clearly make out a purpled cheek.[80] While different readings will no doubt abound, it is possible to detect here the results of an altercation with her Trojan husband, Paris. Whether or not we accept that Helen is the victim of violence, the clearly contrasting sides of her face enable the viewer to reflect on the severe personal consequences of Helen's flight from Sparta, and in turn evoke the rich extra-Homeric mythological tradition on the abduction of Helen, who was seized not only by Paris but also by various other figures including Theseus and Deiphobus.[81]

As these points indicate, Rossetti's portrait of Helen is fundamentally ambiguous. She is certainly a subversive figure – a woman who is dangerously attractive, and whose desirability has devastating consequences. Yet Rossetti raises questions about how far she can be held to account. Some details in the painting suggest callousness and pride, while others simultaneously hint at Helen's possible status as a victim and indicate other causes of the conflict.

This ambiguous depiction of Helen draws from a range of sources. Helen's role in causing the war is explicit in the *Iliad*.[82] Indeed, when Helen appears on the ramparts of Troy in Book 3 of the poem, the assembled Trojans wonder at the combination of her beauty and her destructive potential, making it clear that her terrible power lies in her physical attractiveness (*Il.* 3.156–60). But

---

[78] Donnelly 2015, 10 with n.25.
[79] So especially Swinburne 1875, 99 and Spencer-Longhurst 2000, 42.
[80] Donnelly 2015, 11, noting the degeneration 'on the face of a beautiful woman'.
[81] Edmunds 2015.
[82] References to Helen as the reason for the Trojan War in *Iliad*: 1.159-60; 3.126-28, 156-57; 4.173-74; 6.344-58; 7.350-51; 9.339; 19.325; 22.114-16; 24.762-74; *Odyssey*: 4.235-89; 11.438; 14.68-69; 17.118-19; 22.226-30; 23.218-21. For a deconstruction of Helen as the ultimate *causa belli*, see Herodotus *Histories* 1.1-5, in which Helen is one of a number of mythical women responsible for inter-continental conflict.

while Rossetti's painting reflects the Iliadic representation of Helen, the painting equally speaks to a wider nexus of Helen traditions.[83] The *Odyssey* is even more explicit than the *Iliad* in blaming Helen for the Trojan War (*Od.* 11.436–9),[84] and Rossetti's Helen is Odyssean in that she betrays little regard for her Trojan kin, as illustrated by her disinterest in the catastrophe that occurs in the rear of the painting. The sumptuousness of Helen's golden robe in this painting recalls Hecuba's criticisms in Euripides' *Troades*, too, where Helen is lambasted for her haughty behaviour (*Tro.* 1020–24) and her insatiable extravagances at Troy, in contrast to her modest life back at Sparta (*Tro.* 993–97; see further Chapter 3). Indeed, we have already discussed the image of the firebrand in a Euripidean context. Rossetti's Helen is also generally Homeric, insomuch that she is clearly positioned as directly involved in the Trojan conflict, *contra* the works of other ancient authors, such as Stesichorus and Herodotus, which remove the 'real' Helen from the scene of Troy (see Chapter 4). Furthermore, Helen's salient ambiguity suggests that Rossetti does not fail to recognize her acknowledged status elsewhere in the Trojan War tradition as a victim of the gods' machinations – most famously during the Judgement of Paris. It is clear, then, that in this visual meditation on Helen, her dangerous desirability and ambiguous culpability, Rossetti drew on a range of works both ancient and post-antique.[85]

The Pre-Raphaelite Helen

In the *Helen of Troy*, Rossetti portrayed Helen as a dangerous and subversive individual, destructive through her desirability and beauty, but at the same time of questionable responsibility for the terrible events at Troy. This depiction of Helen is one that can be found more widely, both in Rossetti's other works and in those of his contemporaries.

A trochaic ballad entitled 'Troy Town', published in Rossetti's 1870 collection *Poems*, highlights once more the connected issues of Helen's desirability and her destructive capabilities.[86] The poem concerns an episode before Helen's

---

[83] For a comprehensive survey of Helen in Greek myth, see Edmunds 2015. Suzuki 1989, 12–17 gives a clear and concise overview of the different metamorphoses of Helen in ancient literature.

[84] Blondell 2013, 87–88 and cf. Suzuki 1989, 67.

[85] Blondell 2013, 71 cautions against a too-rigid focus on Helen's status as a victim of divine coercion in *Iliad*, especially given Helen's (self-acknowledged) role in the conflict.

[86] References to the poem are taken from McGann 2003, 41–43; for commentary, 379. There are good discussions of the poem in Howard 1972, 139–43 and Wasko 1987.

sojourn to Troy, namely her offering of a cup in the shape of her breast in the temple of Venus.[87] It constitutes fourteen stanzas, each one split with two parenthetical refrains – the first '("O Troy Town!")' in the second line and the second '("O Troy's down | Tall Troy's on fire!")' at the close of each stanza. While the poem sings of 'heavenborn' (1) Helen's 'heavenly' breasts (3), which are apple sweet (43),[88] and repeatedly refers to 'the heart's desire', the equally insistent repetition of the split refrain paints a sharp contrast with Helen's whimsical and successful appeal to Venus, who permits Cupid to strike his bow towards Paris (78–89). As Wasko notes, the repeated call to Troy's destruction – 'Tall Troy's on fire!' –reinforces palpably the destructive qualities of Helen's erotic power.[89] And yet, just as the poem advocates the idea of Helen as a danger to men, it instantaneously reflects the limitations of Helen as a mortal agent.[90] Although it is Helen who seeks out Venus, it is ultimately the love goddess and her companion Cupid who set in motion the ill-fated union between Helen and Paris ('Cupid took another dart … Drew the string and said, Depart!"', 85, 89).[91] Like the *Iliad* and *Odyssey*, the poem offers a composite mixture of motivations and causes behind Helen and Paris' union, rather than establishing a monolithic rendering of Helen as either dangerous vixen or passive victim. Ambiguity is key here, just as for Rossetti's painted Helen.

The same essential elements can also be seen in depictions of Helen by other artists of the time. The 1860s seem to have been a decade where the figure of Helen was particularly popular in British visual art. Only two years after Rossetti's painting, Frederic Leighton's 1865 painting of Helen presents her as an anguished and solitary figure, shunned by two Trojan women on the ramparts of Troy. By portraying her in the same frame as separate from

---

[87] For this tradition, which does not occur in Homer, see Maguire 2009, 126–27. The poem is also accompanied by a picture, *Troy Town*, which depicts Helen offering a cup moulded like her breasts to the goddess, whilst Venus and Cupid look at Helen from behind a curtain; see further <http://www. rossettiarchive.org/docs/s219.rap.html>. It is possible that the poet Robert Browning proposed the subject to Rossetti; cf. Surtees 1971, 123.

[88] On the Adamic associations in the poem, see Howard 1972, 142.

[89] Wasko 1987, 336 and cf. already Waugh 1928, 157, noting the 'hypnotic effect' of the refrain. On the poem's ominous attitude towards female sexuality and its connections with other Rossettian poems, such as 'Eden Bower', see Howard 1972, 142 Wasko 1987, *passim*, and Bullen 2011, 214.

[90] Howard 1972, 142–43.

[91] Cf. *Il.* 3.442-46.

other figures, Leighton highlights Helen's isolated, even cataleptic nature. Even more crucially, Helen is depicted as a passive subject – undertaking no activity herself, but serving as a feast for the eyes. Like Rossetti's Helen, she is swathed in rich gold cloth; but unlike Rossetti's Helen, this is combined with a glowing white shawl and an angelic white light, which de-emphasizes any taint of culpability.

Helen reappears just one year later in Frederick Sandys' 1866 wood engraving, *Helen and Cassandra*. Here the Trojan princess Cassandra lambasts a pouting Helen, who appears to take no responsibility for the vast conflagration that surges behind them. Once again, Helen is presented as passive. First, the picture presents her as being spoken *to*, rather than taking on any action herself. Secondly, she is clearly depicted in a sexualized and voyeuristic fashion. Sandys draws attention away from her face; he portrays Helen in almost comical fashion with her childlike, churlish frown. Instead, the diaphanous folds of her drapery draw attention to her sexual organs – her pubis, caught in a dark twist of her thin dress, and her breast, cupped and accentuated by the curve of her arm.

One year on again, in 1867, Sandys would return to the same mythological heroine in his painting *Helen of Troy*. In this image, Helen once again pulls a childish grimace, still apparently unperturbed by the consequences of her actions. Like Rossetti's earlier painting, the isolated queen is imagined with long and flowing hair (though Sandys' figure is more obviously flame haired than Rossetti's), pursed lips, and an elaborate necklace, whilst too turning from the viewer's gaze. Although Sandys *contra* Rossetti avoids any visual or verbal reference to the city of Troy, his Helen is nonetheless a morally questionable character, and he reinforces a number of the ideas explored in Rossetti's portrait: Helen's isolation, petulance, desirability, and potential culpability. Sandys' Helen is, nonetheless, more eroticized than Rossetti's – save for her necklace, she appears to be nude (although her body below her décolletage falls tantalizingly outside the frame of the painting).

These three examples from the mid-1860s exhibit a manifold fascination with Helen as a desirable and mostly passive female. Common to these portraits is an interest in the motif of Helen as beauty – a motif that dates back at least as far as Homer's *Iliad* (e.g. *Il*. 3.156–60; 9.139–40), although

Homer avoids referring to specific aspects of Helen's appearance.[92] This feeds into the overwhelming passivity of Helen; where Leighton's Helen is serenely passive for example, Sandys' is frustrated in her lack of agency. In general, Helen is presented as the passive object of the viewer's gaze, her power and her culpability dependent on her visual attractiveness and physical desirability. This trend was to intensify in depictions of Helen over the following decades – including the overtly sexualized images of Helen painted by Evelyn de Morgan (*Helen of Troy*: 1898) and Henri Fantin-Latour (*Helen*: 1892). Therefore, while the Pre-Raphaelite Helen of the 1860s might initially seem to be subversive, dangerous, and threatening, she had no real agency. Her power was bound up with her physical attractiveness and her desirability to others. In the vision of the 1860s, she was a passive object – of heroic desire, of the viewer's gaze, of Cassandra's insults – unable to undertake action in her own right.

The 1860s portrayal of Helen must also be seen in its wider context. In British visual art at this time, there was a broader interest in seductive and dangerous women, whose potent sexuality posed a social threat. For example, when Sandys painted his Helen, he did so as part of a series of pictures, in which he portrayed a range of other subversively sexual women such as Medea and Morgan Le Fey.[93] In all these cases, as with Helen, the sense of female power is inextricably linked to sexuality.

Furthermore, other Greek female mythical heroines became a notable feature of British art during the 1860s, with multiple representations of variously romanticized, torpid, vacant, and scantily clad female figures.[94] In Edward Poynter's 1869 painting *Andromeda*, for instance, the titular heroine is chained nude to the rocks while the sea rages violently in the rear. Serving as a sacrificial victim to the sea monster Cetus, Andromeda gazes downwards, failing to meet the viewer's eye, whilst her lower left leg is swaddled by an artfully floating piece of silken fabric.[95] Similarly, George Frederic Watts' *Thetis* depicts the naked goddess against an altogether more becalmed sea, lazily toying with her golden locks whilst too avoiding the gaze of the viewer.[96]

---

[92] See further Blondell 2013, 54–56.
[93] See Blondell 2013, 248 for the portrayals of Helen by Sandys, de Morgan, and others.
[94] Smith 1996, 117–21; cf. Wood 1999, 181.
[95] Wood 1983, 138–39 and 1999, 215.
[96] Wood 1983, 90 notes that Watts had been painting nudes as early the 1840s, and rightly comments on the way that his *Thetis* anticipates later nudes, such as Frederic Leighton's *Venus Disrobing* and Albert Moore's *A Venus*.

And finally, in *Venus Disrobing* by Frederic Leighton (*c.* 1867) – perhaps the single-most important proponent of the classical revival in Victorian art[97] – the exposed love goddess casts a furtive glance to the floor and leans her left arm downwards, modestly covering her genitalia.[98] In these three images, as in others from the period, there is an unmistakably voyeuristic tone, coupled with a fetishization of the idealized female form. These classical figures have been denuded both literally and metaphorically: not only are they denied raiment, but they are also largely divorced from their traditional narratives.[99] By refusing to focus on the traditional mythic storylines – for instance, Thetis' marriage to the hero Peleus or Andromeda's love affair with the demi-god Perseus – these paintings instead serve as blank canvases upon which the viewer is able to objectify the female figures depicted, and inscribe their own fantasies and ideals – a conscious rejection of the agency displayed by these mythic heroines in their traditional narrative contexts.

This interest in portraying women as powerful only through their sexuality also needs to be seen in its contemporary social context. The mid-nineteenth century was a time of rapid social change in Britain, with increasing urbanization and the forging of a new industrialized society with new social groupings and social norms. Gender roles were in flux at this time, and the 1850s and 1860s in particular saw the emergence of societies and associations across Britain that called for greater rights for women.[100] The 1860s were also a crucial decade for the suffragist movement. There was considerable campaigning in the lead-up to the 1867 Reform Bill, as well as unrest after it when women were excluded from the bill's terms.[101] Indeed, it can be no accident that this very same decade also produced John Stuart Mill's influential treatise 'The Subjection of Women'. Although it was written in 1861, Mill withheld its publication until 1869 when he felt that it would have more impact.[102] The insistence in the visual arts on

---

[97] For Leighton's classical influences, see the contributions of Asleson, Arscott, and Barrow in Barringer and Prettejohn 1999.

[98] For contemporary defences of Leighton's nude, see Wood 1999, 188.

[99] Wood 1999, 181 discusses the notable preference for 'contemplation or reflection of events, rather than the events themselves'.

[100] The bibliography on the changing roles of women and debates around women's rights in the nineteenth century is vast, and includes: Purvis 1995, Caine 1997, 88–130, Smith 1998, Gleadle and Richardson 2000 and Gleadle 2001.

[101] Smith 1998, 7–16.

[102] Caine 1978.

a romanticized, sexualized vision of women must have been in some senses a response to the real-life changes in women's social roles at precisely the same time.

Rossetti's subversive Helen

So far, we have examined the depiction of Helen in the work of Rossetti and his contemporaries, identifying commonalities in the representation of Helen as an ostensibly subversive figure – a dangerously desirable woman with questionable culpability for the destruction of Troy, but whose sole power lies in her role as a passive object of desire. In this final section of the analysis, I want to return to Rossetti's Helen and to highlight one aspect that is different from that of his peers. While Rossetti conforms to the prevailing view of Helen in many ways, in one important way he subverts it, offering a uniquely Iliadic layer to his portrayal of Helen.

In his painting, Rossetti engages with the idea of Helen as an idealized female beauty. He nonetheless eschews depicting her as a passive subject, devoid of agency, as she appears in contemporary portraits by other artists. On the contrary, Rossetti consciously explored the notion of Helen as a dangerous femme fatale,[103] giving her agency not just through her sexuality and desirability, but also by giving her a voice to tell (or in the case of the painting, to indicate) her own version of her story.

Helen's voice comes through most clearly in another of Rossetti's poems in his 1870 collection, the sonnet 'Death's Songsters'.[104] Here Rossetti recounts the moment when the Trojan horse is first presented to the Trojans, who remain dubious about its meaning. For this reason, Helen is sent to investigate and 'sing the songs of home'. Helen proceeds to try to dupe the Greeks, falsely singing 'Friends, I am alone; come, come!'. Although the ruse is not successful, the power of Helen's song is such that she enforces speechlessness on the men inside the wooden horse. We are told that Odysseus had to hold his hands over his men's mouths, and that he 'held them till the voice was dumb'. The story is of course derived from the *Odyssey*, where Menelaus relates to Telemachus that

---

[103] On Rossetti's women as precursors to the 'the endless *femmes fatales* of Art Nouveau', see Wood 1999, 149; cf. Spencer-Longhurst 2000, 42 and Bullen 2011, 158.
[104] McGann 2003, 165–66.

Helen had thrice circled the Trojan horse, misleading the leading chiefs of the Greeks into believing that they were being called by their wives – a deception that would not evade Odysseus (*Od.* 4.271–89).[105] As we have seen in Chapter 1, the portrayal of Helen as a pseudo-poet, engaged in the creation of song and the transmission of *kleos*, is a characteristic of the *Iliad*. Furthermore, the poem pits (the *Iliad's*) Helen against (the *Odyssey's*) Odysseus – a figure deeply connected with verbal wiles and the manipulation of words. 'Death's Songsters' ends with an enigmatic two lines, which might be addressed equally to Helen or to Odysseus: 'Say, soul, – are songs of Death no heaven to thee, | Nor shames her lip the cheek of Victory?'

Returning to his painting, the *Helen of Troy*, it seems that here too Rossetti may have given Helen agency, not just through her destructive beauty, but also in the form of narrative power. The conspicuous positioning of both her hands, with one pointing directly at the firebrand pendant, is a clear direction to the viewer: 'Look here! See this!' Helen is literally indicating what her own version of the story might be and signalling how she might begin to regale these tragic events.

Dante Gabriel Rossetti's conception of Helen is therefore a bold one. Although Rossetti was by no means one of the most prolific proponents of the classical revival during late nineteenth century,[106] it is clear that his painting draws out some of the ideas implicit in Homer's account of the Spartan queen, as well as other portrayals of Helen from classical antiquity. Like other artists of the period, and in keeping with his wider artistic agenda, Rossetti avoids depicting Helen as a classical nude – a notable contrast with the multiple nude representations of other mythical figures (especially Venus) in this period.[107] And yet, this does not attenuate the sense of desirability in his painting; the depiction of Helen with 'masses of long, wavy hair',[108] bedecked in rich fabrics and opulent necklace against a lush background lends a decidedly sensuous feel

---

[105] Cf. *Od.* 4.140, where Helen refers explicitly to her Muse-like ability to speak falsely or truthfully. On this scene, see especially Blondell 2013, 83–84.

[106] Wood 1983, 21: '[Rossetti] made little or no contribution to the classical movement, apart from a brief flirtation with classical subjects in the 1860s'.

[107] Shortly after *Helen of Troy*, Rossetti would paint his own nude Venus, *Venus Verticordia* (c. 1864–1868), for which he published a separate sonnet that sings of her Phrygian boy (i.e. Paris), thus connecting her to Helen of Troy; cf., Bullen 2011, 162. On other nude Venuses in this period, see Smith 1996, 117–34.

[108] Wood 1999, 147.

to the painting. This, compounded with Rossetti's visual and verbal references to Troy's destruction, and his explicit textual references to Helen's ruinous relationship with Troy, ultimately reveals in stark terms the degenerative effects of a powerful female beauty like that of Helen. Helen is therefore given power through her beauty – because of her looks, she has the power to destroy. Rossetti was of course not alone in this portrayal of Helen – there are many ancient antecedents for this as well as other examples from Rossetti's own day.

Where Rossetti's Helen differs most of all from these other Helens, who are subversive through their conformity to the model of female power lying in sexual attraction, is in her power of speech. In Rossetti's poetry, Helen's agency is manifested by her enactment of speech acts and her mastery of words and song – a mastery bested only by Odysseus. In Rossetti's painting, Helen's own version of her story is (literally) pointed out by Helen herself, with the clear gesture to the firebrand locket. Perhaps also significant is what lies at the physical as well as conceptual centre of Rossetti's golden image. Surrounded first by the rich gold of her hair and robe and then more immediately by the sallow paleness of her skin, the viewer's eye is inevitably drawn to Helen's blood-red lips – a bright and lurid splash of vibrant active colour against a passive background. Helen's lip, her mouth, her voice, all remain unshamed by the songs of Death.

3

Staging Conflict

This chapter focuses on another key theme within both the *Iliad* itself and the broader Trojan War tradition: conflict. The *Iliad* explores conflict in many different forms and at many different levels, not only between the Achaeans and the Trojans, but also within communities, and even within the individual psyche. The texts discussed in this chapter are drawn from drama, a medium that has proved fertile ground over the centuries for the Trojan War tradition.[1]

In the first section, Jan considers Euripides' *Troades* (Trojan Women). He examines the play's focus on the speech of its predominantly female characters. The discussion pivots on Cassandra's reflections on the war's true victors, as well as on the famous ἀγών (debate) between Hecuba and Helen. It emphasizes that Euripides' drama has to be read in its late fifth-century context, at a time of considerable intra-Hellenic strife, as well as factionalism and *stasis* within Athens. In the second section, Naoíse examines *Troilus and Cressida*, thought to be one of Shakespeare's more problematic plays. Like the *Troades*, this play dramatizes debate and discussion, depicting a Trojan War where the key battles are fought with words. The staging of verbal conflict in this way may have owed to Euripidean examples, but equally could have emerged from a new engagement with the *Iliad* around the time that the *Troilus and Cressida* was composed. More than any precursor or pattern, however, it must owe to the particular political circumstances of the time, involving unrest and factionalism in the final years of Elizabeth's reign.

In both of these plays, the inherently physical medium of drama is used to explore the significance of verbal, rather than corporeal, conflict. As 'speech

---

[1] For Homer on the ancient and modern stage, see the various contributions in Part VII of Efstathiou and Karamanou 2016.

acts' themselves, the debates staged in both the *Troades* and the *Troilus* are concerned with the efficacy and reliability of other speech acts. Despite showcasing set-piece debates, however, these plays undermine the status of discussion and the trust placed in words. The victory of reason proves to be empty; promises made in earnest are broken; and reports turn out to be lies. Words, it emerges, are dangerous things, and can cause death and destruction just as surely as the point of a sword. This is true, not only of the *Troades* and the *Troilus*, but also of the *Iliad* itself. Perhaps we should not be so surprised to find wordsmiths such as Euripides and Shakespeare engaging in an Iliadic meditation both on the power of their own art and on the limits of that power.

The pairing of the *Troades* and the *Troilus* offers an opposite view from that of the previous chapter. Once more, we present one close reading from a context where the Homeric poems were unquestionably at the heart of the wider Trojan War tradition; and one from a context where the *Iliad* was known, but where it did not dominate perceptions and understandings of the tradition. In contrast to Chapter 2, however, it is the ancient Greek case which corresponds to the former, and the post-antique case that falls into the latter category. The engagement of each of these texts with the *Iliad* is therefore conditioned by the status of and knowledge available about the Homeric poems at the time.

Jan: Euripides' new contests

The surviving corpus of Euripides' works indicates a deep-seated engagement with the Trojan War. Although many of his plays are no longer extant, we still have either full texts or fragments of his *Andromache, Hecuba, Electra, Troades, Iphigenia in Tauris, Helen, Orestes, Cyclops, Iphigenia at Aulis,* and *Rhesus* (though scholars continue to dispute the authorship of this latter play), each of which deals with some aspect of the Trojan War saga (Euripides of course dealt with other mythological storylines in other plays). This discussion will centre in particular on the *Troades* (Trojan Women), which depicts the fates of leading Trojan women after the obliteration of their city, portraying their mournful reflections on their past (the Trojan War) and their future (enslavement in Greece).[2]

The *Troades* is perhaps not obviously Iliadic.[3] It concerns events that fall outside the narrative time of the *Iliad* proper, and commentators have detected only a few instances of specific Homeric phrases or terms in the play.[4] Nonetheless, it is certainly Iliadic in that its female protagonists all feature in the *Iliad*, and in both texts they lament their dismal future following the sack of Troy.[5] It evokes the *Iliad*, too, in its focus on conflict, albeit the *Troades* offers a new vision of war – fought with words rather than with swords and carried out in dialogue rather than in violence. This vision of conflict, as we will see below, owes greatly to the cataclysmic events of the Peloponnesian War (431–404 BC), not least the Athenians' slaughter of adult male citizens and enslavement of women and children on the island of Melos in 416 BCE (an event that plays a crucial role in Thucydides' narrative of the war; Thuc. 5.84–116). What's more, the play deals with conflicts in words, evoking the important role played by public debate and discourse in shaping the events of the Peloponnesian War and Athenian war policy, as is profoundly captured in Thucydides' *History*.

The play originally formed part of a 'Trojan trilogy', following on from two other dramas that also dramatized debate and argument in the context of the Trojan War. The first play, *Alexander*, was concerned with Paris' backstory, and the surviving fragments include a set debate concerning his re-emergence at the royal court after his childhood exile. The second drama, *Palamedes*, centred on internal strife in the Greek camp at the end of the war, with Odysseus and Diomedes accusing Palamedes of consorting with the Trojan

---

[2] The text of the *Troades* used in this section is from Barlow 1986. Note that Euripides also composed the dramas *Andromache*, *Hecuba*, and *Helen*; this bespeaks a particular authorial interest in the fate of Troy's women. For recent responses to this play and its extraordinary popularity from the late twentieth century onwards, see Dunn 1996, 101, Goff 2009, 9–13, 78–135 and Lauriola 2015. For earlier responses, see Michelini 1987.

[3] On the *Troades'* Homeric connections, see principally Croally 1994, 50; Dunn 1996, 113–14; Davidson 1999–2000, 125–28, 2001, Marshall 2011, Torrance 2013, 218–45, Karamanou 2016 and cf. Munteanu 2010–2011, arguing that Euripides deployed epic techniques so as to present tragedy in a different light compared to its epic antecedents. For Euripides' wider relationship with the Homeric corpus, see Goldhill 1986, 138–67, Segal 1993, Croally 1994, 17–21, Mossman 1995, 20–42 and Torrance 2013, 183–265.

[4] See Davidson 2001, 66–68 for a useful summary ('Euripides is certainly not, in the *Troades*, going out of his way to draw attention to details of the Homeric texts', 68).

[5] Davidson 2001, 77. Garvie 2001, 58 comments on the remarkable density of significant female protagonists in this tragedy.

king Priam.[6] Unfortunately, we retain only some fragments of the *Alexander*, and even fewer of the *Palamedes*; the analysis here will therefore centre on the third drama in this 'trilogy'.[7]

In the discussion that follows, I explore the *Troades'* complex relationship with the *Iliad* and the Trojan War tradition, focusing on its treatment of the theme of verbal conflict and oratorical manipulation. The *Troades*, performed at the Great Dionysia in 415 BCE, showcased the results of war for a society that had itself been at war for some sixteen years. At this time, however, the most important war in Athens may not have necessarily been the military conflict with Sparta, but rather the ideological and rhetorical battle for control of the *polis*. The analysis focuses on three key passages of the play. The first is the Trojan princess Cassandra's sophistic analysis of the Trojan War, as well as her own foreboding comments on the Achaeans' ghastly homecomings. The second part looks at the first choral ode, in which the Chorus appeal to the Muses in order to sing of the Trojans' grim destruction following their acceptance of the Trojan horse. The final part of the discussion centres on the blistering ἀγών (a formal set-piece debate) between Helen and her mother-in-law Hecuba – a brutal contest of words that simultaneously highlights the weakness of argument. While Hecuba appears to be victorious in the debate, Euripides' text indicates the questionable value of her triumph.

Cassandra's sophistry

Unusually for Euripidean drama, the *Troades* opens with a dialogue between two gods, Poseidon and Athena.[8] The discussion between the two deities leaves it in little doubt that the Achaeans will suffer in the future for specific

---

[6] See further Scodel 1980, Karamanou 2016, and cf. Torrance 2013, 237–40. These three tragedies were accompanied by the satyr play *Sisyphus*. Dunn 1996, 112–14 well remarks on the unique quality of Euripides' trilogy, insomuch as that it covers the beginning, middle, and end of the Trojan War.

[7] Hall 2010, 270 similarly notes the way that many in antiquity would have encountered the *Troades* as an 'independent artwork'.

[8] Dué 2006, 148 notes that it is Athens' two patron deities that are outraged by the Greeks, intensifying the probability of an implied connection between the events of the play and the atrocities committed by the Athenians against the Scionians and the Melians. In the *Iliad*, however, Poseidon is an enemy of the Trojans; see, e.g., *Il.* 14.357-59; 20.34; 21.435-60. Dunn 1996, 101–14 argues that the prologue acts as a kind of ending to the *Troades*, since the play lacks any formal generic markers of closure; cf. Mastronarde 2010, 179–80.

acts of impiety during the sack of the city (65–66, 73–86; cf. 431–43, 460–61, 1123–30),[9] and evokes the various conversations dotted throughout the *Iliad* in which the capricious gods discuss the fortunes of the poem's human protagonists. Following this divine prologue, the focus shifts to Hecuba, a forlorn figure who, as in Euripides' earlier drama *Hecuba*, mourns her miserable fate ('Aiai! Aiai! What is there for me that I do not mourn with my song, I for whom country, children and husband are gone?', αἰαῖ αἰαῖ. | τί γὰρ οὐ πάρα μοι μελέᾳ στενάχειν | ᾗ πατρὶς ἔρρει καὶ τέκνα καὶ πόσις, 105–07) and remains on stage for the entire performance.[10] The Chorus, consisting of Trojan women, accompany the fallen queen, and they similarly lament their own miserable fates. They sing too of the various places in Greece that they would prefer to be sent to as slaves, listing Athens as their preferred choice, whilst reviling Sparta, 'the most hateful home of Helen' (τὰν ἐχθίσταν θεράπναν Ἑλένας, 211).[11] Finally, the herald Talthybius enters,[12] enumerating the wretched fates of the leading Trojan women; Hecuba, Andromache, and Cassandra are allotted to Odysseus, Neoptolemus, and Agamemnon respectively.[13]

This first part of the play therefore comprises one section in which we are told of the future fate of the surviving Achaeans, and one in which we are told of the future fate of the surviving Trojans. What follows this is an extraordinary intervention by Hecuba's daughter Cassandra, virgin priestess

---

[9] Garvie 2001, 56 and *pace* Goff 2009, 37–38. Kovacs 1997 focuses especially on the gods' role in the destruction of Trojans and Achaeans alike. In a purposeful bit of archaising, Euripides adopts the Homeric term 'Achaean' here and elsewhere in the drama. By the late fifth century BCE, it was commonplace to refer to the Trojan War's Achaeans using the term 'Hellenes'; see below p.113, and especially n.24.

[10] Hall 2010, 269 expands on the uniquely demanding nature of this role; cf. Easterling 1997, 174–76. Although we cannot be certain of the original staging for the play, Poseidon does refer to Troy as a smouldering ruin in his opening speech (lines 8–9); cf. Lee 1976, ad 8.

[11] One notable feature of the Chorus' opening appearance is their preference for Athens and their professed hatred for Sparta. This confirms that the *Troades* cannot be read as a straightforward polemic against Athens and its treatment of the Melians in 415; see further Van Erp Taalman Kip 1987. It is also worth remembering that while the Achaeans are criticized collectively in the play, their leaders Agamemnon and Menelaus are Peloponnesian kings. For similar patriotic sentiments expressed elsewhere in Euripides' works, see Kovacs 1997, 164.

[12] Talthybius similarly functions as Agamemnon's herald in the *Iliad*; see, e.g., *Il.* 1.320-21; 4.193; 23.897.

[13] Torrance 2013, 229 well notes that Hecuba's projected enslavement to Odysseus (278), part of the 'new message' (καινὸν λόγον) conveyed by Talthybius, does not appear in an earlier source. Perhaps we might detect a Euripidean innovation here? See further discussion in Mossman 1995, 34–36.

of Apollo, who emerges as a kind of meta-textual critic, weighing up these two fates and passing judgement on them.[14] Cassandra enters the stage in a bacchanal state[15] and performs a most surprising celebration of her imminent 'marriage' to Agamemnon by delivering an elaborate monody that evokes a wedding song (ὑμέναιος):[16]

> μακάριος ὁ γαμέτας·
> μακαρία δ᾽ ἐγὼ βασιλικοῖς λέκτροις
> κατ᾽ Ἄργος ἁ γαμουμένα
> Ὑμὴν ὦ Ὑμέναι᾽ ἄναξ.

> Blessed is the bridegroom,
> and blessed am I, to a king's bed
> in Argos that I am betrothed,
> Hymen, O lord Hymenaeus.

Euripides, Troades 311–14[17]

The ironic force of Cassandra's song soon becomes apparent when she remarks on the ruin that her marriage will bring to those that she and Hecuba most despise (404–05), thus avenging the Trojans ('I will come bringing victory [νικηφόρος] to the dead, by destroying the house of Atreidae, from whom we perished', ἥξω δ᾽ ἐς νεκροὺς νικηφόρος | καὶ δόμους πέρσασ᾽ Ἀτρειδῶν, ὧν ἀπωλόμεσθ᾽ ὕπο, 460–61).[18] As Dué observes, Cassandra functions here in a manner akin to Athena and Poseidon in the prologue, foretelling the Achaeans' miserable homecomings.[19] Cassandra is offering an assessment of the Trojan War that makes the Greeks the 'losers'.

Cassandra then continues to deliver a candid, even subversive, monologue, arguing that the Trojans are the war's true victors (or, at least on showing how

---

[14] On the play's rich portrayal of different women's voices, see Mossman 2005, 357–62. Euripides' Cassandra is a clear elaboration of the character referred to in the *Iliad* and the *Odyssey*. In the former, she is noted for her special beauty ('the finest of Priam's daughters', *Il.* 13.365) and for her 'resembling golden Aphrodite' ((*Il.* 24.699), while in the latter, the ghost of Agamemnon refers to Cassandra dying at his side (*Od.* 11.421-22).

[15] Goff 2009, 52 sums up the different scholarly views on Cassandra's 'madness' in this episode.

[16] For the generic qualities of ancient Greek wedding songs, see Swift 2010, 245–49.

[17] On the thematic significance of marriage in the *Troades*, see Croally 1994, 84–97 and Mossman 2005, 358.

[18] Barlow 1986, ad 460 points out that by evoking the heroic concept νικηφόρος ('bringing victory'), Cassandra ranks herself with the other leading Trojans, such as Priam and Hector; cf. 353. However, as the discussion below shows, Cassandra in fact outranks herself in the play, since it is she alone that can exact vengeance for the Trojans against Agamemnon.

[19] Dué 2006, 145 and cf. Wohl 2015, 46–47.

Troy is 'more blessed' [μακαριωτέραν] than the Achaeans, 365).[20] According to Cassandra, the Achaeans could hardly be considered the victors, for they succumbed to all of this bloodshed for the sake of one woman who departed from Greece with Paris of her own accord (a reading that clashes with Helen's own version of events later in the *Troades*; see more below). Cassandra continues to pile on reason after reason to bolster her argument on the Achaeans' relative defeat: Agamemnon's destruction of his own family for the sake of a woman that he loathed; the miserable deaths of those Achaean warriors who died away from home without customary burial; and the wretched fates of those back in Greece, many of whom died either childless or after their children, with nobody to attend to the offerings at their tombs.[21] These are brilliant, excoriating lines,[22] which clearly serve to disrupt the epic conception of a heroic death, recasting martial victory as moral ruin.[23] And, while Cassandra's words fail to convince either Hecuba or the Chorus, who regard her speeches as unbelievable, indicative, as Hecuba states, of an unstable mind (350),[24] the external audience, who have already experienced the 'directorial' prologue,[25] are much more inclined to recognise the truthfulness of her account. The scene thus reinforces a wider motif developed elsewhere in the *Troades*: the opacity of words and the limits of effective human communication at times of extremity – a motif that speaks as much to a war-ravaged Athens of Euripides' own day as it does to Cassandra's.[26]

---

[20] For the irony here, see Barlow 1986, ad 308–40 and Swift 2010, 254–55; (more cautiously) Brillet-Dubois 2015, 173 and Karamanou 2016, 356 and cf. Goff 2009, 51–53, who surveys different scholarly approaches to Cassandra's song, some interpreting her speech as insane, rather than being ironical. Cassandra utilizes several different metres throughout her sole appearance in the drama; cf. Brillet-Dubois 2015, 271: 'Cassandra's appearance in the *Trojan Women* results in an eclectic generic collage'.

[21] As Croally 1994, 125 observes, Aristophanes' *Lysistrata* (e.g. lines 508–15) represents another instance in which the destruction of the family was projected as 'the principal horror of war' in fifth-century Athens.

[22] Poole 1976, 278.

[23] Similarly, Poole 1976, 277, Goldhill 1986, 166–67, Barlow 1986, 365ff., Mossman 2005, 359 and Munteanu 2010–11, 140, focusing on the switch of narrative perspective here, and 143: '[Cassandra contends] that traditional poetry *misplaces* fame by giving it to seemingly victorious men'. Croally 1994, 126 agrees that some original audience members might have been swayed by Cassandra's cogent rhetoric, but suggests that those more comfortable with Athens' empire would likely have rejected her radical revisions.

[24] Brillet-Dubois 2015, 175–76.

[25] Easterling 1997, 173. Dunn 1996, 101–14 argues that the prologue acts as a kind of ending to the *Troades*, since the play lacks any formal generic markers of closure; cf. Mastronarde 2010, 179–80.

[26] Goldhill 1997, 149: '[the *Troades*] emphasise[s] the insufficiency of words to deal with the violence and suffering of war'.

Indeed, Cassandra's reinterpretation of the Trojan War explicitly sets out to redefine epic terminology. She argues that the Trojans should receive 'the greatest glory' (κάλλιστον κλέος, 386), having died for their country. Families buried those warriors who died at home, and those who lived got to enjoy the comfort of family life. Hector, moreover, achieved 'the finest reputation' (δόξας ἀνὴρ ἄριστος, 395; cf. 1242–45) following the Achaeans' attack – a subtle revision of the *Iliad*'s presentation of Achilles as the most glorious warrior.[27] Cassandra affords even Paris what is rare praise indeed, since his union with Zeus' daughter Helen saved him from the ignominy of an unknown wife. For all these reasons, Cassandra concludes that while the wise should always avoid warfare (400, a line that elaborates on Poseidon's criticism of those who sack cities in the prologue [95–96]), where war is inescapable, 'it is no shameful crown for a city to die nobly' (στέφανος οὐκ αἰσχρὸς πόλει | καλῶς ὀλέσθαι, 401–02), while an ignoble death is marked as a humiliation.[28]

What should readers make of Cassandra's ingenious rereading of the Achaeans' glorious destruction of Troy? At one level, it is possible to read her speech in conjunction with the prologue of the drama, which hints at the Achaeans' calamitous homecoming, as well as the audience's (intra- and extra-textual) knowledge of Agamemnon's future murder at the hands of his wife and her lover. From this vantage point, Cassandra can be viewed in heroic terms, as the only Trojan able to defeat Agamemnon and avenge Troy.[29] At another level, we might prefer the more ominous view that Cassandra is engaging in the sophistic arts, deploying sophisticated rhetoric in order to argue her case. While she initially destabilizes the myth of glorious warfare, she later resurrects the very terms that she has just laid bare (e.g. κλέος, δόξας). According to this reading, 'these words are corpses, animated only by a false, posthumous galvanism'.[30] While there is evidently an oratorical force in Cassandra's rhetoric, it does not necessarily follow that her statements should be deemed false (indeed, it is worth remembering Cassandra's overarching belief that the wise should oppose warfare).[31] Rather, this speech, along with Cassandra's

---

[27] Clarke 2004, 74–90.
[28] Brillet-Dubois 2015, 172 examines Cassandra's use of several *topoi* in this section of her speech that are found in *epitaphioi logoi*.
[29] Barlow 1986, ad 353ff.
[30] Poole 1976, 278.
[31] Croally 1994, 123: 'she engages in what might be called historical revisionism'; cf. Dué 2006, 140: 'lament often provides a new perspective on the sequencing of events'.

subsequent prophetic statements on Hecuba's death at Troy (428–30), Odysseus' travails following his departure from Troy (431–45),[32] as well as her own bitter death, in which her unburied body will become kibble for wild beasts (448–50), is better read as a response to the portrayal of conflict in the Homeric poems, conditioned by the historical specifics of Euripides' own day.[33]

Athens in 415 BCE was a city deeply concerned about the role of rhetoric in public discourse. Large numbers of sophists were active in the city, offering training in the rhetorical arts – and by extension – the political arts.[34] This led to concern about the power of oratory, and the potential for the manipulation of arguments by skilled speakers. In the years immediately preceding the production of the *Troades*, Aristophanes had written and revised his *Clouds*, a comedy that poked fun at philosophers and sophists.[35] The *Clouds* depicted a world where the power of rhetoric could make an unjust argument preferable to a just one, and a weaker argument appear stronger. Cassandra's speech assumes some ambiguous qualities in this immediate historical context. Her appropriation of Homeric and heroic language is certainly sophistic; but are we meant to see her argument and her value judgement as essentially right or essentially wrong? Is this a case of the weaker argument seeming stronger because it is couched in suitably Iliadic language and because we already know the machinations of the gods? Or is this an example of the stronger argument seeming weak and ridiculous, because it is put into the mouth of a captive woman whose individual fate was never to be believed?

Novel songs

Cassandra's radical speeches are not the only example in which the *Troades* seeks to challenge the Homeric texts by providing a novel perspective on the events at Troy. At the outset of the first choral stasimon (511–67), the Chorus sing:

ἀμφί μοι Ἴλιον, ὦ
Μοῦσα, καινῶν[36] ὕμνων

---

[32] Various scholars have observed that Cassandra's catalogue of Odysseus' struggles reasserts the authority of the *Odyssey*; see, e.g., Barlow 1986, ad 436, Gregory 1991, 180–81, n.21, Torrance 2013, 221 and Brillet-Dubois 2015, 172.

[33] Munteanu 2010–2011, 140.

[34] For the sophists in fifth-century Athens, see Gilbert 2002 and Barney 2006.

[35] For the portrayal of sophists in Attic comedy, see Carey 2000.

[36] On the metapoetic significance of the term 'καινός' in the *Troades*, see Torrance 2013, 229–30.

ἆσον σὺν δακρύοις ᾠδὰν ἐπικήδειον·
νῦν γὰρ μέλος ἐς Τροίαν ἰαχήσω,
τετραβάμονος ὡς ὑπ᾽ ἀπήνας
Ἀργείων ὀλόμαν τάλαινα δοριάλωτος,
ὅτ᾽ ἔλιπον ἵππον οὐράνια
βρέμοντα χρυσεοφάλαρον ἔνο-
πλον ἐν πύλαις Ἀχαιοί·

About Ilium, O Muse,
Sing for me a new-made hymn
of mourning with tears.
For now I will sing a song of Troy,
how that four-wheeled Argive contraption
wrought my destruction and unfortunate enslavement,
when the horse, reaching high heaven
with its clatter, decked with gold cheekpieces and
arms, was left at the gates by the Achaeans.

                                        Euripides, *Troades* 512–21

What emerges from this hymn – aided by the Muses – is not a celebration of
the glory attained by those warriors that had performed best on the battlefield,
or even those like Odysseus who are most crafty in speech; rather, the Chorus
orient the audience's perspective towards the city of Troy itself, specifically at
the fateful moment when the Trojans unwittingly accepted the Greeks' baleful
equine artifice. (In this way, the *Troades* speaks intertextually to Aeschylus'
Persae, which also emphasizes the immediate and disastrous impact of Persian
loss at Salamis and Pysttaleia on Persian society.) In the song that follows,
the Chorus recount in bleak terms their joyful acceptance of the Argives' gift
('Argive' is used in the *Troades*, as in the *Iliad*, interchangeably with 'Achaean');
for instance, the Chorus refer to the songs and dances they performed in
honour of Artemis (552–55).[37] They continue by relating a 'murderous shout'
(φοινία … βοά, 555–56) that possessed the city, which left the children of
Troy in a state of terror, as the Greek men emerged from the Trojan horse
('the work of maiden Pallas', κόρας ἔργα Παλλάδος, 561; cf. 46–47, 72)
and committed unspeakable atrocities against the Trojans at their altars and
in their homes.

---

[37] Cf. *Il.* 5.447, which places Artemis on the side of the Trojans.

Many scholars have rightly emphasized the differences between this tragic hymn and epic poetry. For instance, Kevin Lee has argued that in performing this new tragic lament for Troy, the Chorus appeal to and refresh epic themes by delivering a new kind of epic account, one that reifies not glorious warfare, but the women's experience of Troy's destruction.[38] Eirene Visvardi has written similarly of the Chorus' performance of a tragic epic that eschews celebrating 'the glorious deeds of men' (κλέα ἀνδρῶν, *Il* 9.189).[39] More recently, Isabelle Torrance has fruitfully explored the passage's intertextual relationship with *Odyssey* 8, specifically when the bard Demodocus sings a *hymnos* concerning the wooden horse (8.426–534). As Torrance notes, this is the only occasion in the Homeric poems that we encounter this particular term for a song, and it can hardly be coincidental that the *Troades'* Chorus deploy this same term for their ode,[40] which also concerns the Achaeans' equine 'gift'. The connections between the two texts are further enriched when we consider that just as the Chorus' ode is one sustained with tears (513), Demodocus' song reduces Odysseus to tears – tears that become the subject of a famous, extended simile on a female victim's tears (*Od.* 8.523–32).[41] In this sense, this scene is indeed, as Davidson suggests, 'thoroughly Homeric',[42] by capitalizing on a set of motifs already operative in the *Iliad*.

What this ode does, therefore, is to offer an alternative *Iliad*, from the perspective of Trojans rather than Achaeans.[43] Euripides presents here a song that could have been part of the wider set of Trojan War traditions, acknowledging the breadth of this tradition. He is also writing himself into the role of the Homeric poet – as the composer of an alternative *Iliad*. This sets up a kind of meta-competition, pitting Euripides against Homer as the poet of Troy and its commemoration. We already saw in Chapter 1, how the *Iliad* sought to position itself within a wider poetic tradition – here, we can see Euripides' Iliadic attempt to position his own play

---

[38] Lee 1976, ad 511–14. On lamentation as the unifying theme of the *Troades*, see Suter (2003) and cf. Dué 2006, 139.

[39] Visvardi 2011, 283–84, cf. too Barlow 1986, ad 511ff, Croally 1994, 245 and Munteanu 2010–11, 137–38 ('the Muse ... sings in tears a new repertoire about the Trojan War ... they immortalize female suffering, not male conquest', 137); Torrance 2013, 228: 'sufferings are [made] an appropriate subject for poetic performance'.

[40] For other terms used to denote 'song' in the *Troades*, see Torrance 2013, 220.

[41] Torrance 213, 220–21.

[42] Davidson 2001, 78.

[43] Bachvarova 2016b argues that such a Trojan *Iliad* must indeed have existed in the Iron Age.

within the wider Trojan War tradition. Doing this, however, seems to have meant placing himself in relation to – or perhaps more accurately *in the position of* – Homer. By this time, to engage with the Trojan War tradition was to engage with the *Iliad*.

Agonal conflict

One of the most crucial scenes in the *Troades* comes near the climax of the play, involving a dramatic ἀγών (a formal verbal contest) between Hecuba and Helen.[44] This debate scene has generated considerable scholarly discussion, not least because of the extraordinarily sophistic defence offered by Helen, as well as the unsatisfying outcome of the debate, which leaves the scene's (arguably) shallowest characters (Helen and Menelaus) as the eventual victors.[45] The scene opens with a jarringly cheerful Menelaus ('O how bright the radiant light of the sun is', 860), who defends his decision to attack Troy, not in order to reclaim Helen but rather to avenge Paris (864–66). Menelaus then insists that he can no longer take pleasure in enunciating his wife's name (869–70)[46] and proclaims that he has come to transport her back to Greece, where she will be murdered in order to satisfy those whose loved ones died in Troy (876–79). Hecuba instantaneously responds in hopeful expectation, praying to 'Zeus, whether you are the necessity of nature or the mind of mortals' (Ζεύς, εἴτ᾽ ἀνάγκη φύσεος εἴτε νοῦς βροτῶν, 886) to deliver justice by ensuring the death of Helen.[47] Hecuba continues by advising Menelaus to avoid Helen's gaze, 'for she captures the eyes of men, destroys cities, and burns homes' (αἱρεῖ γὰρ ἀνδρῶν ὄμματ᾽, ἐξαιρεῖ πόλεις, | πίμπρησιν οἴκους, 892–93), a trio of evils

---

[44] On this scene, see Amerasinghe 1973, Barlow 1986, 205–08, Lloyd 1992, 99–112, Croally 1994, 134–62, Meridor 2000, Goff 2009, 63–71, Marshall 2011, 38–43, and Blondell 2013, 182–20. For a useful summary of different scholarly interpretations of the debate, see Davidson 2001, 75–76 and Goff 2009, 70–71. For the ἀγών elsewhere in Euripides, see Loyd 1992.

[45] Cf. MacNeice 2002, 36: 'the whore and the buffoon | Will come off best'.

[46] Blondell 2013, 130–31 suggests that Helen's name itself exercises a kind of supernatural power, hence Menelaus' reluctance to repeat it. Most editors excise lines 862–63, in which Menelaus utters Helen's name.

[47] Amerasinghe 1973, 103 notes that Hecuba's prayer indicates the brief resurrection of her hope for revenge. It is notable that elsewhere in the drama Hecuba expresses deep scepticism in the reality of divine justice (469, 1240–41). On the sophistic quality of Hecuba's prayer, see, for example, Griffin 2001, 69, Goff 2009, 64, and Mastronarde 2010, 220–22, who characterizes the prayer as 'an ironic marker of a high point of illusory confidence and futile construction of order' (222). On vengeful Hecuba already in the *Iliad*, see *Il.* 24.212-14.

that operates as a modified form of Aeschylus' famous pun on Helen's name: 'destroyer of ships, destroyer of men, destroyer of cities' (ἑλένας, ἕλανδρος, ἑλέ- | πτολις, Aesch. *Ag.* 689–90; cf. p.64 above).

It is at this moment of profound denigration of Helen that she finally enters the tragic stage – perhaps for the first time[48] – dressed in royal splendour (1022–28; cf. 1107–09), though fearful for her life. This Helen instantly proves a stark visual contrast with the other Trojan women, who are dressed in rags with heads shaven. She asks to defend herself, in order to show that her death would be unjust (903–04); although Menelaus initially rejects her pleas, Hecuba (somewhat improbably) incites him to permit Helen's discourse, since '[Helen's] entire speech will kill her' (ὁ πᾶς λόγος | κτενεῖ νιν, 909–10). The audience, however, might already perceive a bleak irony in these lines, since Hecuba has just referred to Helen's bewitching charms.[49] Even before the contest begins properly, the playwright intimates that Helen will emerge unscathed, and that woe will continue to pile on woe for Hecuba.

Unusually for a debate, Helen begins with her defence speech, which, as other have acknowledged, is highly sophistic in nature, evoking in particular Gorgias' famous *Encomium of Helen* (for which see p.117 below).[50] Unlike the Helen of the *Iliad*, who, as we saw in Chapter 1, explicitly blames herself for Troy's troubles (e.g. *Il.* 3.344–48; 6.356), the *Troades*' Helen develops a multipronged speech that implicates various individuals, but not herself. To blame are: Hecuba, for rearing Paris, 'the beginning of evils' (ἀρχὰς … τῶν κακῶν,[51] 919); the old man (either the retainer of Paris or Priam) who failed to expose the baby Paris, a story that had already been covered in the first drama of this trilogy, the *Alexander* (920–22); Paris, who is characterized as 'resembling a firebrand' (δαλοῦ πικρὸν μίμημ᾽, 922; see p.65 above for a later

---

[48] Blondell 2013, 168. Note too Aristophanes *Frogs* 1043–56, which signals Euripides' tendency to stage disreputable women.

[49] Cf. Blondell 2013, 187: 'Helen therefore wins her first victory … suggesting, on his [Menelaus'] part, a certain weakness of resolve'.

[50] Thus, e.g., Barlow 1986, 207–08, Michelini 1987, 158, Lloyd 1992, 304, Croally 1994, 136, 144, Goldhill 1997, 146, Goff 2009, 67–68, Blondell 2013, 187, 193–95, and Karamanou 2016, 365.

[51] Compare the *Iliad*, which uses the same phrase somewhat differently *Il.* 5.62-64: '[Phereclus] also built for Alexander the seemly ships, *the beginning of evils*, those [ships] that were the affliction of all Trojans, and of his own self' (ὃς καὶ Ἀλεξάνδρῳ τεκτήνατο νῆας ἐΐσας | ἀρχεκάκους, αἳ πᾶσι κακὸν Τρώεσσι γένοντο | οἷ τ᾽ αὐτῷ).

appearance of this image); Hera, Athena, and Aphrodite, who instigated the Judgement of Paris; Menelaus, who she outrageously casts as 'most evil' (κάκιστε, 943),[52] for sojourning to Crete while Paris was at Sparta (943–44); Aphrodite, who enslaves even Zeus (949–50); the Trojans, for denying Helen flight from the battlements of Troy; and, finally, her new husband, Deiphobus,[53] who kept her by force, against the wishes of the Trojans.[54] In a spin on Cassandra's speech earlier in the play, Helen suggests that by eloping with Paris, she helped Hellas (Greece) avoid human bondage;[55] the Hellenes' victory, however, she casts as her ruin, since she is reproached for the very thing that should have secured a 'crown on her head' (στέφανον ἐπὶ κάρᾳ, 937).[56]

At first sight, Euripides' unapologetic Helen appears to be a far cry from the Helen of the *Iliad*, who repeatedly blames herself for the events that have ensued. That being said, Euripides' account does not entirely depart from the Homeric poem; in some senses, his account develops ideas already implicit in the *Iliad*.[57] First, true to the traditional character of Helen's remarks concerning Aphrodite's power in the *Troades*, when the *Iliad*'s Helen attempts to snub Aphrodite's command for her to enter Alexander's chamber, the goddess issues such a threat that Helen swiftly heeds her words, fearful and in silence (*ll.* 3.389–410). Secondly, while the *Iliad*'s Helen is more forthcoming about her own culpability, she too boldly casts aspersions on Paris, charging him as being inferior to Menelaus in valour and questioning his soundness of mind (*ll.* 3.428–36; 6.349–53), as well as implicating him in the terrible fate of the Trojans (*ll.* 6.356; 24673–74). Finally, in her lament for slaughtered Hector at the close of the *Iliad*, Helen remarks explicitly on her loneliness at Troy, since all shudder at the sight of her (*ll.* 24.674–75), which the *Troades* confirms

---

[52] Similarly, Blondell 2013, 188.

[53] Note that it is Deiphobus who accompanies Helen when viewing the Trojan horse in the *Odyssey* (4.274–76).

[54] Most editors, following Wilamowitz, excise lines 959–60, which refer to Helen's new husband; for a defence, however, see Lee 1976, ad 959–60, who argues that the reference to Deiphobus makes sense in the light of the play's connection to the *Alexander*, in which Paris and Deiphobus are bitter rivals; cf. too Scodel 1980, 143.

[55] In this speech, Helen refers repeatedly to the Greeks using the word Hellas, rather than employing the Homeric terms 'Achaean' or 'Argive', which are used elsewhere in the drama. This illustrates further the contemporary qualities of her speech, which offers a sophistic reinterpretation of Helen's role in the conflict.

[56] Goff 2009, 66.

[57] Some of the ideas developed here intersect with those of Karamanou 2016, 364–66.

throughout with the various invectives that are delivered against her (e.g. Andromache's brutal attack at 766–73). Clearly, then, Euripides' fifth-century Helen is not a complete reimagining of her Iliadic counterpart; she constitutes a more extreme form of the *Iliad*'s already-conflicted Helen, attempting to persuade Menelaus of her own innocence (cf. *Il.* 6.360, where Hector rebuffs her request to sit down, stating that 'you will not persuade me').[58]

In Hecuba's response to Helen, the fallen queen delivers an extended, multilayered attack that thoroughly refutes Helen's *apologia*. Hecuba denies the Judgement of Paris ever took place (869–82; *contra* 23–24); she proposes that Helen transformed her lust for beautiful Paris into an Aphrodite-led infatuation (987–88); she denigrates Helen for craving Troy's luxuries (993–97); she denies that Helen was led to Troy by force (998–1001); and she reproaches her for failing either to flee Troy or to commit suicide (1010–19). The viciousness of Hecuba's reprimand comes to full force at the close of the speech, where she urges Menelaus to kill Helen, so that she functions as a negative paradigm for all adulterous women (1029–32). One of the most remarkable features of Hecuba's speech is its consciously Hellenic texture:[59] she twice refers to the Trojans as barbarians (973, 1021), calling to mind contemporary Athenian political discourses on the foreigner;[60] she characterizes Troy as a seat of oriental luxury, in contrast to modest Argos (Helen's former home); and she suggests that Menelaus will win a crown for Hellas by killing Helen (1030–31). In Hecuba's use of rational argumentation and familiar panhellenic ideology, Euripides thus destabilizes the distinctions between self and other, and, remarkably enough, enables the audience to empathize with a vanquished, foreign woman.

As much as Menelaus' concluding verdict on Helen's guilt (1036–41) and the force of Hecuba's indignant attack has satisfied some commentators that she is the ἀγών's clear victor,[61] Euripides in fact presents a debate that is more concerned with exploring the multiple causes of the Trojan War than

---

[58] *Pace* Gellie 1986, who views Helen as a childish figure that subjects the Homeric myths to an outdated reading. The nuances of Helen's characterization in both texts demonstrate that this is too simplistic.

[59] Goff 2009, 67–69.

[60] See references in see below p.113, and especially n.24. The classic work on the portrayal of 'barbarians' on the tragic stage is Hall 1989.

[61] For instance, see Lee 1976, xxiii, Dover 2001, 4 (more cautiously) Barlow 1986, 205.

delimiting a conclusive answer on the architect of the war. Like the *Iliad*, the debate leaves the audience unclear as to who is ultimately responsible for what has occurred (see further Chapter 2), not least because of the way that the complex mixture of divine and mortal causations (particularly in Helen's speech) become impossible to disentangle.[62]

Helen is a powerful figure of blame in this episode, as she is elsewhere in the *Troades* (e.g. 134–37, 373, 498–99, 780–81). And yet, as if to underline the inconclusiveness of the contest, it is plainly clear in the lines which follow that Euripides encourages his audience to appeal to their knowledge of *Odyssey* 4, in which the Spartan queen is back at home with Menelaus.[63] For Menelaus initially claims that she will be stoned to death straightaway, but after Helen supplicates the king, he commands his servants to take her to the ships, from where she will be conveyed back to Greece (1046–48). Hecuba's faith in retribution has now clearly dwindled, and the playwright underscores this point when Menelaus, advised by Hecuba not to embark on the same ship as Helen, responds bemusedly 'is she heavier than she was previously?' (μεῖζον βρῖθος ἢ πάροιθ' ἔχει; 1050).[64] Indeed, the theme of Hecuba's hopes being dashed is a motif repeated throughout the play, such as when Andromache informs her of Polyxena's death, quashing her earlier hopes that she may still be alive (626–27, 260–71), or when Talthybius relates that Astyanax is to be killed, thus thwarting Hecuba's hopes that her grandson might refound the city of Troy (719, 701–05). The failure of the ἀγών is poignant, not only in the pathos it generates for Hecuba but also in its comment on contemporary Athens. Debate and discussion have been proved futile, and logical argument has been rendered valueless. In the ἀγών, the themes touched on in Cassandra' speech are taken to their logical conclusion, with chilling effect. Indeed, the tragic ἀγών of the *Troades* eventually reaches the same conclusion as Aristophanes' comic ἀγών of the *logoi* in the *Clouds*, revised for publication only a few years before the first performance of the *Troades*.[65] In both cases,

---

[62] Cf. Amerasinghe 1973, 103: '[we cannot] unravel the complex of causes that were responsible for the fate of Troy'; Croally 1994, 159–60, Goldhill 1997, 148, Goff 2009, 39, and *pace* Marshall 2011, 40.

[63] Thus Gregory 1991, 174, Scodel 1980, 98, Goldhill 1997, 147, Davidson 2001, 76, Dover 2001, 3, Mastronarde 2010, 79, 222, Marshall 2011, 42, Blondell 2013, 197–98, 200–01, Torrance 2013, 228, Rabinowitz 2016, 208, and *contra* Lloyd 1992, 112. Croally 1994, 157–59 and Goff 2009, 71 are somewhat non-committal on this point.

[64] Green 1999, 110.

[65] See Papageorgiou 2004 for the '*Agon of the Logoi*'.

the Unjust Argument (᾽Ἄδικος Λόγος) won out over the Just Argument (Δίκαιος Λόγος).

Conflicts old and new

Like other texts that we encounter in this volume, the *Troades* is no straightforward adaptation of the *Iliad*; not only does much of the storyline of the drama differ from that of the Homeric poem, but Euripides' tragedy adopts a reading of the events at Troy that bespeaks a wide intertextual framework.[66] As the discussion has illustrated, this is a drama that is fundamentally concerned with the utterly bleak effects of a city's annihilation, profoundly depressing in its unrelenting depiction of the Trojans' misery, in contrast to other Euripidean Trojan texts such as *Hecuba*, in which the former queen manages to exact vengeance on Polymestor for the murder of her son Polydorus.[67] The fall of a city would have an especially redolent topic at this time, given recent atrocities conducted by the Spartans against Plataea (Thuc. 3.68), Hysiae (Thuc. 5.83), and Iasos (Diod. 13.104.7), as well as by the Athenians against Scione (Thuc. 5.32) and Melos (Thuc. 5.116).[68]

The last of these in particular would have been at the forefront of the audience's mind when it was first performed in 415 BCE. Just one year before, the ἀνδραποδισμός of the Melians (the slaughter of adult male citizens and enslavement of women and children) had been ordered after a debate between the Melians and the Athenians – a kind of political ἀγών where the stakes were life and death for an entire community. The so-called 'Melian Debate' (Thucydides 5.84–116) was evidently written some time after the *Troades*, but it too depicts debate, rhetoric, and oratory as an arena of war. Indeed, in the very same year as the *Troades* was produced, Thucydides sets another of his dramatic set-piece political debates – the debates surrounding the decision to launch the Sicilian Expedition (Thuc 6.8–26). Taken together with

---

[66] Wright 2010 explores Euripides' relationship with his literary predecessors.

[67] Cf. Marshall 2011, 33–34 and Torrance 2013, 228. In the *Iliad*, by contrast, Polydorus is murdered by Achilles (*Il.* 20.407-18).

[68] Dover 2001, 8, Clay 2010, 237–39, Burian 2010, 154–57, Torrance 2013, 235–36. For the *Troades* as a thorough critique of Athenian imperialism, see Croally 1994 and cf. Gregory 1991, 155–83. For a sceptical reading, which downplays any Euripidean allusions to and critique of these contemporary events, see Green 1999.

Aristophanes' *Clouds* and Thucydides' portrayal of contemporary political discourse, Euripides' *Troades* suggests a deep anxiety in Athens over debate, rhetoric, and the power of words.

In addition, while it is necessary to appreciate the play's specific contemporary contexts, it is essential to recognize, too, the complexity of Euripides' engagement with the Homeric texts. Where women lament in the *Iliad* at just a few crucial junctures (see pp.19–23 above), in the *Troades* we find numerous women lamenting *en masse* and individually throughout, ultimately showing that the suffering of the defeated is worthy of poetic commemoration (cf. 1242–45, where Hecuba observes the terrible irony that her own destruction has ensured the fame of Troy amongst future generations, lines that, interestingly enough, largely echo the sentiments expressed by Helen in the *Iliad* [6.357–58]).[69] Where the *Iliad* explored the different reasons for the war's causes, suggesting through the figure of Helen that she herself was responsible, while elsewhere underlining the role of the gods (e.g. *Il.* 3.164–65; 14.85–87), the *Troades* elaborates on the various overlapping, yet conflicting, reasons to explain the conflict, while also magnifying Helen's culpability (a particular strand of Iliadic reception that we have already met in Chapter 2).

It would be a mistake, however, to reduce Euripides' drama to a kind of 'protest play', serving as a narrow critique of events from the very recent past (chronological considerations only accentuate the unlikelihood of such an intention on the part of the author in the case of Melos) and the political culture of the time.[70] For the *Troades* is a drama that exposes the hollow core of glorious warfare; as Poole has richly put it, the drama exposes how 'the nutritive elements of the past are related to, and in this case perhaps annulled by, the toxic'.[71] The drama's different characters repeatedly question our underlying assumptions about the true victors of the war, just as the playwright opens up new contexts for celebration and commemoration in dramatic poetry.

---

[69] Cf. Munteanu 2010–2011, 138.
[70] See especially Van Erp Taalman Kip 1987 and cf. Mastronarde 2010, 77, n.27; *contra* Karamanou 2016, 360: 'Euripides seems to have aimed at conveying a strong anti-war message'.
[71] Poole 1976, 277.

Naoíse: Shakespeare's empty arguments

HECTOR:

Paris and Troilus, you have both said well,
And on the cause and question now in hand
Have glozed, but superficially: not much
Unlike young men, whom Aristotle thought
Unfit to hear moral philosophy:
The reasons you allege do more conduce
To the hot passion of distempered blood
Than to make up a free determination
'Twixt right and wrong, for pleasure and revenge
Have ears more deaf than adders to the voice
Of any true decision.

Shakespeare, *Troilus and Cressida*, Act 2 Scene 2.163–73[72]

Hector's criticism of his brothers comes midway through the second act of *Troilus and Cressida*, one of Shakespeare's most notoriously problematic plays. The brothers have been locked in debate over whether Helen should be returned to the Greeks (for in Shakespearean English the Homeric Achaeans have become 'Greeks', cf. Prologue, line 21), thereby ending the war. Troilus, Helenus, and Paris have offered heated arguments in favour of keeping Helen, while Hector maintained it was in the best interests of the city to return her to Menelaus. In the section of his speech quoted above, Hector anachronistically evokes classical Greek models of debate, attributing to Aristotle the notion that young men are not suited to philosophy because of their hot tempers.

Hector's appeal to Aristotle may clang uncomfortably in our ears, but it might not have been so jarring for Shakespeare's contemporary audiences. For many of the play's original viewers, both Hector and Aristotle may have belonged to the same vague and generalized timeframe of 'antiquity'. Few would have been aware that the Trojan War was thought to have happened some four centuries before the composition of the *Iliad*, and that this was

---

[72] There are several versions of the text of *Troilus and Cressida*. The text used here is that of the Arden Shakespeare, edited by Bevington 1998.

itself separated from Aristotle by another four centuries.[73] For Shakespeare, as in the painting by Rembrandt featured on the cover of this book, the idea of dialogue and engagement between Homer and Aristotle may have posed no conceptual problems. Perhaps more importantly, historical accuracy does not seem to have been a prime concern for Shakespeare in the composition of this scene – it was far more important to communicate the heat of the debate.

Conflict and debate in the *Troilus*

Debate, persuasion, and rhetoric are central to the plot of *Troilus and Cressida*, in a way that mirrors their centrality in Euripides' *Troades*. In each of the play's five acts, the rhetorical arts are crucially important in moving the plot forward. In Act 1 (Scene 3), the Greek leaders discuss what to do in the face of Achilles' ongoing refusal to fight. In Act 2 (Scene 2), Hector argues with his brothers about whether or not to return Helen. In Act 3 (Scene 2), the young lovers Troilus and Cressida exchange rhetorically charged promises of fidelity. In Act 4 (Scene 4), Troilus attempts to persuade Cressida to accept her fate as a hostage amongst the Greeks. And in Act 5 (Scene 3), Hector's family argue with him unsuccessfully that he should not go out to battle, in a scene which bears only limited similarities with the *Iliad* (6.369-493 and 22.1-89; see for contrast p.43 above). Beyond these key moments that focus on discussion, the play is also shot through with references to the use and misuse of the rhetorical arts. Ulysses muses on the nature of reputation to goad Achilles (Act 3, Scene 3); Diomedes and Paris revisit the debate about the true value of Helen (Act 4, Scene 1); Thersites reports the words of others to Achilles (Act 2, Scene 3); Patroclus reports the words of Achilles to Agamemnon, and those of Agamemnon to Achilles (Act 2, Scene 3); and a silent letter penned by Hecuba reports the words of Polyxena to the lovelorn Achilles (Act 5, Scene 1). Throughout the play, then, power is shown to reside in words, and in their rhetorical deployment.

---

[73] This is true even of a more learned audience. It has been suggested that *Troilus and Cressida* was originally performed at the Inns of Court, implying an audience with a particularly high level of education. This theory has now been questioned: Bevington 1998, 87–90. For the generalized sense of the ancient past in Tudor times, see Burrow 2013, 7–8.

As a play so deeply concerned with the political power of words, *Troilus and Cressida* was perhaps a victim of its own central message. The play has a chequered early history, and there is evidence that it was originally suppressed – not necessarily by the authorities, but perhaps by Shakespeare himself. The play was first entered into the Stationer's Register in 1603, but does not seem to have been published until 1609, when it appeared simultaneously in two quarto versions. Although one of these versions makes reference to the performance of the play at the Globe Theatre, the second implies that the play had never been performed, claiming that it was 'a new play, neuer stal'd with the Stage'. When it appeared in the first collected folio edition of Shakespeare's plays in 1623, there was some uncertainty as to where it should be placed – it ended up being inserted between the histories and the tragedies, excluded from the pagination of both and unlisted in the table of contents.[74]

The confusion around the play during its early years may have been due in part to its controversial nature. *Troilus and Cressida* must have been written during 1601–1602, in the immediate aftermath of a major political scandal. In these twilight years of Elizabeth I's reign, disillusionment and unrest were everywhere, and had found expression in the 1601 rebellion of the Earl of Essex. The charismatic Essex had previously enjoyed both royal favour and popular support, and occupied a position of prominence at court. The elevation of a rival in 1597, however, prompted him to leave court in a sulk, furious with the queen at the perceived slight. He staged a coup in 1601 which failed. This led to his capture and execution, but it also stirred up a wider sense of political disaffection.[75] Any play that dramatized either the making of political decisions or the strife of factionalism would have touched a nerve in such troubled times. *Troilus and Cressida*, with its deliberate and unswerving examination of these sensitive issues, might have been judged 'too hot to handle' after its initial composition. The play would also have been politically sensitive simply because it was written by Shakespeare. Shakespeare's company had staged *Richard II*, a play that questioned royal power, on eve of Essex' rebellion in February 1601, and the entire company was mired in controversy as a result.

---

[74] Indeed, the cover page of one of the quarto versions gives its title as: *The Famous Historie of Troylus and Cresseid*, while the cover page of the folio records the title as: *The Tragedie of Troyus and Cressida*.
[75] For a detailed study of the life of Essex, see Hammer 1999. For a recent thematic reinterpretation, see Dickinson 2012.

There are yet more reasons why *Troilus and Cressida* would have been controversial. The myth of British descent from Troy was widely promoted by the Tudor dynasty.[76] Elizabeth herself oversaw an explosion of interest in the myth,[77] from Spenser's extended poem *The Faerie Queene* (1590–1596)[78] to Marlowe's tragic play, *Dido, Queen of Carthage* (1594); and from George Peele's narrative poem, *The Tale of Troy* (1589), to jurists such as Edward Coke seeking to establish the origins of English common law in a Trojan past.[79] In the political and literary discourse of the time, the Tudor monarchs were the rightful heirs of the Trojan hero Brutus, and the city of London was 'Troynovant'.[80] Any literary work which dealt with the ancient story of Troy could scarcely avoid being seen, therefore, as a commentary on contemporary political claims to be the 'new' Troy.

There were yet further parallels between the story of the Trojan War and late Elizabethan politics. The Earl of Essex had been likened to Achilles at several points over the years, and when Robert Greene published his *Euphues His Censure to Philautus* at the height of Essex's popularity in 1587, he dedicated it to the Earl. *Eupheus* described a contest of storytelling between Hector and Achilles, through which it meditated on the true essence of heroism and masculinity. As in Shakespeare's *Troilus and Cressida*, it was words and rhetoric, rather than martial deeds, which were the focus. A decade later, when Essex had withdrawn from court, comparisons between Essex and Achilles became even more widespread. Indeed, when George Chapman published the first translation of the *Iliad* from Greek into English in 1598, he too dedicated it to the Earl, describing him as the 'living instance of the Achileian vertues' [*sic*].[81] If Essex was Achilles, then Elizabeth might be compared to the bullish

---

[76] The myth was in circulation as early as the twelfth century, in Geoffrey of Monmouth's *Histroria Regum Britanniae*, see p.150 and n.5 below.

[77] As one modern scholar has put it: 'No traditional story was so popular in the Elizabethan age as that of the siege of Troy' (Tatlock 1915, 673).

[78] For example, descent claimed from Paris: 'From him my Lineage I derive aright, | Who long before the ten Years Siege of Troy, | Whiles yet on Ida he a Shepherd hight, | On fair Oenone got a lovely Boy:' (Spenser, *The Faerie Queene* 3.9 stanza 36). Also: 'For noble Britons sprang from Trojans bold, | and Troynovant was built of old Troye's ashes cold' (Spenser, *The Faerie Queene* 3.9 stanza 38).

[79] For example: 'Brutus, the first king of this land, as soon as he settled himself in his kingdom, for the safe and peaceable government of his people, wrote a book in the Greek tongue, calling it the Laws of the Britons, and he collected the same out of the laws of the Trojans': Coke, 3 *Reports* 4 (1602), Preface viii a.

[80] See papers in Shepard and Powell 2004.

[81] Chapman dedicated the first instalment of his translation to Essex when it was published in 1598, entitled the *Seaven Bookes of the Iliades*. For Chapman and Essex, see Briggs 1981. For Chapman and his celebrated translation of the *Iliad* more generally, see Sowerby 1992.

Agamemnon, and given that this play explored factionalism in the Greek camp at Troy, would likely have been seen as making a comment on both Elizabeth's treatment of Essex and on Essex' failed rebellion.[82]

There is an apparent incompatibility here of the British being cast on both the Trojan side (by descent) and the Greek (by politics). This seems to have been solved by Shakespeare through the repackaging of the Trojan War as a factional struggle between kin. When Hector faces Ajax in single combat, he discovers that they are cousins, and muses on the merging of bloodlines:

> Were thy commixtion Greek and Trojan so
> That thou couldst say, 'This hand is Grecian all,
> And this is Trojan; the sinews of this leg
> All Greek, and this all Troy; my mother's blood
> Runs on the dexter cheek, and this sinister
> Bounds in my father's.
>
> Shakespeare, Troilus and Cressida, Act 4 Scene 5.125–30

Shakespeare's play therefore depicts factionalism within factionalism – not just internal strife tearing apart the body politic, but also as threatening to dismember the body itself. With its heady combination of a politically charged theme, setting, and characters, in 1603 *Troilus and Cressida* would have been political dynamite. Elizabeth's death in the same year would have added further complications, and it is hardly surprising that the play remained unpublished for another six years.

Shakespeare's Homer

Shakespeare, according to his contemporary and eulogist Ben Jonson, had 'small Latine and lesse Greeke'.[83] Jonson's comments may have been aimed

---

[82] It is worth noting that in *Troilus and Cressida*, neither Achilles nor Agamemnon comes off particularly well. Achilles, although he styles himself as a great warrior and chivalric lover, is obsessed with his own reputation, and after the death of Patroclus goes against the wishes of his beloved Polyxena to murder Hector in the most dishonourable fashion – ambushing him while he is unarmed and setting a platoon of Myrmidons on him. Agamemnon, in contrast, is unimpressive from the outset. While deeply concerned with status and hierarchy, he fails to offer leadership, instead following the suggestions of Ulysses. Indeed, when Aeneas arrives to treat with the Greek host, he does not recognize Agamemnon as a great king, and instead speaks to him as he would a common soldier.

[83] Jonson's words were published in a poem entitled 'To The Memory of My Beloved the Author, Mr. William Shakespeare and What He Hath Left Us', which Jonson prefixed to the first folio edition of Shakespeare's plays (1623).

more at elevating his own standing as a classicist than accurately documenting Shakespeare's, but the comment has nonetheless stuck. It was traditionally assumed that Shakespeare knew little of the Classics, and drew instead from medieval and early modern sources in his depictions of the ancient world. In the case of *Troilus and Cressida,* medieval texts certainly provided much of the source material for Shakespeare's Trojan War,[84] as they did for the central romantic plot of the play.[85]

Nonetheless, *Troilus and Cressida* also seems to have some specifically Homeric resonances. Several details of the narrative action, for example, appear to have come directly from Homer. These include how Achilles surveys Hector's body, seeking the best place to strike him (Act 4, Scene 6; cf. *Il.* 22.317–27); and the dragging of Hector's body behind Achilles' chariot (Act 5, Scenes 8 and 10; cf. *Il.* 22.395ff). These details are particularly significant because they occur in parts of the *Iliad* that had not yet been translated into English at the time that *Troilus and Cressida* was written. The first instalment of Chapman's translation of the *Iliad* had indeed been published in 1598, some three years prior to the composition of *Troilus,* but this included only seven books – Books 1, 2, and 7–11. Similarly, Arthur Hall's 1581 publication of *Ten Books of Homer's Iliades,* an English rendering of Salel's French translation from the Greek, covered only the first ten books of the *Iliad* and did not include these later episodes. In order to learn about these Iliadic details of the duel between Hector and Achilles, Shakespeare must have consulted either the *Iliad* itself in the original Greek, or a translation of the poem in Latin.[86]

A more extended allusion to the *Iliad* can be found in Act 1, Scene 2. In this scene, Cressida watches a procession of leading Trojans as it wends through the streets of Troy, discussing those who pass first with her manservant and later with her uncle Pandarus. The scene is a comedic

---

[84] For the transmission of the Trojan War myths from antiquity through the medieval period, see Aerts 2012 and Desmond 2016, 253–57; and Chapter 5 below. For Shakespeare's use of these sources, see Presson 1953.

[85] Troilus first appears as a romantic hero in the twelfth-century French romance poem the *Roman de Troie* by Benoît de Sainte-Maure, and originally is depicted as a lover of Briseis. Cressida replaces Briseis as Troilus' lover in Boccaaio's *Filostrato,* and the story of the pair was popularized in England most famously by Chaucer. See papers in Boitani 1989 for the development of the Troilus and Cressida story through medieval and early modern European literature; and also Desmond 2016, 258–61; Pearsall 2015, 35–43.

[86] For a list of the available Latin translations at the time, see Tatlock 1915, 742.

parody of the *Iliad*'s Teichoscopia, with a gender role-reversal in Cressida taking the place of Priam as the questioner and Pandarus assuming the role of Helen, naming each of the Trojan warriors and extolling their virtues as they pass. The comedy of the scene derives from Pandarus' none-too-subtle attempts to elevate Troilus in Cressida's eyes, comparing him favourably to each man. If the similarities with Book 3 of the *Iliad* were not plain enough, Shakespeare adds a helpful signpost at the start of the scene for those in the know. The first notables to pass in the procession are Hecuba and Helen. When Cressida asks her manservant where they are going, he replies: 'Up to the eastern tower, | Whose height commands as subject all the vale, | To see the battle' (Act 1, Scene 2.2–4). What we are being treated to is a Shakespearean Hodoscopia (view from the road) on the way to the Homeric Teichoscopia (view from the wall; see pp.13–4 above for Helen's role in the Homeric Teichoscopia). In contrast to Homer's (literally) elevated overview of heroes and kings, Shakespeare's is a (literally) more down-to-earth perspective over the desirability of different men. Once more, Shakespeare cannot have relied on Chapman's new translation of the *Seaven Bookes of the Iliades* for this episode, as the Teichoscopia occurs in Book 3 of the *Iliad* – beyond the seven books published by Chapman in his first Iliadic instalment. The formulation of Shakespeare's Hodoscopia, then, likely owes to Hall's English rendering of the Teichoscopia, one of the available Latin translations, or even to the Greek text of the *Iliad* itself.

There has been much scholarship on extent of Shakespeare's knowledge of and engagement with ancient texts. Despite Jonson's characterization, it is now well established that Shakespeare was profoundly influenced by a number of ancient texts, including the works of Ovid and Plutarch.[87] Recent research has also highlighted that Shakespeare also drew broadly from Greek tragedy, although he may well have encountered much of this indirectly, through a variety of mediating texts and translations.[88] The state of the debate over Shakespeare's relationship to Homer is similar – it is evident that he made use of Homeric themes and motifs, but it remains uncertain whether this engagement was facilitated by a direct reading of the Greek text or through

---

[87] Arnold 1984, Martindale and Taylor 2004, and Burrow 2013.
[88] Arnold 1984, Silk 2004, Pollard 2012, Demetriou and Pollard 2017.

mediating texts, such as the many Latin translations of the *Iliad* that would have been available, or the various partial translations into English, most notably those of Chapman and Hall.[89] What we do know, however, is that Shakespeare's Iliadic allusions must have been the result of a deliberate set of choices: a choice to deviate from more familiar medieval precedents; and a choice to allude to Homer and the *Iliad*. By carefully working Homeric echoes and themes through the play, Shakespeare was signalling something – but what?

At some level, the Homeric resonances are partly a demonstration of Shakespeare's education and classical learning. Although they may have been lost on a wider audience, for the Elizabethan literary elite these Iliadic references would have been obvious. Shakespeare's deployment of Homeric allusions must therefore, at least in part, have been directed at his literary peers – perhaps a repost to the charge of 'small Latine and lesse Greeke'. Around the time that *Troilus and Cressida* was written, there was much rivalry and conflict in literary circles over the methods, techniques, and principles of drama. It is possible, then, that Shakespeare's conspicuous display of classical knowledge may have been amongst the milder expressions of this broader tension.

Indeed, although Shakespeare does not seem to have engaged directly in this 'War of the Theatres' (1599–1602),[90] there is a clear reference to it in the prologue of *Troilus and Cressida*. The actor tells us: 'And hither am I come | A prologue armed, but not in confidence | Of author's pen or actor's voice, but suited | In like conditions as our argument' (Prologue 23–5). This is a direct reference to Johnson's 'Armed Prologue' in *The Poetaster* (1601), itself a lampoon of Marson's 'armed epilogue' in the *Antonio and Mellida*.[91] But Shakespeare's armed prologue also has another function. The prologue in the *Troilus and Cressida* is not armed confidently with the words of either the author or the actor, but rather 'in like conditions as our argument'. This description focuses the audience's attention on the nature of the argument in question – if the prologue is armed in the same way as the argument, then how is the argument

[89] For the availability of Greek tragedy and Homeric poetry, and its cultural status in Early Modern England, see Demetriou and Pollard 2017. For the question of Shakespeare's knowledge of Homer either directly or through various mediating texts, see Presson 1953, Braden 2017, and Schein forthcoming.

[90] Bednarz 2001.

[91] For the 'War of the Theatres' and *The Poetaster*, see Bevington 1998, 6–11.

armed? This is a subtle clue of things to come in the rest of the play, a herald of how argument, debate, and the clash of words will be placed at centre stage.

'All argument is a whore and a cuckold'

Thus speaks Thersites in Act 2, Scene 3. The scene opens in the Greek camp, outside Achilles' tent, and Thersites has just been engaging in a humorous exchange with Achilles and Patroclus about their collective foolishness. Thersites has, as his role requires, been playing the fool for the amusement of his superiors, crafting his words and his argument so that he can conclude that he and all around him are also fools:

> Agamemnon is a fool to offer to command Achilles;
> Achilles is a fool to be commanded of Agamemnon;
> Thersites is a fool to serve such a fool, and
> Patroclus is a fool positive.
>
> Shakespeare, *Troilus and Cressida*, Act 2 Scene 3.59–62

This kind of circular word play is common in the mouths of Shakespearean fools, offering a moment of humour and entertainment in between more serious episodes. And yet, Thersites is painfully aware of how crafty words can lead to more than mere entertainment. As the other Greek leaders draw near and Achilles withdraws into his tent, Thersites highlights the very real dangers that lurk behind words:

> Here is such patchery, such juggling and
> such knavery! All argument[92] is a whore and a
> cuckold; a good quarrel to draw emulous factions
> and bleed to death upon. Now, the dry serpigo[93] on
> the subject! And war and lechery confound all!
>
> Shakespeare, *Troilus and Cressida*, Act 2 Scene 3.68–72

---

[92] In some versions of the text, this phrase reads 'All the argument' rather than 'All argument'. The former implies more of a comment on the immediate argument – the cause of the Trojan War; while the latter implies a broader comment on argument and debate as a whole. As mentioned at the start of this section, I am following the text of the Arden Shakespeare, edited by Bevington (1998), which has opted for the latter.

[93] Serpigo was a term for a creeping skin disease.

The famous line: 'All argument's a whore and a cuckold' can be taken as a reference to the central conflict that led to the Trojan War – the breakup of the marriage between a cuckold (Menelaus) and a whore (Helen). It is possible, however, to see the line as commenting on the nature of argument and debate itself. An argument can be a whore – sold when convenient, motivated by a desire for gain and profit. The arguments and appeals made to Achilles by the Greek leaders are whores in this sense – insincere and dissembling, they are made with the sole aim of securing Achilles' service on the battlefield. An argument can equally be a cuckold – it can be cheated on, gone back on, invalidated. The arguments and promises made by Cressida to Troilus are cuckolds in this sense – made in earnest at the time, but abrogated by later actions. The result of these dangerous arguments is factionalism and blood; and Thersites wishes war, lechery, and the pox on the whole enterprise.

Thersites' comments come into sharper relief once we consider their timing within the play. They occur just before the arrival of the Greek leaders, who are hoping to persuade Achilles to re-enter the fray. But they also occur just after the Trojan debate scene with which we opened this chapter. Thus, we have just been witness to a lengthy and highly stylized ἀγών – a set-piece scene which showcases rhetoric, discussion, and argument. It would have been all but impossible to hear Thersites' barbed words in this scene without recalling the verbal jousting in the scene that immediately preceded it.

The Trojan debate scene (Act 2, Scene 2) can indeed be seen as a kind of ἀγών, and the key elements of the Euripidean ἀγών are clearly present here: a pair of opposing speeches, setting out conflicting perspectives on a central question, of comparable length, separated by a few lines of briefer interjections.[94] These paired speeches are those given by Hector (lines 8–24) and Troilus (lines 37–50) towards the start of the scene. Their paired nature is evident from their comparable structures, and the way in which Troilus' speech is designed to mirror and answer Hector's:

HECTOR:
Though no man lesser fears the Greeks than I
As far as toucheth my particular,
Yet, dread Priam,

---

[94] For the Euripidean ἀγών, see Lloyd 1992.

There is no lady of more softer bowels,
More spongy to suck in the sense of fear,
More ready to cry out 'Who knows what follows?'
Than Hector is. The wound of peace is surety,
Surety secure; but modest doubt is called
The beacon of the wise, the tent that searches
To th' bottom of the worst. Let Helen go.
Since the first sword was drawn about this question,
Every tithe soul, 'mongst many thousand dismes,
Hath been as dear as Helen – I mean, of ours.
If we have lost so many tenths of ours,
To guard a thing not ours, nor worth to us,
(Had it our name) the value of one ten,
What merit's in that reason which denies
The yielding of her up?

[13 lines – including an interjection from Helenus]

TROILUS:
You are for dreams and slumbers, brother priest;
You fur your gloves with reason. Here are
your reasons:
You know an enemy intends you harm;
You know a sword employed is perilous,
And reason flies the object of all harm.
Who marvels, then, when Helenus beholds
A Grecian and his sword, if he do set
The very wings of reason to his heels
And fly like chidden Mercury from Jove,
Or like a star disorbed? Nay, if we talk of reason,
Let's shut our gates and sleep. Manhood and honour
Should have hare hearts, would they but fat their
thoughts
With this crammed reason; reason and respect
Make livers pale and lustihood deject.

Shakespeare, *Troilus and Cressida*, Act 2 Scene 2.8–50

Both speeches begin with an introductory preamble of two and a half lines,
before launching into the main body of the argument. Hector uses his speech

to claim his own fearlessness and to address his father Priam, while Troilus uses his to address his brother scornfully and to introduce what he considers to be Hector's motives. Both speeches have two further sections. In Hector's, the second section takes the form of a very physical description of fear – he speaks of soft and spongy bowels, as well as wounds – and an exhortation to 'modest doubt' and wisdom. In his third section, he elaborates on that wisdom, questioning what value has been placed on the lives of each individual who has been sacrificed for the sake of Helen. The rationality of this final section is heightened by the precise language of numbers: the first sword, many thousand dismes (i.e. tens), many tenths, the value of one ten – and completed by an explicit appeal to reason.

The final two sections of Troilus' speech mirror and invert those of his brother. Matching Hector's second section on the physicality of fear and picking up from his rational third section, Troilus' third section offers a calm and reasoned assessment of cause and effect. Three brief statements of knowledge are made about knowledge of combat and the nature of reason. These are followed by four and a half lines of logical consequence – why should we therefore be surprised if men flee from battle? The third section of Troilus' speech returns to the emotional, advocating the abandonment of reason. The language once more returns to raw physicality of body parts, with hare-hearts, fat, and livers. The mirrored structure of these two speeches binds them together, marking them out as the two key statements in the ἀγών: on the one side, reason dictates that we should give Helen up; on the other side, reason undercuts honour and so we should not give Helen up.[95] For the remainder of the scene, interjections are made on both sides, but no new arguments are introduced. On the side of reason stand Hector, Cassandra, and in a brief few lines Priam. On the side against reason stand Troilus, Paris, and, in four short lines, Helenus.

The form of this debate scene deviates somewhat from the scheme of the classical Greek ἀγών, as it involves several speaking characters in addition to the two main opponents. In addition, the remaining discussion following the two key speeches is long and includes further extended speeches by both main

---

[95] Interestingly, when Hector incites Paris to single combat with Menelaus in the *Iliad*, he does so using similar arguments to those deployed here by Troilus, focusing on honour and shame (*Il.* 3.39–57).

characters. That Shakespeare does not adhere to the strict rules of the classical Attic ἀγών should not be surprising. As mentioned above, Shakespeare's engagement with Greek drama was likely mediated by a number of other texts and translations. But even an indirect encounter with Attic drama would have revealed that the staging of formal debate scenes was a key feature of the genre, and the introduction of the Trojan ἀγών into the *Troilus and Cressida* may well owe to this influence. We cannot know if Shakespeare had read Euripides' *Troades* specifically – although this is certainly possible, given that the play was first published in England in 1575 (albeit in the original Greek).[96] We certainly cannot suggest that the ἀγών of the *Troades* was the precursor for the ἀγών in the *Troilus*. What we do know, however, is that Shakespeare was influenced by a number of Euripides' other plays,[97] and that the centrality of a war of words to both the *Troilus* and the *Troades* is remarkable.

An alternative model for the Shakespeare's Trojan ἀγών may have come from the *Iliad* itself. His dramatic staging of an impassioned debate, ostensibly focused around the possession of a woman but actually concerned with the preservation of masculine honour and status, finds an easy parallel in Book 1 of the *Iliad*, which had been conveniently translated into English by Chapman only a few years before. Indeed, at the start of what he called *The First Book of Homer's Iliads*, Chapman offers a brief prologue to explain the plague on the Achaean army under the heading: 'ARGUMENT'. The main body of the translation then begins below under a second heading: 'ANOTHER ARGUMENT'. If, as is usually assumed, Shakespeare relied heavily on Chapman in the *Troilus and Cressida*, it is unsurprising that he conceived of the Trojan War as a tale fundamentally concerned with debate, discussion, and argument.

Where does this leave us with Thersites' statement: 'All argument is a cuckold and a whore'? Thersites addresses his comments in this speech to the audience in much the same way as a chorus would have done in Attic tragedy. He is alone on stage at the time, and offers us an opinion, not just on the immediate action of the moment, but also on a broader issue: the state and status of rhetoric as a whole. His remarks have the sense of authorial comment

---

[96] Demetriou and Pollard 2017, 15.
[97] Arnold 1984 and Pollard 2012.

about them – do we have in this short speech a window into the heart of the play? *Troilus and Cressida* is a play about war. Not war at the point of a sword, but war by the pointed word. Oratory and persuasion are showcased at every turn, formal debates are staged, and the characters frequently reflect on both the power and the limits of words. But while this is a play deeply concerned with debate, it is also a play that is deeply cynical about it. At every turn, words prove false. Promises are not kept; assertions turn out to be untrue; and arguments are empty. For all his lengthy expounding on the virtues of reason, in the Trojan ἀγών Hector eventually caves in and agrees to abandon both rationality and truth in favour of manly honour:

> Hector's opinion
> Is this in way of truth; yet ne'ertheless,
> My spritely brethren, I propend to you
> In resolution to keep Helen still;
> For 'tis a cause that hath no mean dependance
> Upon our joint and several dignities.
>
> Shakespeare, *Troilus and Cressida*, Act 2 Scene 2.188–93

Hector had never really been in favour of giving Helen up, and all the debate, discussion and argument had been for nothing. The Trojan ἀγών has been staged in more way than one. As well as a scene staged as part of the play, it is also a scene staged by Hector within the play, a conflict simulated rather than real. Who can blame Thersites for his cynical perspective on the play from the play, uttered just minutes after Hector's disavowal? As Euripides might well have agreed, all argument is indeed a whore and a cuckold.

4

Seeking Truth

In this chapter we address one of the most pervasive strands in the Trojan War tradition and Iliadic receptions – the issue of the historical truth behind the Trojan War. In order to explore this, we have considered two prose texts that might be broadly considered as historiographical, in that they claimed to set down the truth concerning the ancient past.

In the first section, Jan investigates the work of the fifth century BCE historian Herodotus, who offers his readers an alternative account of the events at Troy, notably concerning Helen's 'true' whereabouts. Herodotus was not the first to reject Helen's physical presence at Troy, but he was perhaps amongst the first to subject the Homeric poems to a rigorous set of inquiries, exposing the subtle limitations of the *Iliad* as a document suitable for conveying historical matter, yet simultaneously reasserting the essential historicity of the Trojan War as related by the Homeric narrator. Naoíse then moves on to look at Heinrich Schliemann, who also set out to establish the 'truth' of the Trojan War, this time by discovering the physical remains of the Homeric city. Schliemann sought to position his research between the new science of archaeology and the traditional discipline of classical philology, while still appealing to a popular audience. Like Herodotus, he tried to apply notions of objective truth and rationalism to the Homeric poems and found them lacking; and like Herodotus, he nonetheless upheld their cultural significance and their central position within the Trojan War tradition.

As is the case with the receptions that have already been considered, these two authors and their works are divided on both chronological and cultural grounds, but this chapter will nonetheless show how they adopted some similar approaches to the *Iliad*. Both sought to mine the text for useable facts and historical information, deploying textual references and analysis of poetic details in the service of this goal. Both were concerned with issues of discipline and genre – they were keen to highlight what distinguished their own work from epic poetry in terms of form and content. Both also sought to bring a new objectivity to their work and to claim reliability based on first-hand inquiry or *autopsy*. Ultimately, Herodotus and Schliemann aimed to offer a corrective to Homeric epic by presenting their own research in dialogue with the poem, in which the dormant historical 'truths' of the Trojan War are ready to be illumined. For while these authors developed highly nuanced challenges to the *Iliad*'s commitment to historical accuracy, they were careful not to question the poem's status as an artistic or cultural icon. This separation of the factual and the artistic is a central feature of a particular strand in Iliadic receptions – the strand that aims to identify what, if any, historical truth may be extracted from the epic.

This historicizing approach to the *Iliad* is extremely popular today – indeed, perhaps more so at the end of the twentieth and start of the twenty-first centuries than it has been previously. Such interest comes not so much from academia as from the popular sphere. Amongst researchers, agreement has largely been reached that the Trojan War as it is framed in the *Iliad* is not an historical event, although we now know that there were several wars at Troy around the end of the Bronze Age, some of which seem to have involved groups from the Aegean (intriguingly sometimes fighting alongside the Trojans rather than against them).[1] The historicity of the *Iliad* is still a live question, however, in the popular discourse, particularly in popular books, television programmes, and magazine articles.[2] Indeed, as we will see in Chapter 5, this was one of the key areas of discussion surrounding the release of the 2004 Hollywood film, *Troy*. Herodotus and Schliemann, as key proponents of this

---

[1] Cline 2013 and Mac Sweeney 2018, 29–36.

[2] Examples of the topic in recent popular books include: Strauss 2006 and Alexander 2009. In terms of television programmes, the BBC alone has produced a series: *In Search of the Trojan War* (aired in the United Kingdom in 1985), with its accompanying popular book (Wood 1986, reprinted in a new edition in 1996), as well as the documentary, *The Truth of Troy* (first aired in the United Kingdom in 2004). National Geographic has produced: *The True Story of Troy; Troy* in Season 1 of the *Unforgettable Histories* series and *Troy: Behind the Movie* (2004); as well as *Troy* in Season 1 of the *Unforgettable Histories* series. The History Channel filmed *The Battle of Troy* as part of its *Ancient Mysteries* series (first aired in 1995) and also released a documentary called *The True Story of Troy* on DVD in 2007. For a particularly recent magazine article on the historicity of the Trojan War, see: 'The Search for the Real Troy' (*The Guardian Newspaper,* 9 August 2016).

historicizing approach, helped to lay the foundations for debates on the Trojan War that are still carried out today.

Herodotus and Schliemann both wrote in periods where the Homeric poems occupied a central, and almost indeed an unassailable position at the core of the Trojan War tradition. This is evident in their writings, in which the *Iliad* was the primary reference point for their analysis. When Herodotus seeks to challenge ideas about the Trojan War, he offers us a reimagined *Iliad*, rather than a reworking of the *Cypria*, the *Aethiopis*, or another other poem from the Epic Cycle. Similarly, when Schliemann wanted to discover the truth about physical environment of Troy, he started with the *Iliad* as his essential guide, rather than the later (and potentially more accurate) descriptions of the city in Strabo, Pliny, or Quintus Smyrnaeus. Both Herodotus and Schliemann hoped to 'correct' their contemporaries' understanding of the Trojan War. To do this, both felt that the key authority that they had to look to was the *Iliad*.

Jan: Herodotus' Trojan truths

One of the signal developments of the fifth century BCE was the emergence of what is now recognized as the genre of historiography, heralded by Herodotus' *Histories* – a text that emerged in both written and oral forms towards the end of the century.[3] As indicated in the proem of the work, Herodotus sought to commemorate and to glorify the achievements of Hellenes and 'barbarians' alike, as well as to explain the chain of events that would lead to the war between Greece and Persia (1.1.0). Herodotus' focus was thus on the more recent past, primarily on events that occurred no more than two generations before his time,[4] though this did not inhibit him from including several accounts that in some way related to a more remote, sometimes mythical, past. For instance, following an extended digression in which Xerxes and his comrades discuss whether or not to invade Hellas, Herodotus reports that Xerxes marched out towards the Hellespont.

---

[3] The compelling arguments developed by Fornara 1981 have convinced many (though by no means all) that Herodotus lived throughout the Archidamian War; for other works on Herodotus' publication date, see Asheri 2007, 51, n.12.

[4] See Thomas 2001.

ἐπὶ τοῦτον δὴ τὸν ποταμὸν ὡς ἀπίκετο Ξέρξης, ἐς τὸ Πριάμου Πέργαμον
ἀνέβη ἵμερον ἔχων θεήσασθαι. θεησάμενος δὲ καὶ πυθόμενος ἐκείνων
ἕκαστα τῇ Ἀθηναίῃ τῇ Ἰλιάδι ἔθυσε βοῦς χιλίας, χοὰς δὲ οἱ Μάγοι τοῖσι
ἥρωσι ἐχέαντο.

When Xerxes arrived at this river [i.e. the Scamander], he ascended the
citadel of Priam, having a desire to see it. After he saw it and he learnt about
each of the things that occurred there, he sacrificed one thousand oxen to
Athena Ilias, and the Magi poured libations to the heroes.

Herodotus, Histories 7.43.1–2

Xerxes' somewhat surprising pilgrimage to the ruins of Troy on his march to
Greece might not appear credible for some readers, unconvinced that a Persian
king could be so engaged with Greek cultural narratives,[5] but what is important
here is the implicit connection that is established – by both the narrator and
the Persian King – between Xerxes and the Trojan king Priam.[6] Such appeals to
mythic/heroic predecessors by Herodotus and his protagonists are pervasive in the
Histories, and help to illustrate the remarkably broad nature of Herodotus' spatial-
chronological perspective.[7] Indeed, as a cornerstone of Greek culture, Herodotean
appeals to Homer are particularly frequent in the *Histories* (see further below).

Responses to Herodotus' relationship with myth and Homeric epic
have a decidedly antique provenance – possibly even as early as his broad
contemporary Thucydides, who besmirches those whose accounts are
suffused with 'the legendary' (τὸ μυθῶδες).[8] Most famously, [Longinus] would
claim that Herodotus was 'most-Homeric', while an anonymous author of a
(probably) second-century inscription regards Herodotus as 'the prose Homer
of history'.[9] These examples form part of a much wider set of discourses in
antiquity on Herodotus' Homeric persona – both flattering and scornful.[10]

---

[5] Haubold 2007, 55–56, following Georges 1994, 59–63, places complete faith in this episode, arguing
  that it forms part of a thoroughly Xerxean reading of Greek epic; *pace* Grethlein 2009, 123. Erskine
  2001, 84–85 appears to accept the visit, but discerns no evidence in Herodotus to assume that Xerxes
  saw a Trojan-Persian parallel.

[6] Erskine 2001, 85, who is more sceptical about any Trojan-Persian parallel in this 'low-key' scene.
  Rose 2014, 144–45 accepts the historicity of the visit, yet posits that Xerxes' sacrifice was not so
  much an acknowledgement of the site's legendary foundations, but rather an attempt to secure meat
  for his army.

[7] See especially Cobet 2002.

[8] Thus Hornblower 1991, ad loc.

[9] Most-Homeric: [Longinus] *On the Sublime* 13.3; prose Homer: Lloyd-Jones 1999.

[10] Priestley 2014, 187–219.

This section is thus concerned with Herodotus' relationship with Homer. It explores his innovative, if playful, approach towards the Trojan War, examining in particular his forensic analysis of the contexts and causes of the war in his account on Helen's true location (2.112–20).[11] The discussion commences with a survey of some of Herodotus' references to Homer and individuals associated with the Trojan War. The second part examines the wider cultural and literary contexts of Herodotus' Helen account, and introduces other attempts to undermine Homer's version of Helen's role in the war, notably in Stesichorus' earlier *Palinode* and Euripides' roughly contemporary tragedy, *Helen*. The third section moves on to examine the Helen *logos* in more detail, an account in which Herodotus applies the characteristic elements of ἱστορίη ('inquiry'):[12] ὄψις ('personal observation'), γνώμη ('judgement'), and ἀκοή ('hearsay'),[13] while the fourth section offers some brief remarks on Thucydides' similar approach to the Trojan War. I finish with some concluding remarks on the intellectual-cultural impact of Herodotus' historiographic analysis of the Homeric texts, arguing that the growing tendency to question or rebuff Homer's account of the war in the fifth century would both question Homeric authority and, simultaneously, cement Homer and his Trojan War in an historical framework.

An historical war

As many readers have already noted, Herodotus opens and closes his work with marked references to individuals involved in the Trojan War.[14] In the 'historicizing' prologue, he famously reports allegedly Persian versions of a series of tit-for-tat exchanges between the Hellenes and what he terms 'barbarians' – the Greeks seizing Medea and Europa and the barbarians seizing Io and Helen (1.1–4.1).[15] Herodotus adds, somewhat remarkably, that

[11] Fornara 1971, 19–20, who regards this account as ironic, humorous, and superficial; Vandiver 1991, 130, is correct to discern more sophisticated themes at work (see below).
[12] On the meaning of to discern more sophisticated Thomas 2000: 161–67, 262–74 and Bakker 2002: 13–19, 29–32.
[13] As recognized by Neville 1977, 9, Hunter 1982, 52–61, Munson 2001, 142–44, and de Jong 2012, 127–28.
[14] Ayo 1984.
[15] The bibliography on this passage and its relationship with epic traditions is gargantuan; see further Vandiver 2012, 152, n.33 and Saïd 2012, nn.58–65 with text. Note, however, the especially valuable contributions of Fornara 1971, 35, Ayo 1984, Nagy 1990, 218–21, Vandiver 1991, 114–24, Moles 1993, 92–98, Węcowski 2004, 150–53, 155–58, Chiasson 2012, Saïd 2012, 102–05, Blondell 2013, 143–50, and Branscome 2013, 178–86.

in the Persians' eyes 'the beginning of the hostility towards the Greeks was a consequence of the capture of Ilium' (καὶ διὰ τὴν Ἰλίου ἅλωσιν εὑρίσκουσι σφίσι ἐοῦσαν τὴν ἀρχὴν τῆς ἔχθρης τῆς ἐς τοὺς Ἕλληνας, 1.5.1). The Trojan War is therefore transformed from a major historical event in its own right into merely one of a series of precursory episodes leading up to the Persian Wars. The Hellenes of Herodotus' day are cast as Homeric Achaeans, while contemporary Persians are cast as Homeric Trojans.[16] It is important to note, of course, the way that Herodotus concludes this account:

> ταῦτα μέν νυν Πέρσαι τε καὶ Φοίνικες λέγουσι. ἐγὼ δὲ περὶ μὲν τούτων οὐκ ἔρχομαι ἐρέων ὡς οὕτως ἢ ἄλλως κως ταῦτα ἐγένετο, τὸν δὲ οἶδα αὐτὸς πρῶτον ὑπάρξαντα ἀδίκων ἔργων ἐς τοὺς Ἕλληνας, τοῦτον σημήνας προβήσομαι ἐς τὸ πρόσω τοῦ λόγου,

> Now this is what the Persians and Phoenicians say. I for my part am not going to speak about these matters that they happened in this way or another. Instead, I will signal the man whom I myself know first instigated unjust deeds (*adikōn ergōn*)[17] against the Greeks,[18] and I will proceed forwards with the account
>
> Herodotus, *Histories* 1.5.3

While Herodotus, like the epic poet, is particularly concerned with the preservation of Greek and non-Greek glory (*kleos*; see further pp.17–19 above), as well as excavating the *aitia* ('reasons') behind a human conflict,[19] it is clear from this passage that he presents himself as unwilling to pass judgement on a series of skirmishes that are ultimately beyond the purview of *his* historical inquiry.[20] This explicit declaration – that he will begin his account with the man whom 'I myself know' to have committed unjust deeds against the Greeks – instigates a clear shift from the largely effaced epic poet, who relies on the all-knowing Muses in order to bring forth his story

---

[16] For the post-Homeric emergence of collective Hellenic identity, see Hall 2002.

[17] Similarly, Herodotus uses the formula ἀρχὴ κακῶν at 5.97.3, for which see Pelliccia 1992, 79; Munson 2007, 152-3; cf. *Il.* 1.6, 5.62-3, 11.604; Thuc. 2.12.3.

[18] This interest in tracing firsts reverberates throughout the *Histories*: 1.5.3, 6.2, 23, 94.1, 163.1, 2.188.2, 6.112.3, cf. Harrison 2000, 75; and, in early prose works more generally, Fowler 1996, 73–74.

[19] Cf. *Il.* 1.7f. with Gould 1989, 48–49.

[20] Momigliano 1966, 114: 'he definitely decided that if you want to know something about the causes of the Persian Wars, you must not look at Greek myths, you must not look at Homer'; see also Ayo 1984, 32, Lateiner 1989, 38, 42, Thomas 2000, 268, Luraghi 2001, 156, and Węcowski 2004, 154, n.64.

(see p.12 above).[21] And just as the *Histories* begins by looking back to the Trojan War story, so too the work closes somewhat ominously with an account of the Persian Artÿactes who plundered the temple of Protesilaus in Eleaus, ostensibly avenging the first Achaean to step foot on the plains of Troy.[22] These appeals to the Trojan War are a clear indication, then, not only of Herodotus' potential to distance himself from events that occurred at some point in the remote or legendary past, as is the case in the first passage, but equally, as the second passage shows, his widespread attempts to forge a profound connection between the ancient Trojan War and the more recent Persian Wars.[23] Such a response is not altogether surprising, of course; as Andrew Erskine, amongst others, has demonstrated, the 'Trojan-Persian analogy' was a convenient political tool that could be used across a wide range of media produced in and beyond classical Athens.[24]

In addition to this bookending of the *Histories* with references to Troy, Herodotus offers a wide range of allusions to events and figures related to the Trojan War throughout his work. Chief amongst these, Herodotus proposes that Homer (and Hesiod) flourished no more than 400 years before his own time (2.53.2) and that Helen never really went to Troy (2.112-20, see further discussion below), later declaring that the god Pan was born some 800 years ago, after the Trojan War (2.145.4).[25] The date of the war is further refined in Book 7, when Herodotus states that the Trojan War took place in the third generation following the death of Minos (7.171.1). In Book 7, too, Herodotus remarks candidly that Xerxes' campaign was by far the greatest on record, certainly compared with reports of the Atreidae's expedition

[21] *Il.* 2.485-86; *Od.* 1.1-3. On Herodotus' use of ἐγώ, see de Jong 1999, 228. On the similarities and differences between the Homeric and Herodotean narrator, see de Jong 1999, 220–29. Cf. de Jong 2012, 141–42, comparing the authority of the Egyptian priests in the Helen *logos* to that of the Muses in the *Iliad* (e.g. *Il.* 2.485).

[22] On this closing passage as a commentary on fifth-century Athenian imperialism, see especially Fornara 1971, *passim*, Boedeker 1988 and Moles 2002.

[23] Pelling 2006, 78–79.

[24] The Persian-Trojan-barbarian equation seems to have developed in the political rhetoric and ideology of mid-late fifth-century Athens, partly in response to the Persian Wars and partly as a tool of Athenian imperialism. This phenomenon has been widely discussed in the existing literature: see variously Hall 1989, 102, Boedeker 2001, 126, Erskine 2001, 61–92, J. Hall 2002, 172–89, Castriota 2005, Pallantza 2005, Vlassopoulos 2013, 61, 189–95 with references, and Priestley 2014, 191. The wider cultural impact of the Persian Wars on classical Greece is discussed in Rhodes 2007.

[25] Graziosi 2002, 112–13 draws attention to the way that Herodotus includes these hypothetical dates in order to forge a gulf between his own contemporary history and Homer's narration of 'a remote, mythical and ultimately unknowable era' (112).

to Ilium (7.20.2).[26] These narratorial remarks illustrate the considerable space that Herodotus dedicates to Homer's poetry, a stark contrast with the much more scanty allusions he makes to other poets.[27]

Herodotus' protagonists are also capable of making allusions to Troy. In the so-called embassy scene, when the Spartans, Athenians, and Syracusans are all contending for leadership of the Hellenes, the Spartan and Athenian envoys cite the achievements of Agamemnon and Menestheus respectively in order to buttress their argument (7.159, 161.3). Similarly, in the Athenians' and Tegeans' dispute over the projected battle formation at Plataea in 479 BCE (9.26–28), the Athenians describe a number of their more ancient deeds, including their significant contribution at Troy (although subsequently dismissing all of these deeds as 'ancient matters' [παλαιῶν ἔργων] in a rhetorical flourish).[28] Herodotus clearly took it for granted that Homer's Trojan War was deeply embedded within Greek culture during the fifth century BCE, playing a fundamental role in the formation of Greek identity.[29] As my discussion will demonstrate, his narrative would push this one step further, making Homer's Troy part of the *discourse* of History.

Relocating Helen

One of the ways in which Herodotus positions himself in relation to Homer most explicitly is his exposition on Helen's true whereabouts in Egypt during the Trojan War. The succeeding section will show how his account fundamentally challenges Homer's version of the Trojan War, and raises profound questions on the ability of epic poetry to convey historical truth. Of course, Herodotus was by no means the first to question Homer's authority or to call into question the verifiability of his account. The epinician poet Pindar muses in *Nemean* 7:

ἐγὼ δὲ πλέον' ἔλπομαι
λόγον Ὀδυσσέος ἢ πάθαν διὰ τὸν ἁδυεπῆ γενέσθ' Ὅμηρον·
ἐπεὶ ψεύδεσί οἱ ποτανᾷ τε μαχανᾷ

---

[26] Cf. Thuc. 1.1.2-3. On the complex mixture of Homeric and epic allusions in Book Seven of the *Histories*, see Carey 2016.
[27] On Herodotus and the poets, see West 2004 and Marincola 2006.
[28] 9.27.2-5. On this and the previous scene in Book 7, see Grethlein 2010, 160–86 and cf. Pelling 2006.
[29] See further Skinner 2012 and cf. Graziosi 2002, 195. On fifth-century audiences' knowledge of Homer in an Athenian context, see Baragwanath and Foster 2017, 4–5.

σεμνὸν ἔπεστί τι: σοφία δὲ κλέπτει παράγοισα μύθοις· τυφλὸν δ᾽ ἔχει
ἦτορ ὅμιλος ἀνδρῶν ὁ πλεῖστος.

I expect the *logos* on Odysseus
exceeds his experiences, due to sweet-voiced Homer;
for in his lies and winged contrivances there is
something reverent, and his skill deceives, leading others astray with *mythoi*.
Indeed, the heart of the great throng of men is blind.

Pindar, *Nemean* 7.20–24[30]

For Pindar, then, Homer is able to convince his listeners on account of his poetic skill, even though his stories are exaggerated to the point that they are endowed with 'lies' (ψεύδεσί). Surely Homer's seminal influence on the Greeks is at the root of Heraclitus' ire too; the late sixth-century philosopher reportedly bemoaned that 'Homer is worthy of being chased out of the competitions and thrashed' (τόν τε Ὅμηρον ἔφασκεν ἄξιον ἐκ τῶν ἀγώνων ἐκβάλλεσθαι καὶ ῥαπίζεσθαι, D.L. 9.1).[31]

Herodotus' criticisms of Homer were similar but more subtle, effected by calling into question his presentation of Helen. Once again, however, Herodotus was not the first to do this. One early challenger of Homer on this point was the lyric poet Stesichorus,[32] active in the first half of the sixth century BCE. His elliptical *Palinode* (literally a 'running-back') appears to have offered a panegyric for the goddess Helen, in the hope of curing the poet's blindness.[33] Although Stesichorus' poem exists only in fragments preserved by later authors, it is clear that his poetry provided a distinct rupture with Homeric thought. Helen, it would seem, had never been to Troy:

ἔστι δὲ τοῖς ἁμαρτάνουσι περὶ μυθολογίαν καθαρμὸς ἀρχαῖος, ὃν Ὅμηρος
μὲν οὐκ ᾔσθετο, Στησίχορος δέ. τῶν γὰρ ὀμμάτων στερηθεὶς διὰ τὴν Ἑλένης
κακηγορίαν οὐκ ἠγνόησεν ὥσπερ Ὅμηρος, ἀλλ᾽ ἅτε μουσικὸς ὢν ἔγνω τὴν
αἰτίαν, καὶ ποιεῖ εὐθὺς–

---

[30] Cf. *Nemean* 8.32-33, and (later) Aristotle *Poetics* 1460a18-19, 1460a35-b1-5.

[31] Marincola 1997, 219.

[32] Stesichorus may not have been the first to question the Homeric Helen. There is a reference to Hesiod as the inventor of this tradition, Hesiod frag. 358 MW: 'Hesiod first introduced the *eidōlon* to the story concerning Helen', πρῶτος Ἡσίοδος περὶ τῆς Ἑλένης τὸ εἴδωλον παρήγαγε; see further West 2002, 33–36. It is also possible that the sixth-century prose writer Hecataeus of Miletus also narrated a revised account on Helen of Troy, see Lloyd 1988, 47 with references.

[33] For a critical discussion on Stesichorus' *Palinode*, see Davies and Finglass 2014, 299–343 and cf. Blondell 2013, 117–22, focusing on Stesichorus' break from, and compliance with, Homeric tradition.

οὐκ ἔστ' ἔτυμος λόγος οὗτος,
οὐδ' ἔβας ἐν νηυσὶν εὐσέλμοις,
οὐδ' ἵκεο Πέργαμα Τροίας·
καὶ ποιήσας δὴ πᾶσαν τὴν καλουμένην Παλινῳδίαν παραχρῆμα
ἀνέβλεψεν.

For those who make mistakes in *mythologia*, there is an archaic technique of purification that Homer did not know, though Stesichorus did. For when he was deprived of his eyesight on account of his slander of Helen, he did not fail to understand, like Homer; but since he was *mousikos* he knew the cause, and at once creates the following verses:
'This story is not true,
You did not go on board the well-decked ships,
You did not arrive at the citadel of Troy.'
And after composing all of the so-called *Palinode* he recovered his sight immediately.

Plato *Phaedrus* 243a2–3b3

Stesichorus is presented in a decidedly competitive light in this passage, not only by rebuffing the Homeric version of Helen's role in the war, but also in his ability to overcome his blindness, unlike the ignorant Homer. The passage's agonistic flavour clearly hints at the poet's especial, often polemical, interest in Homeric epic.[34] Indeed, in a separate fragment, we are also informed: 'Stesichorus says that the *eidōlon* of Helen was fought over at Troy, due to an ignorance of the truth' (τὸ τῆς Ἑλένης εἴδωλον ὑπὸ τῶν ἐν Τροίᾳ Στησίχορός φησι γενέσθαι περιμάχητον ἀγνοίᾳ τοῦ ἀληθοῦς, Plato *Republic* 9.586c).[35] So for Stesichorus, a Helen of sorts was present at Troy, though not the mortal Helen that surfaces in *Iliad*. Rather it was a 'phantom' (εἴδωλον) that went on the goddess' behalf. There are some intriguing similarities between Stesichorus' and Herodotus' Helen,[36] but it is sufficient to note here that by the time that Herodotus came to author his *Histories*, there was an established tradition that questioned the authority of Homer's version of Helen's whereabouts.

This tradition seems to have been especially strong in the late fifth century, and some of Herodotus' contemporaries were also sceptical about Helen's

---

[34] See further Kelly 2015.
[35] For problems and inconsistencies with Stesichorus' εἴδωλον, see Blondell 2013, 96–98.
[36] Blondell 2013, 154.

supposed journey to Troy. In the drama *Helen*, the tragic poet Euripides wove an alternative story in which the errant Helen had in fact spent the previous seventeen years holed up in Egypt under the protection of king Proteus (on Euripides' engagement with Homer, see Chapter 3). Like Stesichorus' *Palinode*, Euripides' drama proposes *contra* Homer that it was a phantom of Helen that was in Troy.[37] And in prose, too, the sophist Gorgias of Leontini expressed similar reservations regarding the poetical Helen, appealing to his 'reasoning' (λογισμόν) in order to reclaim Helen and her sullied reputation by demonstrating her true innocence (2). According to Gorgias, it was one from of a whole variety of causes that was truly to blame for Helen's behaviour: chance, necessity, and the gods' stratagems; or abduction by force; or persuasion by *logos*; or the submission to *erōs* (6). While Gorgias' quasi-forensic encomium does not seek to elide Helen's sojourn in Troy à la Stesichorus and Euripides, his exculpation of the goddess nevertheless serves to question the efficacy of Homer's characterization of Helen.[38]

As these examples illustrate, Helen had become a powerful heuristic for thinking through the problems of Homer's account of the war more broadly by the time of Herodotus.[39] Nevertheless, as we shall see, Herodotus' unique take on Helen's role in the war foments new hermeneutic challenges to the authority of the epic poet and their ability to convey the past accurately. For as the *Iliad* and *Odyssey* make patently clear, Helen's presence at Troy is crucial for the unravelling of the conflict (and is even presented as an explanation for the war); in removing her from the scene of that conflict, Herodotus makes a powerful case about the ability of historiography to explain human actions better than epic poetry.

Inquiry and the Trojan War

The discussion above has addressed Herodotus' uneasy relationship with mythical time coupled with a pre-historiographical tradition of questioning different aspects of Homer's version of the Trojan War. These themes will recur in 2.112–20 – Herodotus' own archaeology of competing Trojan

---

[37] On the *Helen*, see Blondell 2013, 202–21.
[38] The tradition continued even after Herodotus; see Isocrates *Helen* 64 (Graziosi 2002, 148).
[39] This was also true in poetry. See Blondell 2010 and Boedeker 2012 on early Greek lyric responses to Helen.

War traditions.[40] In this passage, the historian makes repeated nods to the constituent parts of his inquiry process, and in an extraordinary section, he consults the Homeric texts in order to affirm his own innovative reading of the war.[41] For Herodotus will attempt to demonstrate that the 'real' Helen was never held captive in Troy, arguing that Homer showed this true version of events within his poetical retelling.[42] As we shall see, the passage will bring into question crucial aspects of Homer's *Iliad* and its relationship with historical truth.[43]

The narrative begins with an explicit reference to Herodotus' source: the Egyptian priests, those most learned individuals whom he consults for much of his Egyptian account (2.113.1, cf. 2.118.1–20.1).[44] The priests relate that the Trojan Alexander had seized Helen from his host Menelaus in the hope of taking her back to his fatherland; however, the couple faced violent winds en route and were forced to land in Egypt. The Egyptian king Proteus proceeded to arrest Alexander, and, having interrogated the deceitful Trojan and uncovered his outrageous behaviour against Menelaus, he sent Alexander away whilst detaining Helen (2.115).[45] The Helen of Herodotus, like Stesichorus and Euripides, is thus absented from Troy to Egypt; but unlike the poets, Herodotus offers no phantom or otherwise in her place at Troy.

[40] On this passage, see variously Fornara 1971, 19ff., Neville 1977, Hunter 1982, 52–65, Lloyd 1988, 43–52, Fehling 1989, 59–65, Vandiver 1991, 124–32, Austin 1994, 118–36, West 2002, 31–39, Graziosi 2002, 113–18, Grethlein 2010, 151–58, Sammons 2012, and the contributions of de Jong and de Bakker in Baragwanath and de Bakker 2012b.

[41] Ford 2002, 148 notes the way that Herodotus provides a close reading of the epic texts. Herodotus seldom quotes texts verbatim; the majority of quotations that he does include are from inscriptions or, notably, oracles; see further Haywood 2013, *passim*.

[42] Sammons 2012, 55–57 discusses Herodotus' confident assertion that Homer intentionally showed this to his audience, rather than, for example, implying this. It is worth remembering, however, that challenging long-held assumptions held by the Greeks is one of Herodotus' chief motivations to write his *Histories*; cf. Cartledge and Greenwood 2002, 363: '[Herodotus'] innovative research sometimes cuts across or directly contradicts the received assumptions of his Greek audience'.

[43] On Herodotus' steadfast belief in the Trojan War, affirmed by his Egyptian sources, see, inter alia, Hunter 1982, 53–4, Vandiver 1991, 127, Stadter 2004, 33–38, Grethlein 2010, 153, Saïd 2012. For other Homeric/epic themes and reminiscences in Book 2, see Lloyd 1990, 227–28.

[44] Fehling 1989, 59–65 argues that Herodotus has fabricated this entire story, since the Egyptians could hardly have invented a story concerning Helen's sojourn in Egypt; cf. West 2002, 36. Note, however, Lloyd 1976, 89–113, which offers a number of useful insights into the long-standing cultural interactions between Greeks and Egyptians; cf. Moyer 2002. In the end, whatever the truth of Herodotus' inquiries, we cannot accept that he offers a verbatim report of his interviews with the Egyptian priests, for de Jong 2012 well illustrates how Herodotus' distinct authorial voiceprint infuses this narrative.

[45] For the contrast between the Helen of Homer and Stesichorus and Herodotus' 'distinctively imperial Helen', see Austin 1994, 127–36. Given the plethora of inquiring terms in this account (see below), West's view that Herodotus' account is 'quite plainly a version of Stesichorus' seems much too reductive (2004, 89).

Having established Helen's 'true' location during the Achaean-Trojan conflict, Herodotus subsequently sets out to demonstrate the various processes that he has undertaken in order to verify this account. First, he makes explicit appeals to the (probably written) *Iliad* (and possibly two passages from *Odyssey*),[46] one of our earliest citations from the Homeric corpus.[47] The passage from the *Iliad* centres on a scene in which Hecuba ascends to her chamber:

ἔνθ᾽ ἔσαν οἱ πέπλοι παμποίκιλα ἔργα γυναικῶν
Σιδονίων, τὰς αὐ᾽τὸς Ἀλέξανδρος θεοειδής
ἤγαγε Σιδονίηθεν, ε᾽πιπλὼς εὐ᾽ρέα πόντον,
τὴν ὁδὸν ἣν Ἑλένην περ ἀ᾽νήγαγεν εὐ᾽πατέρειαν·

and there were all-embroidered robes, the productions of Sidonian women,
whom God-like Alexander himself
led from Sidon, sailing over the broad sea,
on that journey on which he brought back the noble-born Helen.

Iliad 6.289–92

Alexander's connection in 'these verses' (τοῖσι ἔπεσι) with the Syria-dwelling Sidonian women convinces Herodotus that Homer knew of his journey to Egypt; 'for Syria borders upon Egypt, and the Phoenicians, to whom Sidon belongs, dwell in Syria' (ὁμουρέει γὰρ ἡ Συρίη Αἰγύπτῳ, οἱ δὲ Φοίνικες, τῶν ἐστι ἡ Σιδών, ἐν τῇ Συρίῃ οἰκέουσι, Hdt. 2.116.6).

Through what appears to be a rather strained reading of the Iliadic passage,[48] Herodotus argues that Homer was in fact 'well informed' of Helen's sojourn in Egypt, though he was compelled to offer an account that was 'fitting' (εὐ᾽πρεπὴς) for epic poetry. What does Herodotus mean by his suggestion that Helen's stay at Troy is 'fitting' for epic poetry? Earlier in Book 2, he remarks that 'the story' (τὸν μῦθον)[49] surrounding Ocean is 'beyond proof' (οὐκ ἔχει ἔλεγχον), surmising: 'I think that Homer or some older poet fabricated the name and inserted it into his poetry' (Ὅμηρον δὲ ἤ τινα

---

[46] The *Odyssey* passages are 4.227-30 and 4.351-52. As Lloyd 2007, 325 notes, the final remarks in 2.116.6 proceed as though the *Odyssey* citations were not there; cf. further discussion in Sammons 2012, 57, n.12.

[47] Anderson 1997, 11.

[48] Lloyd 2007, 325 speaks of the passage as 'suspect evidence for Herodotus' purpose'; cf. Vandiver 1991, 126 ('an essay in applied literary criticism').

[49] On the meaning of μῦθος in Herodotus, see Baragwanath and de Bakker 2012a, 10–19; for the fifth century more broadly, see Fowler 2011.

τῶν πρότερον γενομένων ποιητέων δοκέω τοὔνομα εὑρόντα ἐς ποίησιν ἐσενείκασθαι, 2.23).[50] Several chapters later in the same *logos* he states that Homer and Hesiod 'created the Greeks' theogony and gave the gods their names, allotted their honours and skills, and indicated their appearances' (οὗτοι δέ εἰσι οἱ ποιήσαντες θεογονίην Ἕλλησι καὶ τοῖσι θεοῖσι τὰς ἐπωνυμίας δόντες καὶ τιμάς τε καὶ τέχνας διελόντες καὶ εἴδεα αὐτῶν σημήναντες, 2.53.2). In Book 3, too, Herodotus concludes that the name river Eridanus is clearly a Greek one, 'made up by some poet' (ὑπὸ ποιητέω δέ τινος ποιηθέν, 3.115.2). With this broader context in mind, it is clear that Herodotus regards Homer as a creator of stories (designated *mythoi* at 2.23) that in some ways cannot be proven. The implication for Herodotus' comments at 2.116 is that Homer was not primarily concerned with unvarnished truth when composing his poem. Herodotus' point is primarily a historiographical one: Homer's account must be denuded; only then will the historical and poetical become disentangled.[51] In his remarks on Homer's version of Helen's role, then, Herodotus at once divorces his work from that of Homer, the latter clearly not bound by the same generic principles as Herodotus, whilst simultaneously reasserting *a* truth value to the Homeric account. Perspicuous readers of Homer, Herodotus intimates, can indeed recover the historical events at Troy.[52]

Clearly not satisfied with his scrutiny of the Homeric texts alone, however, Herodotus deploys a second strategy to convince the reader that his own version of the war is the authoritative one: the application of inquiry techniques. At the midpoint of Herodotus' digression on Egyptian history, politics, and culture, he asserts:

μέχρι μὲν τούτου ὄψις τε ἐμὴ καὶ γνώμη καὶ ἱστορίη ταῦτα λέγουσά ἐστι, τὸ δὲ ἀπὸ τοῦδε Αἰγυπτίους ἔρχομαι λόγους ἐρέων κατὰ τὰ ἤκουον· προσέσται δὲ αὐτοῖσι καὶ τῆς ἐμῆς ὄψιος.

---

[50] Lloyd 2007, 256 and Fowler 2011, 46–48, 59.

[51] Similarly West 2002, 47: 'it might be possible to strip off fabulous and fictional accretions and expose a sound historical core'; *contra* Lateiner 1989, 99 and Austin 1994, 123 ('Homer is being relegated to no more than a poet'). de Jong's view that '[Herodotus is] enlisting [Homer] as much as possible in the historiographical camp' 2012, 133, n.24 is surely a step too far, since Herodotus explicitly demarcates Homer as an epic poet; cf., however, [Plutarch] *On the Life and Poetry of Homer* 74–90, which credits Homer as the inventor of the ἱστορικὸς λόγος ('Historical Work').

[52] Cf. Sammons 2012, 56: 'Homer indicates the true account could only be properly interpreted by an expert, indeed someone like Herodotus'.

Until now, all I have spoken of is the record of my own personal observation (*opsis*) and judgement (*gnōmē*) and inquiry (*historiē*). From here I will speak of Egyptian matters, according to what I have heard (*kata ta ēkouon*), though supplemented with something of what I myself have seen (*tēs emēs opsios*).[53]

Herodotus, *Histories* 2.99.1

This roster of general research principles regarding Herodotus' Egyptian material (and perhaps his work more broadly?)[54] will soon resurface in his account on 'the matters concerning Helen'. Indeed, near the start of the *logos*, Herodotus notes that there is a *temenos* of Aphrodite the Stranger in the precinct of Proteus. He surmises (συμβάλλομαι) that it is actually a temple for Helen, (1) because it is said to be dedicated to foreign Aphrodite (a form of the goddess honoured in no other Egyptian temple) and (2) because of the story he had *heard* (ἀκηκοὼς) regarding Helen's entreaty to Proteus (2.112.2). In the succeeding chapter, Herodotus repeats that his knowledge of Helen's whereabouts derives from *inquiry* conducted with the priests ('the priests told me, when I inquired [*historeonti*], that the events concerning Helen happened as follows', ἔλεγον δέ μοι οἱ ἱρέες ἱστορέοντι τὰ περὶ Ἑλένην γενέσθαι ὧδε, 2.113.1).

Following the claims made against the Trojan prince, the Egyptian king Proteus is not content only with others' reports (i.e. hearsay); Proteus submits him to an inquisition (2.115.2–6), bringing together the essential tools outlined in 2.99: observation, hearsay, and judgement. Seeking to verify what he had heard from Thonis (2.114),[55] Proteus brings Alexander before his eyes and asks him about his background and how it was that he came to acquire Helen. Alexander, we are told, equivocated and did not convey 'the truth' (τὴν ἀληθείην, 2.115.3); at this very moment, a group of suppliants confute Alexander's account, exposing his heinous crimes ('recounting the entire story of the wrong done', ἐξηγεύμενοι πάντα λόγον τοῦ ἀδικήματος, 2.115.3). Through inquiry, a process that distils truths and falsehoods, Proteus reveals his quasi-Herodotean judgement,[56] setting out in detail Alexander's moral

---

[53] For other instances of autopsy in Book 2, see Lloyd 2007, 229.

[54] Cf. 2.123.1, 147.1; 7.152.3.

[55] Lloyd 2007, 324 notes here the 'accumulation of detail, a standard Herodotean device for creating verisimilitude'; cf. 1.23.7, where Periander interrogates the crew that flung the poet Arion overboard.

[56] de Bakker 2012, 115 on Proteus' revelation of truth. Blondell 2013, 152 compares Herodotus' Proteus with Homer's Priam.

turpitude, whilst reinforcing his own impeccable treatment of guest-friends. Hence, Herodotus' Proteus scene reinforces how the inquiring techniques referred to in 2.99 can evince the truth – even concerning matters that, at least for Herodotus, are antique.

Yet again, once Herodotus has served to uncover the true account of Helen in Homer, along with the arcane authorship of the *Cypria* (a text that, Herodotus surmises, cannot be Homeric, given its narrative of Alexander and Helen's favourable journey direct to Ilium, 2.117),[57] Herodotus signals further research processes at work in his *logos*. Seeking to confirm all that has been reported, Herodotus narrates that he asked the priests whether or not the Greeks (i.e. Homer) told a foolish story about the matters concerning Troy ('I asked the priests whether or not it is a foolish account which the Hellenes speak of concerning the events at Ilium', εἰρομένου δέ μευ τοὺς ἰρέας εἰ μάταιον λόγον λέγουσι οἱ Ἕλληνες τὰ περὶ Ἴλιον γενέσθαι ἢ οὔ, 2.118.1). The priests confidently asserted their knowledge, 'having made *inquiries* and acquired knowledge from Menelaus himself' (ἱστορίῃσι φάμενοι εἰδέναι παρ᾽ αὐτοῦ Μενέλεω, 2.118.1). Shortly after this, once the Greeks found no Helen at Troy, Menelaus was sent to Proteus – an important detail, further corroborating Menelaus' status as a direct, hence authoritative, witness to the priests' account. In Egypt, 'the truth' (τὴν ἀληθείην) was revealed to Menelaus, and he was subsequently reunited with his wife (2.119.1). Finally, after relating Menelaus' most impious sacrifice of two Egyptian children (recalling Agamemnon's sacrifice of his daughter Iphigenia),[58] Herodotus concludes that '[the priests] said that they knew some of these things from *inquiry*; the things which happened in their own country they knew precisely' (τούτων δὲ τὰ μὲν ἱστορίῃσι ἔφασαν ἐπίστασθαι, τὰ δὲ παρ᾽ ἑωυτοῖσι γενόμενα ἀτρεκέως ἐπιστάμενοι λέγειν, 2.119.3). Throughout the Helen *logos*, therefore, Herodotus repeatedly indicates the forensic quality of his analysis and the *bona fide* quality of his information, which, rather than being fitting for an epic context, is suited to an account concerned with unadorned historical truths.[59]

---

[57] Cf. 4.32, where Herodotus proffers that 'Hesiod has spoken about the Hyperboreans, just as Homer has done in the *Epigonoi*, if at any rate he composed that poem' (ἀλλ᾽ Ἡσιόδῳ μέν ἐστι περὶ Ὑπερβορέων εἰρημένα, ἔστι δὲ καὶ Ὁμήρῳ ἐν Ἐπιγόνοισι, εἰ δὴ τῷ ἐόντι γε Ὅμηρος ταῦτα τὰ ἔπεα ἐποίησε). Graziosi 2002, 193–95 shows how this serves a dual function of challenging Homeric authority whilst simultaneously reinforcing the superior skill of the Iliadic poet.

[58] Fehling 1989, 62 and Lloyd 2007, 325–26.

[59] Hunter 1982, 55, Vandiver 1991, 127, and Munson 2012, 200–01.

The extent to which Herodotus' analysis of competing Trojan War traditions wholly (or even partially) conveys the precise techniques that he applied in composing his *Histories* is, of course, forever unknowable.[60] Yet this account reveals much about those methodologies that he wished his audience to perceive as being crucial in the publication of his work.[61] Herodotus' ultimate message is that, no less than the recent events of the Persian Wars, the much more ancient Trojan War must be subjected to the rules of historiographical inquiry. A demonstrably historical event is clearly recovered from such a process, even if the shape and texture of that event is not as the epic poet Homer would have it.

This particular medley of written texts, oral traditions, autoptic evidences, and logical deductions all lend authority to the Herodotean voiceprint. The narrator is then able to finish his analysis with a final flourish, judging that:

οὐ γὰρ δὴ οὕτω γε φρενοβλαβὴς ἦν ὁ Πρίαμος οὐδὲ οἱ ἄλλοι <οἱ> προσήκοντες αὐτῷ, ὥστε τοῖσι σφετέροισι σώμασι καὶ τοῖσι τέκνοισι καὶ τῇ πόλι κινδυνεύειν ἐβούλοντο, ὅκως Ἀλέξανδρος Ἑλένῃ συνοικέῃ.

surely Priam, or those others closest to him, were not so crazy that they would wish to endanger their own lives and their children and their city, just so that Alexander could live with Helen.

Herodotus, *Histories* 2.120.2

This logical deduction adds further proof for Herodotus that the war was ultimately a divinely ordained catastrophe, in which the gods sought to punish those that had committed great wrongs (2.120.5).[62]

Herodotus' account by no means creates an irreparable gulf with that of Homer – he envisages the divine playing a no less substantive role than his epic predecessor did,[63] but it nonetheless poses deeply troubling questions about the Homeric account. How does one square, for instance, Homer's presentation of Helen and Priam at the walls of Troy in *Iliad* 3 (the so-called Teichoscopia) with Herodotus' insistence that Helen was never there? And how to account

---

[60] According to Fehling 1989, Herodotus is no historian: 'there are no sources other than [Herodotus] for entire accounts, only for individual items of data' (259). For a response, see now the various discussions in Dunsch and Ruffing 2013.

[61] de Bakker 2012, 122ff., de Jong 2012, 128, cf. already Fornara 1971, 19–20, Neville 1977, and Hunter 1982, 56–61.

[62] ὡς μὲν ἐγὼ γνώμην ἀποφαίνομαι, τοῦ δαιμονίου παρασκευάζοντος.

[63] Harrison 2000, 105 and Munson 2001, 185–86 and 2012, 200.

for Herodotus' assertion that Priam and his advisers would not be so crazy as
to fight such a war merely for Helen and Alexander (2.120.1–3)[64] with Homer's
Priam, who accedes that there is no shame in warring over a woman as beautiful
as Helen (*Il.* 3.156–60)? Several Iliadic episodes and whole narrative strands
(such as Helen's status as an outsider amongst the women of Troy) are rendered
implausible according to Herodotus' interpretation,[65] a gulf that reinforces his
view that one of Homer's principal concerns was to present an account that
was fitting for his genre. Truth, Herodotus suggests, is the ultimate marker of
historiography, distinguishing it from epic and other genres.

   As has become clear from our reading of this passage, Herodotus is
concerned with correcting currently held views – and not just on Helen's
whereabouts, but equally Greek attitudes towards foreigners, in this instance
the Egyptians.[66] As several scholars have already recognized, Herodotus'
Proteus is an unimpeachable host throughout the Helen *logos*, indiscriminately
welcoming all of his guests – a characterization that contrasts sharply with
the scandalous behaviour of the Trojan Alexander and the impious Achaean
Menelaus.[67] To note just one more significant instance here, in another account
that strives to overturn current views on Egyptian culture, Herodotus reports a
misguided 'story' (μῦθος) concerning Heracles when he reached Egypt (2.45).
Some Greeks state (λέγουσι) that, having arrived in Egypt and been crowned,
Heracles slew all those Egyptians who subsequently attempted to offer him
as a sacrifice to Zeus. Codswallop, declares Herodotus, 'for how should [the
Egyptians] sacrifice men when they are forbidden to sacrifice beasts except for
swine and oxen and bull-calves, if they are uncontaminated, and geese?' The
Greeks' Heracles *logos* is ultimately designated 'ill-considered' (ἀνεπισκέπτως),
'naïve' (εὐήθης), symptomatic of a blanket ignorance of the Egyptians' nature
and customs ('Now it seems to me that when the Hellenes repeat this account
they are altogether ignorant of nature of customs of the Egyptians', ἐμοὶ μέν
νυν δοκέουσι ταῦτα λέγοντες τῆς Αἰγυπτίων φύσιος καὶ τῶν νόμων πάμπαν
ἀπείρως ἔχειν οἱ Ἕλληνες, 2.45.2). As this parallel case shows, Herodotus often

---

[64] Similarly 1.4.3: 'And the Persians say that they, the people of Asia, when their women were seized
     by force, had made it of no account' (σφέας μὲν δὴ τοὺς ἐκ τῆς Ἀσίης λέγουσι Πέρσαι ἁρπαζομένων
     τῶν γυναικῶν λόγον οὐδένα ποιήσασθαι); see further Węcowski 2004, 152–53.
[65] Blondell 2013, 154.
[66] Cartledge and Greenwood 2002.
[67] Munson 2001, 141–44, de Bakker 2012, 113–14, and Vandiver 2012.

draws upon characters and events from myth in order to reject contemporary Greek traditions and beliefs.[68] Herodotus' appeals to the Trojan War in the Helen *logos* thus contribute towards the polemical spirit that undergirds his narrative.

Antique vs. recent pasts

A final, brief look at the historian Thucydides, an author broadly contemporary with Herodotus,[69] reveals a great deal of continuity between the two historians in terms of their approach towards the Trojan War. Just as Herodotus displays marked concern with Homer's ability to convey what was already a 400-year-old conflict, so too Thucydides begins his *History* by observing, 'For in the preceding time and in the period still more ancient, the amount of time that had passed made it impossible to discover clearly what occurred' (τὰ γὰρ πρὸ αὐτῶν καὶ τὰ ἔτι παλαίτερα σαφῶς μὲν εὑρεῖν διὰ χρόνου πλῆθος ἀδύνατα ἦν, 1.1.3). Thucydides' reticence towards the deep past is reinforced throughout his work, and on a number of occasions via explicit reference (either by the narrator or by one of his protagonists) to Homer:

ὡς Ὅμηρος τοῦτο δεδήλωκεν, εἴ τῳ ἱκανὸς τεκμηριῶσαι.

Homer has showed this [i.e. the power of Agamemnon], if one is to consider such testimony adequate.

Thucydides, *History* 1.9.4

τῇ Ὁμήρου αὖ ποιήσει εἴ τι χρὴ κἀνταῦθα πιστεύειν, ἣν εἰκὸς ἐπὶ τὸ μεῖζον μὲν ποιητὴν ὄντα κοσμῆσαι, ὅμως δὲ φαίνεται καὶ οὕτως ἐνδεεστέρα.

... if we may place trust in Homer's poetry again here; for it is likely that as a poet he elaborated the expedition for effect, though it still appears to have been smaller than our own.

Thucydides, *History* 1.10.3

καὶ οὐδὲν προσδεόμενοι οὔτε Ὁμήρου ἐπαινέτου οὔτε ὅστις ἔπεσι μὲν τὸ αὐτίκα τέρψει, τῶν δ' ἔργων τὴν ὑπόνοιαν ἡ ἀλήθεια βλάψει.

---

[68] Herodotus was regarded by Plutarch as a *philobarabros* ('barbarian-lover') in his *On the Malice of Herodotus*; see further Marincola 1994 and Baragwanath 2008, 9–22.

[69] Scholarship on the connections between these two authors continues to flourish; for a provocative reading, which sees Herodotus responding to Thucydides, see Irwin 2013.

[Pericles:] ... and neither do we need a Homer to sing our praise nor another
who pleases for the moment with his epic verses, but for whom the truth will
dispel the conjecture of the deeds.

                                                    Thucydides, *History* 2.41.4

These passages signal a profound mistrust of things from the ancient past
(cf. 1.20.1) – an age that is largely beyond the grasp of even the most credulous
of inquirers, according to Thucydides. It is for this reason that in his opening
section Thucydides rejects the exaggerations of the poets (as well as the
λογογράφοι or 'story-makers'), since they work with evidence that is 'beyond
disproof' (ἀνεξέλεγκτος), a point that renders their works devoid of value and
shrouded in 'the legendary' (τὸ μυθῶδες, 1.21.1).

Yet there is no indication that Thucydides ultimately rejected the idea of the
Trojan War as an historical event. On the contrary, Thucydides remarks near
the beginning of his *History*: 'one must accept that [the Trojan War] was the
greatest [conflict] up to now, though small by modern standards' (νομίζειν δὲ
τὴν στρατείαν ἐκείνην μεγίστην μὲν γενέσθαι τῶν πρὸ αὐτῆς, λειπομένην δὲ
τῶν νῦν, 1.10.3).[70] Such a position aligns Thucydides rather closely with his
contemporary Herodotus. Both authors regard the Trojan War as a monumental
conflict in its own historical context, and both appeal to that conflict in order to
(1) underscore the magnitude of their own wars and (2) throw into sharp relief
the difference between epic poetry (concerned with the creation of fitting stories)
and historiography (concerned with the critique of authoritative evidence).

Thinking through Homer

This analysis of the Helen *logos* has revealed how Herodotus makes use
of the Trojan War story in order to reinforce a number of principal themes
that recur elsewhere in his *Histories*. The story enables him to reinforce: (1)
the authoritative nature of his own inquiry, a radical form of discourse that
constitutes elements which all feature explicitly in this account ('observation'
[ὄψις], 'judgement' [γνώμη], 'hearsay' [ἀκοή]);[71] (2) the ignorance of other

---

[70] Thucydides also refers to Homer at 3.104.4, where he cites the Homeric *Hymn to Apollo* as proof of
    the ancient festival and assembly at Delos.
[71] On Herodotus' radical 'monumental historical narrative' written in prose, see Chiasson 2012 (quote
    at p.137); cf. the measured caveats in Clarke 2008, 189.

Greeks concerning their traditional stories;[72] (3) the importance of establishing a more relativist framework when approaching other cultures; (4) the inescapable place of the divine and δίκη ('justice') within any causal explanation of human affairs;[73] and, finally, (5) the vital role played by the Egyptians in the commitment to writing 'of great and wondrous deeds' – the very stuff that make up his own historical record.[74] Readers should not underestimate the especially controversial nature of that final point: Herodotus' λόγιοι ('learned') priests even trump Greeks on their own ancient history.[75]

There is no indication in the *Histories* that Herodotus in any way questioned the historical reality of the Trojan campaign, nor indeed that he doubted the existence of the war's chief protagonists; however, his engagement with the story of Troy exposes acutely the limits of Homer's epic world from the vantage point of a fifth-century historian writing in prose. As Lloyd puts it, Herodotus is no 'latter-day Homer';[76] his masterful synthesis of multiple accounts related to the Trojan War throws into sharp relief the *Iliad*'s (in)ability to function as a historical document, pointedly its ability to convey *wie es eigentlich gewesen*. So while Herodotus may have somewhat ironically acquired a reputation in later antiquity for his most-Homeric persona,[77] his own examination of the Trojan War reveals the considerable gap between historical inquirer and epic poet.

Nevertheless, there can be little doubt that Herodotus' analysis served to strengthen his contemporaries' faith in the essential historicity of the Trojan War, a war that would even stand up to his idiosyncratically 'meticulous enquiry'.[78] And indeed, this faith in the war as an historical event transcends Herodotus' immediate context. For as Naoíse demonstrates in the succeeding section, this admixture of faith and scepticism concerning

---

[72] Fornara 1971, 19: '[Herodotus pursues] destructive criticism of the general and unconsidered assumptions of his parochial contemporaries'.

[73] Herodotus provides similar sentiments on divine punishment as a response to criminal or profane acts at 4.205; 6.84.3, 91, 139.1; 7.134-37; 8.129.3. See further Harrison 2000, 102–21 and Lloyd 2007, 232–34.

[74] 2.3.1, 77.1; Munson 2001, 143.

[75] Vandiver 1991, 129.

[76] Lloyd 2007, 325; cf. Baragwanath 2008, 54, remarking on the mixture of 'Homeric aspects alongside those that seem more fifth century and sophistic' in Herodotus.

[77] Priestley 2014, 217: 'There is a certain irony that Herodotus came to be associated with the very writer that he accuses of intentional fictions'. It is worth bearing in mind, of course, that Herodotus strives throughout his work to forge a clear union of magnitude with Homer and his great war, even if not a hermeneutical union.

[78] Munson 2012, 200.

Homer's *Iliad* chimes rather closely with that of Schliemann, who hoped his archaeological excavations would serve as concrete proof of the historicity of a Trojan War.

Naoíse: Schliemann's physical proofs

Hinter der letztern legte ich ... stiess beim Weitergraben auf dieser Mauer und unmittelbar neben dem Hause des Priamos auf einen grossen kupfernen Gegenstand höchst merkwürdiger Form, der um so mehr meine Aufmerksamkeit auf sich zog, als ich hinter demselben Gold zu bemerken glaubte. ... Um den Schatz der Habsucht meiner Arbeiter zu entziehen und ihn für die Wissenschaft zu retten, war die allergrösste Eile nöthig, und, obgleich es noch nicht Frühstückszeit war, so Hess ich doch sogleich 'paidos' ... ausrufen, und währed meine Arbeiter assen und ausruhten, schnitt ich den Schatz mit einem grossen Messer heraus was nicht ohne die allergrösste Kraftanstrengung und die furchtbarste Lebensgefahr möglich war, den die grosse Festungsmauer, welche ich zu untergraben hatte, drohte jeden Augenblick auf mich einzustürzen. Aber der Anblick so vieler Gegenstände, von denen jeder einzelne ainen unermesslichen Werth für die Wissenschaft hat, machte mich tollkühn und ich dachte an keine Gefahr. Die Fortschaffung des Schatzes wäre mir aber unmöglich geworden ohne die Hülfe meiner lieben Frau, die immer bereit stand, die von mir herausgeschnittenen Gegenstände in ihren Shawl zu packen und fortzutragen.

In excavating this wall further and directly by the side of the palace of King Priam, I came upon a large copper article of the most remarkable form, which attracted my attention all the more as I thought I saw gold behind it ... In order to withdraw the Treasure from the greed of my workmen, and to save it for archaeology, I had to be most expeditious, and although it was not yet time for breakfast, I immediately had *'paidos'* called ... While the men were eating and resting, I cut out the Treasure with a large knife, which it was impossible to do without the very greatest exertion and the most fearful risk of my life, for the great fortification-wall, beneath which I had to dig, threatened every moment to fall down upon me. But the sight of so many objects, every one of which is of inestimable value to science, made me foolhardy, and I never thought of any danger. It would, however, have been impossible for me to have removed the Treasure without the help of my dear wife, who stood ready to pack the things which I cut out in her shawl and to carry them away.[79]

Schliemann 1874, 289–90

A priceless ancient treasure is discovered, and a dedicated scholar risks his life to save it from theft and confiscation. This story of adventure and derring-do comes from the final climactic chapter of *Trojanischer Alterthümer* (Trojan Antiquities), Heinrich Schliemann's first major work chronicling his discoveries at the site of Hisarlık, the location of the ancient city of Troy/Ilium. In his breathless account, Schliemann describes the excavation of a glittering hoard of gold, silver, and copper objects, which included metal vessels, weapons, and jewellery. This hoard was later styled as the 'Treasure of Priam' and to this day continues to stimulate both popular excitement and scholarly controversy.

Schliemann's quest to discover the archaeological remains of Troy was, like Herodotus' Helen *logos*, a means of seeking the truth behind the *Iliad*. Like Herodotus, Schliemann sought to use the latest methods and tools to uncover that truth and to establish himself as an authority on the 'real' Trojan War. In this section, I will consider how Schliemann constructed authority in relation to Homer in *Trojanischer Alterthümer*, focusing in particular on Chapter XXIII and the description of the 'Treasure of Priam'.

Schliemann's Trojan controversy

Controversy surrounded both the personal life and the archaeological career of Heinrich Schliemann. Schliemann was a German businessman who amassed a vast fortune in questionable circumstances, first during the Californian gold rush of 1849 and later during the Crimean War of 1853–1856. By 1863, his financial success was such that he was able to retire from business and devote himself to his private passion – Homeric archaeology.[80] Schliemann's first

---

[79] This translation of the German text is taken from the English edition of *Trojanischer Alterthümer*, translated and edited by Philip Smith, and published as *Troy and Its Remains* in 1875 (Schliemann 1875, 323–24). Throughout this section, I have used this translation as it was a popular and well-known book in its own right.

[80] For biographical information about Schliemann and an assessment of his archaeological work, see Traill 1995. For problems with the sources for Schliemann's life and his own autobiographical writings, see Calder 1972. For an apologist treatment which presents Schliemann as a romantic figure and which downplays his misdeeds, see Moorehead 1994.

major archaeological project was to establish the location of Homeric Troy. After visiting several sites in the Troad, he was eventually convinced by the results of Frank Calvert's early investigations at the mound of Hisarlık.

Calvert had bought much of the land around the site with the aim of conducting major excavations, but had been unable to fund archaeological work on a substantial scale. He therefore enthusiastically supported the idea of Schliemann sponsoring new excavations, which started in 1870. The two had fallen out by 1872, however, with Calvert voicing public disapproval of both Schliemann's destructive methods and his problematic interpretations. Unabashed, Schliemann published stinging responses in print and aggressively promoted his own interpretation of the material.[81] He believed that the remains of Homeric Troy would lie close to the bottom of the mound and so drove the excavations forward at breakneck speed, recording relatively little about the objects, pottery, and architecture that he destroyed along the way. By the time Schliemann concluded his work in 1873, he had identified five successive cities amongst the remains, the second of which he argued to be the Troy of the *Iliad* – the city of Priam.[82] While most scholars accept that Hisarlık is indeed Troy, it is now recognized that the site has no fewer than nine distinct levels; that Schliemann's second city dates to the Early Bronze Age; and that if any of these cities did offer historical inspiration for the myth of the Trojan War, it is most likely to have been that destroyed at the end of the Late Bronze Age (Troy VIa-VIIb$_1$), rather than Troy II as Schliemann suggested.[83] During the 1870s, however, Schliemann's claims caused a popular sensation.

Public interest in the discovery of Homeric Troy was stoked not only by Schliemann's findings but also by the ensuing controversy. At the time, there was substantial scepticism about the existence of an historical Troy, as it was argued amongst professional classicists that the *Iliad* should be read as

---

[81] For Calvert and the relationship between Calvert and Schliemann, see Heuck Allen 1999.

[82] Schliemann triumphantly announces in the preface to *Trojanischer Alterthümer*: 'Meine driesjährigen Ausgrabungen haben zur Genüge bewiesen, dass die zweite Nation, die auf diesem Berge, auf den 4 bis 6 Meter oder 13 bis 20 Fuss hohen Trümmern der erstern Ansiedler, eine Stadt erbaute, die von Homer besungenen Trojaner waren' (Schliemann 1874, x): 'The excavations made this year (1873) have sufficiently proved that the second nation which built a town on this hill, upon the *debris* of the first settlers (which is from 13 to 20 feet deep), are the Trojans of whom Homer sings.' (Schliemann 1875, 16). Schliemann eventually returned to dig at Hisarlık again in 1878–1879.

[83] For current perspectives on the archaeology of the site of Troy, see Korfmann 1997 and 2006, Rose 2014 and Mac Sweeney 2018.

literature, rather than as history (see below). In his preface to the English edition of *Trojanischer Alterthümer*, published under the title *Troy and Its Remains* in 1875, Schliemann's editor and translator Philip Smith dismissed these views as 'sentimental objection' and claimed that Schliemann's discoveries added 'the interest of truthfulness to those poetic beauties which remain the pure creation of Homer'.[84]

In addition to this principled opposition about the historicity of Homer, Schliemann also attracted criticism on a more practical level relating to his methods and findings. Archaeologists condemned the speed of excavation and scale of destruction, as well as the poor quality of recording and the frequent contradictions in Schliemann's claims.[85] One of Schliemann's most vocal early critics was his erstwhile friend, Frank Calvert, who disputed several of Schliemann's claims about his discoveries. Indeed, Schliemann dedicated a substantial section of *Trojanischer Alterthümer* to refuting an article published by Calvert in the *Levant Herald* in 1873.[86] Taking recourse to Homer for historical verification, he casts aspersions on the quality of Calvert's scholarship, claiming that Calvert would have a better grasp on antiquity: 'Wenn Herr Calvert sich aber die Mühe gemacht hätte, im Homer nachzusehen' ('If Mr Calvert had taken the trouble to look into Homer').[87] He also denies building directly on Calvert's work, saying: 'er bemerkt irrthümlich, dass ich seine Ausgrabungen fortgesetzt habe' ('he is wrong in saying that I have continued his excavations').[88] While Calvert had censured Schliemann for what he saw as exaggeration and misinterpretation, other critics went further, accusing him of outright deceit and the falsification of evidence.[89] While many of these accusations have since been proved true, in the mid- to late 1870s Schliemann's infamy and the controversy surrounding his discoveries only served to make

---

[84] Smith 1875, xvii.
[85] Schliemann attempts to forestall these latter complaints in the preface to *Trojanischer Alterthümer*: 'Wenn meine Aufsätze hin und wieder Widersprüche enthalten, so hoffe ich, dass man mir diese zugute halten wird, wenn man berücksichtigt, dass ich hier eine neue Welt für die Archäologie aufgedeckt' (Schliemann 1874, v): 'If my memoirs now and then contain contradictions, I hope that these may be pardoned when it is considered that I have revealed a new world for archaeology' (Schliemann 1875, 12).
[86] Schliemann 1874, 235–41 (English edition: Schliemann 1875, 270–75).
[87] Schliemann 1874, 235 (English edition: Schliemann 1875, 270).
[88] Schliemann 1874, 237 (English edition: Schliemann 1875, 272).
[89] For a sketch of the various scholarly responses to Schliemann's claims, see the account of Newton in Traill 1995, 126. For Schliemann's many critics in the academy, see Calder 1972, 347–48 and Marchand 1996, 120–22.

the excavations at Hisarlık all the more sensational.[90] Schliemann's first major publication on the Hisarlık excavations therefore sought both to answer his critics and to play to the crowd.

Autopsy and adventure

Schliemann chose to structure his book in the form of journal entries, each labelled with a date and location. In doing so, he presents his reader, not with an account of the material remains in historical order, but rather with a dramatic chronicle of discovery casting himself as the protagonist. This structure heightens the drama of the piece, placing the archaeologist rather than the archaeology centre stage.

The diary style also served to construct Schliemann's claim to truthfulness and authority. The preface begins with a conspicuously Herodotean statement about autopsy, with Schliemann asserting that the vividness of his descriptions proved the genuine nature of his diary entries: 'Das vorliegende Werk ist eine Art von Tagebuch meiner Ausgrabungen in Troja, den alle Aufsätze, woraus es besteht, sind, wie die Lebhaftigkeit der Schilderungen es beweist, an Ort und Stelle, beim Fortschreiten der Arbeiten, vor mir niedergeschrieben' ('The present book is a sort of Diary of my excavations at Troy, for all the memoirs of which it consists were, as the vividness of my descriptions will prove, written down by me on the spot while proceeding with my works').[91] Schliemann was certainly familiar with Herodotus, and the *Histories* had indeed proved useful for Calvert in his early explorations of the Troad.[92] In *Trojanischer Alterthümer*, however, Schliemann referred to Herodotus only six times, mostly in relation to Xerxes' visit to Troy and the appearance of the site in the classical period.[93] In comparison, Strabo appears no less than twenty-seven times, again mostly concerning the preservation of the site later in antiquity.[94] Schliemann's debt

---

[90] For the public interest in Schliemann's Trojan excavations, particularly in Britain, see Moorhead 1994, 151–54.

[91] Schliemann 1874, v (English edition: Schliemann 1875, 12).

[92] Heuck Allen 1999, 61.

[93] Schliemann 1874, v, 5, 14, 125, 133, 189.

[94] Schliemann 1874, xl, xli, 5, 16, 20, 32, 39, 77, 101, 102, 126, 130, 131, 132, 133, 134, 135, 136, 142, 153, 154, 192, 206, 264, 309, 320.

to Herodotus therefore lay less in the content of the *Histories* and more in his rhetoric of authority.

The diary style of the book also has the effect of making it into a story. It is a tale that begins with Schliemann's arrival on site, and describes his activities through the 1871, 1872, and finally the 1873 seasons. As with any good story, there are moments of triumph and catastrophe, from plagues of scorpions and outbreaks of fire, to startling discoveries and remarkable local characters.[95] The climax of the story, however, is unquestionably the discovery of the 'Treasure of Priam' in the concluding chapter of the book, Chapter XXIII.[96]

The chapter opens with Schliemann expressing his anxiety over his slow progress and claiming this slow pace made it necessary to excavate a 'tiefen Einschnitt' ('deep cutting'), and to break through several ancient walls in order to reach the early periods.[97] This destruction, we soon hear, was more than vindicated by the discovery of the Treasure of Priam. The unearthing of the treasure itself is described in dramatic terms, as we saw in the passage quoted at the start of this section. According to this account, it was Schliemann alone who was responsible for the treasure's detection and excavation, with only his wife to help with its packing and storage. In the story that we are told, once he has recognized the glint of gold through the dirt, our hero must work against the clock in order to save the treasure from his greedy workmen, labouring in imminent physical danger with the ancient fortification wall threatening to collapse on him at any moment.[98]

This narrative of discovery recalls the drama of the adventure novels that were popular across Europe and the United States at the time.[99] Schliemann is known to have enjoyed these stories and, by his own admission, even to

[95] Plagues of insects and scorpions: Schliemann 1874, 155. Fire: Schliemann 1874, 241–42. The discovery of the 'Scaean Gate': Schliemann 1874, 271–72. The unexpected encounter with the crippled owner of the local shop, whose natural ability with languages, appreciation of Homer, and business acumen is described in terms comparable with Schliemann's own: Schliemann 1874, 135–36.
[96] For the account of the discovery of the Treasure of Priam, see Schliemann 1874, 289–302 (English edition: Schliemann 1875, 323–40).
[97] Schliemann 1874, 288 (English edition: Schliemann 1875, 322).
[98] Schliemann 1874, 298–90 (English edition: Schliemann 1875, 323–24).
[99] The genre was extremely popular in the late nineteenth century and often featured intrepid explorers undertaking heroic feats in faraway lands (Phillips 1996, Markovitis 2006, 171–78). For example, the decades immediately before and after the publication of *Trojanischer Alterthümer* saw the appearance of such adventure classics as: Jules Verne's *Voyage au centre de la Terre* (1864); Baludin Möllhausen's *Die Mandanenwaise: Erzählung aus den Rheinlanden und dem Stromgebiet des Missouri* (1865); Robert Louis Stevenson's *Treasure Island* (1881); and H. Rider Haggard's *King Solomon's Mines* (1883).

have memorized them.[100] It has even been suggested that Schliemann's various autobiographical writings[101] may have followed the pattern of the 'rags-to-riches' tale that was popularized in the mid-nineteenth century by the American novelist Horatio Alger.[102] While it is impossible to know whether Schliemann deliberately drew from adventure novels when crafting his autobiographical reflections or his archaeological description, the parallels with the genre are nonetheless striking. This is particularly true of the passage in which he describes the discovery of the treasure – the elements of environmental danger (the nearly collapsing wall), dastardly natives (the greedy workmen), hidden mysteries (the lost city of legend), and fabulous riches (the treasure) are all classic hallmarks of the genre.[103]

Archaeology: An Homeric science

If Schliemann sought to beguile his readers with a combination of vivid autopsy and exciting adventure, he also sought to reassure them by constructing a clear sense of himself as a reliable archaeological authority. His strategy for this was twofold. Most obviously, Schliemann appealed to the idea of archaeology as an emerging scientific discipline, and sought to give his account an air of scientific precision and objectivity. In his description of the treasure itself, Schliemann methodically details each object in turn, with each description conforming to a standard pattern. We are first presented with a description of the item's physical form and material, several measurements, and then an interpretation of the object's function based on Homeric epic. For example, the description of six particularly mysterious silver items runs thus:

> Ich fand dort ferner sechs mit dem Hammer getriebene Stüke allerreinsten Silbers in Form von grossen Klingen, deren eines Ende abgerundet, das andere in Gestalt eines Halbmondes ausgeschnitten ist. Die beiden grössern sind 21½ Centimeter lang und 5 Centimeter breit, und wiegt eins davon 190, das andere 183 Gramm. Die darauffolgenden zwei Stücke sind 18½

---

[100] Calder 1972, 352.

[101] These can be found in the Preface to *Ithaque, le Péloponnèse, Troie: Recherches archéologiques* (1869), the Introduction to *Ilios* (1880), and in his posthumous *Selbtsbiographie* (1892).

[102] Marchand 1996, 118. Alger's most famous book was *Ragged Dick* (1867), published only two years before Schliemann began to include autobiographical elements in his books, and seven years before the publication of *Trojanischer Alterthümer*.

[103] See n.99 above for the adventure novel genre.

Centimeter lang und 4 Centimeter breit, und wiegt eins davon 174, das
andere 173 Gramm; die beiden übrigen Stücke sind 17¼ Centimeter lang
und 3 Centimeter breit, und wiegt eins davon 173, das andere 171 Gramm.
Höchst wahrscheinlich sind dies die homerischen Talente (τάλαντα),
welche nur klein sein konnten, da z. B. Achilles (Ilias, XXIII, 269) als ersten
Kampfpreis eine Frau, als zweiten ein Pferd, als dritten einen Kessel und als
vierten zwei goldene Talente aufstellt.

I also found in the Treasure six pieces of the purest silver in the form of large
knife-blades, having one end rounded, and the other cut into the form of
crescent; the two larger blades are nearly 8½ inches long and 2 inches broad,
and weigh respectively 190 and 183 grammes. The next two pieces are about
7½ inches long and 1½ broad, and weigh respectively 174 and 173 grammes.
The two other pieces are nearly 7 inches long and 1⅕ inches broad, and
weigh respectively 173 and 171 grammes. It is extremely probably that these
are the Homeric *talents* (τάλαντα), which could only have been small, as, for
instance, when Achilles offers for the first prize a woman, for the second a
horse, for the third a cauldron, and for the fourth two gold talents.[104]

Schliemann 1874, 292–93

This passage is peppered with numerical measurements, lending a sense
of objectivity to the descriptions and bolstering claims that Schliemann's
work was a serious contribution to 'Wissenschaft' ('science'). Details offered
about the nature of the materials had a similar effect – the silver of these
objects is described as 'allrreinsten' ('the most pure'). The final items of the
treasure described are some 8750 small gold objects – mostly, wire rings,
buttons, studs, and pegs. These are presented with even more attention to
detail, rounding off the section on the treasure as a whole with an apparently
objective and scientific fashion.[105] For several of these objects, Schliemann
offers measurements exact to half a millimetre (converted into hundredths
of an inch in the English edition), and specifies that he examined the finds
scientifically with a magnifying glass. In addition to conducting his own
analysis, Schliemann then also mentions that he had the finds examined by
an independent and well-respected metallurgical expert, who corroborated
Schliemann's own opinions about materials and manufacture:

[104] English edition: Schliemann 1875, 328.
[105] Schliemann 1874, 301 (English edition: Schliemann 1875, 338-40).

Mein geehrter Freund, der durch seine Entdeckungen und Schriften bekannte Chemiker Landerer in Athen, welcher alle im Schatze enthalten kupfernen Gegenstände aufs genaueste untersucht und Bruchstücke davon analysirt hat, findet, dass alle, ohne jegliche Beimischung von Zinn oder Zink, aus reinem Kupfer bestehen, welches, um es haltbarer zu machen, geschmiedtet worden (σφυρήλατον) ist.

My esteemed friend M. Landerer, of Athens, a chemist well known through his discoveries and writings, who has most carefully examined all the copper articles of the Treasure, and analysed the fragments, finds that all of them consist of pure copper without any admixture of tin or zinc, and that, in order to make them more durable, they had been wrought with the hammer (σφυρήλατον).

Schliemann 1874, 301–2[106]

Science was not the only source, however, upon which Schliemann based his claims of authority – classical texts and especially the *Iliad* were equally important. For example, he calls the silver weights described above as 'talents', deliberately using Iliadic terminology and offering a textual reference to the *Iliad* (although in the English edition, these textual references are usually included in footnotes – an interesting point of divergence between the German and English editions). Not only are the 'talents' named according to Iliadic terminology, they are also ascribed a function and a relative value according to their Iliadic precedent. In the case of the small gold studs and pegs, these too are interpreted with reference to ancient Greek terms: a tube of 6 millimetre length is a αὐλίσκος ('little pipe'); a peg of the same length was a ἔμβολον (a word meaning anything wedge shaped); and the studs were ornaments for the leather τελαμῶνες ('strap' or 'band') of shields.[107] Even Schliemann's mention of the independent metallurgical specialist includes the Greek term for an object that has been worked with a hammer. While this use of ancient Greek, and in particular Homeric Greek, can be found throughout the book (consider, for example, the names Schliemann assigned to major architectural features: the Scaean Gate, Priam's Palace), this practice is conspicuous in the description of

---

[106] English edition: Schliemann 1875, 341. It is also interesting that Schliemann, like Herodotus, appealed to specialists and experts while for Herodotus, these were the *logiotatoi* ('most-learned') Egyptian priests (Hdt 2.77.1 and above p. 118 and 121–2), for Schliemann, these were scientific experts.

[107] Schliemann 1874, 301 (English edition: Schliemann 1875, 3–40).

the treasure. It seems there was a Homeric precedent for almost every item. Given the crucial role played by the treasure in Schliemann's overall argument about Hisarlık (for which see below), it was especially important to link each item of the hoard to the *Iliad*.

The catalogue of the treasure is given in two sections: the first presents the vessels, weapons, and other objects; the second describes the jewellery.[108] The division of the objects into two groups was ostensibly because Schliemann claimed that he excavated the objects first, and only found the jewellery later inside a large silver vase. This structure also serves, however, to raise tension and build the narrative dramatically to a climax. We are presented with a mouth-watering parade of precious items, and just when things could not get any more sensational, we are confronted with the biggest of all the vases encountered so far.[109] Hidden inside this largest and grandest of the

Figure 4.1 Sophia Schliemann wearing gold jewellery from the 'Treasure of Priam'.

[108] Vessels, weapons, and other objects: Schliemann 1874, 290–95. Jewellery: Schliemann 1874, 296–301.
[109] Schliemann 1874, 297.

metal vessels is an even more bewildering array of treasures than has hitherto been described – diadems, rings, earrings, headbands, necklaces, and other ornaments. This jewellery, made internationally famous in a photograph where it was modelled by Schliemann's wife Sophia (Fig. 4.1), soon came to represent the treasure as a whole.

Between the description of the larger artefacts and that of the jewellery, Schliemann inserts a brief digression to speculate on the circumstances of the treasure's deposition.[110] All the items, including the large silver vase containing the jewellery, are said to have been found within 'einer hölzernen Kiste (φωριαμός) lage, wie solche in der Iliad (XXIV, 228) im Palast des Priamos erwähnt warden' ('a wooden chest (φωριαμός), such as those mentioned by Homer as being in the palace of King Priam').[111] Schliemann suggests that the treasure would most likely have been packed by a member of the Trojan royal family but later abandoned during their flight. The treasure is thus explained with reference to the myth of the Trojan War – its collection into a single assemblage, the particular find context, and also the circumstances of its deposition. Schliemann here uses his standard strategy for supporting his interpretations – the combination of Homeric and scientific arguments. The location of this imaginative explanation halfway through the catalogue of objects serves a purely literary function. It offers a break in the monotony of description, punctuating the list at a crucial point and acting as a narratological drumroll before the presentation of the jewellery.

An exclusively Iliadic treasure

It is significant that in his description of the treasure, Schliemann does not refer to any ancient text besides the *Iliad* to bolster his arguments. As we have already seen, references to Herodotus and Strabo can be found elsewhere in *Trojanischer Alterthümer*. They do not, however, appear in this particular section of Chapter XXIII. Similarly, we can find Aelian, Arrian, Cicero, Dio Cassius, Herodian, Pausanias, Philostratus, Pliny, Plutarch, and, of course, the *Odyssey* elsewhere in the book – but not in this particular section. This

---

[110] Schliemann 1874, 295–96 (English edition: Schliemann 1875, 333).
[111] Schliemann 1874, 296 (English edition: Schliemann 1875, 332–33).

is perhaps surprising. Schliemann's theory concerning the deposition of the treasure, for example, might have been strengthened by a reference to the *Posthomerica* of Quintus Smyrnaeus – a text that would have been easily accessible in the late nineteenth century and which had been the focus of several scholarly works in the decades prior to the Hisarlık excavations.[112] Indeed, in the English edition of *Trojanischer Alterthümer*, Schliemann's editor Philip Smith adopted precisely this approach, using his footnotes to add further references to other ancient texts and make additional comparisons. For example, in his footnote to this section on the silver talents quote above, Smith adds first in Schliemann's original textual reference to the *Iliad*, before commenting:

> *Iliad*, XXIII. 262–70 (cf. vv. 612–16) The passage furnishes other striking parallels to Dr. Schliemann's discoveries ... The passage seems to confirm Schliemann's interpretation of δέπας ἀμφικύπελλον, for what sort of a vessel can we conceive of as a double dish joined bottom to bottom? We know side-dished with their covers can be used as two dishes, but what would be the use of joining them? Aristarchus, indeed, explained ἀμφίθετος as *double*, i.e. *standing on both ends*, after the supposed analogy of ἀμφικύπελλον, but Eustathius interpreted it was *with handles on both sides*, after the sounder analogy of the ἀμφιφορεύς. These cumulative analogies between Hiassarlik [*sic*] and Homer, gathered incidentally to a climax at the end of each work, are very striking. – [Ed.]
>
> Schliemann 1875, 328 [all italics original]

Elsewhere, Smith also uses footnotes to make comparisons between items from the treasure and objects mentioned in the *Odyssey* (325 and 335); 'modern travelling flasks' (329); and Chinese bronze vessels (326–27). Given Smith's more liberal use of comparative material in the English edition, Schliemann's failure to employ any comparisons beyond the *Iliad* in this section of the original German edition is notable. It had the effect of presenting the treasure purely in Iliadic terms, as a coherent entity that could be interpreted and compared exclusively to the *Iliad*. For Schliemann (although evidently not for Smith), there was no other way of thinking about the treasure apart from in Iliadic terms.

---

[112] E.g. Dyce 1821, Spitzner 1839, Köchly 1843, and Struve 1864.

There can be little doubt that such a rhetorical sleight of hand was deliberate. The account of the Treasure of Priam was the grand climax of *Trojaner Alterthümer*.[113] It was not only a dramatic showcase for his approach and method, as we have seen above, but, as Schliemann argued, it was a crucial piece of evidence that Hisarlık was indeed the location of Homeric Troy. In June 1873, at the time Chapter XXIII was reportedly written, Schliemann was in a difficult position: he was reaching the end of his permitted excavation period; he had suffered vigorous criticism of his work in print; and he still lacked the conclusive proof he needed to connect Hisarlık with Homer. At this point, Schliemann needed something new and dramatic, something which unquestionably confirmed Hisarlık as the seat of a great and wealthy king. Schliemann needed the 'Treasure of Priam'. Presenting this crucial find only as Homeric was a means of directing its interpretation. If the treasure was so obviously Iliadic, the entire settlement at Hisarlık must have been Homeric Troy.

This connection is made clear, not only by the unusual treatment of the treasure in Chapter XXIII, but in the introduction to the book as a whole, four pages of which were devoted to the treasure. [114] Schliemann claimed that the violent destruction of the city and the wealth of that city, were proved, 'vor allen Dingen, durch den … reichen Schatz' ('above all other things, by the rich Treasure').[115] The iconography of certain decorative elements on the treasure provided, Schliemann argued, unassailable proof that they belonged to the Homeric city:

> Leider finde ich auf keinem der Gegenstände des Schatzes eine Inschrift, auch kein anderes religiöses Symbol als die an den beiden Diademen (κρήδεμνα) und an den vier Ohrgehängen prangenden 100 Idole der homerischen 'θεὰ γλαυκῶπις Ἀθήνη', welche uns aber den unumstösslichen Beweis geben: dass der Schatz der Stadt und dem Zeitalter angehören, welche Homer besingt.

> Unfortunately upon none of the articles of the Treasure did I find an inscription, nor any other religious symbols except the 100 idols of the Homeric 'θεὰ γλαυκῶπις Ἀθήνη' which glitter upon the two diadems and

---

[113] The section on the Treasure of Priam is followed by a brief presentation of other remarkable finds including an inscription and coins (Schliemann 1874, 302–4 and 312–18); a discussion about the overall size of Troy (*idem.* 304–11); and a concluding vote of thanks to particular workmen, the site draftsman, and God for the overall success of the enterprise (*idem.* 318–19).

[114] Schliemann 1874, xvii–xx (English edition: Schliemann 1875, 20–24).

[115] Schliemann 1874, xiv (English edition: Schliemann 1875, 20).

the four ear-rings. These are, however, irrefragable proof that the Treasure belongs to the city and to the age of which Homer sings.

Schliemann 1874, xxi[116]

The centrality of the treasure for the overall argument about Hisarlık is evident from the debates that sprang up as soon as Schliemann began to publicize his dramatic discovery in the autumn of 1873. In January 1874, the very same month that *Trojanischer Alterthümer* was first published, the first serious challenge to Schliemann's account of the treasure was also printed. In the *Levant Herald*, a notice described the discovery of a cache of gold jewellery which had been illicitly smuggled from Hisarlık by two of Schliemann's workmen. These items bore many similarities to those of the Treasure of Priam, but were uncovered in a different location and at a different time from the treasure, leading to the suggestion that Schliemann had misreported his findings.[117] The charge of misreporting was soon confirmed, with evidence emerging to invalidate Schliemann's claims about the findspot of the treasure, the presence of his wife at its discovery, and the coherence of the treasure as a single assemblage.[118] The treasure proved controversial, not only archaeologically but also politically. Schliemann had secretly shipped it to Athens in defiance of an official agreement to divide all finds equally with the Ottoman government. This resulted in a high-profile international lawsuit, much diplomatic wrangling, a scotched plan to hire a Paris jeweller to make forged copies of the treasure to give to the Ottomans, and clandestine negotiations to sell the treasure to various museums around Europe.[119]

The quest for truth

Schliemann's approach to the myth of the Trojan War in general, and to the *Iliad* in particular, was like Herodotus' – primarily a quest for historical truth.

---

[116] English edition: Schliemann 1875, 23.
[117] Traill 1995, 125–26.
[118] Traill 1995, 112–20. It is now thought that the various items of the treasure were discovered in different parts of the site over the three seasons of excavation between 1871 and 1873.
[119] See Traill 1995, 125–40. Schliemann eventually decided to donate the treasure to the Ethnographic Museum in Berlin, in return for various honours and awards. Along with other artworks and museum pieces, it was carried away by Russian troops at the end of the Second World War, and has since been held at the Pushkin Museum in Moscow. For the recent debates over the ownership of the treasure, see Blake 2015, 17.

In his introduction to *Trojanischer Alterthümer*, Schliemann acknowledges that he began work at Hisarlık with an almost religious belief in the accuracy of the Homeric epics,[120] but claims that he later recognized that 'Homer is aber nun einmal kein Historiker, sondern ein epischer Dichter, und muss man ihm die Uebertreibungen zugute halten' ('Homer, however, is no historian, but an epic poet, and hence we must excuse his exaggerations').[121] Without questioning the fundamental basis of the Trojan War story or Homer's cultural authority, Schliemann positions himself in relation to Homer in a remarkably similar way to Herodotus, as Jan has shown in the previous section. Schliemann is the historian, the seeker of truth, employing scientific methods of autopsy and archaeology.

Once more like Herodotus, Schliemann nonetheless maintained the *Iliad* faithfully reported ancient 'tradition' (Überlieferung), and that his own work had proved this tradition to be correct in many of its details.[122] He reminds his readers, for example, that the Scaean Gate was described by Homer as a double gate, and that this matched the double gate uncovered at Hisarlık.[123] Indeed, Schliemann claims, the events of the Trojan War as a whole had been proved largely true by the Hisarlık excavations.[124] Schliemann's perspective on the myth of the Trojan War therefore was that while some elements of the Homeric epics might not be accurate, they contained an essential kernel of historical truth – a core of hard fact around which later exaggerations and poetic inventions had accumulated.

Schliemann did not pioneer this approach to Greek myth, but he was one of its most vocal proponents. The approach was not de rigeur amongst professional classicists, who argued that literary texts such as the Homeric

---

[120] 'Auf die Angaben der Ilias vertrauend, an deren Genauigkeit ich wie ans Evangelium glaubte', Schliemann 1874, xi ('Trusting to the data of the Iliad, the exactness of which I used to believe in as in the Gospel itself', Schliemann 1875, 17).

[121] Schliemann 1874, xi (English edition: Schliemann 1975, 18).

[122] 'Homer stellte keine Excavationen an, um jene Denkmäler ansucht zu bringen; er kannte sie aber aus der Ueberlieferung, denn seit Jahrhunderten war Trojas tragisches Ende im Munde aller Sänger, und das Interesse, was sich daran knüpfte, war so gross, dass, wie meine Ausgrabungen erwiesen haben, die Tradition selbst in vielen Einzelheiten genau die Wahrheit berichtete', Schliemann 1874, xiii ('Homer made no excavations so as to bring those remains to light, but he knew of them from tradition; for the tragic fate of Troy had for centuries been in the mouths of all minstrels, and the interest attached to it was so great that, as my excavations have proved, tradition itself gave the exact truth in many details': Schliemann 1875, 19).

[123] Schliemann 1874, xiii.

[124] Schliemann 1874, 305.

poems were shaped more by artistic concerns and social context than by the passive reportage of a received tradition. One such critic of Schliemann was Ulrich von Wilamowitz-Moellendorff.[125] Wilamowitz dismissed Schliemann's historicist approach as naïve, mocking Schliemann in person and in print. It is telling that perhaps Wilamowitz's sharpest lampoon of Schliemann focused on the cornerstone of Schliemann's argument – the discovery of the Treasure of Priam. This took the form of a theatrical skit at the German Archaeological Institute in Rome in Christmas 1873, at which he appeared dressed as Sophia Schliemann, and performed a mock epic poem he had composed in hexameter entitled 'das Epos von der Findung des Schatzes' ('The Epic of the Discovery of the Treasure').[126] Similar criticisms were made by students of comparative mythology and linguistics.[127] The prominent scholar Max Müller, for example, argued that seeking to prove the details of the Homeric poems was ridiculous. Once more, his objection was phrased in terms of an attack on the central piece of 'proof' in Schliemann's argument – the Treasure of Priam. Müller is widely reportedly to have said 'to look for the treasure of the Homeric Priamos at Hissarlik [*sic*] would be like looking for the treasure of the Niebelunge at Worms'.[128]

Schliemann's historicizing approach to Homer was therefore out of step with disciplinary trends both in classics, which favoured 'scientific' philology, and in the study of mythology, which favoured 'scientific' comparative studies. Wilamowitz was better aligned, however, with contemporary movements in the new discipline of archaeology. Reacting against the antiquarianism of the enlightenment era, two major trends were emerging in archaeology.[129] First, there was a growing interest in the prehistoric as opposed to the classical past,

---

[125] Wilamowitz argued a line more representative of scholars today – that the Homeric poems may have made use of some traditional material but were also very innovative, and that their composition owed greatly to the contemporary context of Hesiod, the lyric poets, and archaic Greek society. Wilamowitz's argument regarding Homer and the composition of Homeric poetry were first laid out with primary reference to the *Odyssey* in Wilamowitz-Moellendorff 1884, and later expanded upon with primary reference to the *Iliad* in Wilamowitz-Moellendorff 1916. For the different impacts of Wilamowitz and Schliemann on the field of Homeric scholarship, see Myres 1958, 123–222.

[126] Calder 1980, 146–48.

[127] For this approach to Greek myth, see Graf 1993, 22–34. Key proponents of the approach in the nineteenth century included Karl Otfried Müller, Jane Ellen Harrison, and James George Frazer.

[128] Anon 1874, 296. Müller here refers to the Niebelunge, a dynasty of mythical kings featuring in traditional German myth and epic poetry.

[129] Trigger 1989, 80–87.

with the development of the three-age chronological system for prehistory in Scandinavia (i.e. the stone, bronze, and iron ages). Secondly, there was a focus on scientific methods in excavation, recording, and interpretation, in contrast to the more descriptive and aesthetic approaches of eighteenth-century art historians.[130] Schliemann's aims at Troy, with their prehistoric focus and its emphasis on empirical proof, fitted both trends. But while his aims may have been aligned with contemporary archaeological thinking, his methods were not. As already illustrated above, Schliemann's excavations at Hisarlık were widely criticized both for their destructive nature and for the poor quality of the recording.

Scholarly responses to Schliemann therefore varied between disciplines, and also between countries. He faced substantial hostility in Germany, for example, while in Britain he was widely feted.[131] Schliemann's legacy in the twenty-first century is similarly mixed. In general, while his discoveries at Troy and elsewhere are celebrated, his methods, mendacity, and underhand dealings are condemned. His historicizing approach to the *Iliad* continues to have widespread appeal in the popular sphere,[132] while in academic circles such approaches have by now been thoroughly debunked.[133]

Schliemann's engagement with the *Iliad* was, like that of Herodotus, primarily focused on a quest for historical truth. Yet in Schliemann's quest for an ancient truth, he was willing to tell some very modern lies. Nowhere is this more obvious than with the Treasure of Priam. The account of the treasure's discovery, the claims about its findspot, and its very identity as a coherent hoard: it is now clear that these were all deliberate fictions, shrewdly presented using a range of rhetorical and literary strategies. The incongruity of engaging in a series of falsehoods in pursuit of truth does not seem to have bothered Schliemann, who perhaps felt that, like Homer, his own 'exaggerations' should be overlooked while the central kernel of his text should be believed. Indeed,

---

[130] Increasing professionalism and the greater use of scientific approaches characterizes not only mainstream archaeology at this time (see Trigger, *op. cit.*), but also classical archaeology, and in particular in Germany where there was a refinement of stylistic analysis developing from Winkelmann's more subjective aestheticism (Marchand 1996, 75–115).

[131] Traill 1995.

[132] E.g. Moorehead 1994.

[133] For the 'Homeric Question' and issues concerning the historicity of the Trojan War, see Mac Sweeney 2018. For a concise statement of the problems with a historicist approach to myth, see Osborne 2014, 36.

towards the end of Chapter XXIII, Schliemann made his final claim for a Homeric truth:

> die Wahrheit geht mir über alles, und ich freue mich, durch meine dreijährigen Ausgrabungen, wenn auch nur in verkleinertem Massstabe, das homerische Troja aufgedeckt und bewiesen zu haben, dass die Ilias auf wirkliche Thatsachen basirt ist.

> I value truth above everything, and I rejoice that my three years' excavations have laid open Homeric Troy, even though on a diminished scale, and that I have proved the Iliad to be based on real facts.

Schliemann 1874, 305[134]

---

[134] English edition: Schliemann 1875, 344.

5

Claiming Identities

In the final chapter of this volume, we consider another key theme running through the Trojan War tradition and Iliadic receptions – that of heritage, identity, and claims of cultural ownership. We explore this theme in two composite texts that derive from the post-antique Trojan War tradition: Godfrey of Viterbo's *Speculum Regum* (*c.* 1183) and the Hollywood film *Troy* (2004), directed by Wolfgang Petersen. Both of these case studies employ mixed artistic forms – in the case of the *Speculum*, this constituted poetry and prose; while in the case of the film, *Troy*, this is the mixed medium of cinema.

In the first section, Naoíse explores Godfrey of Viterbo's *Speculum Regum* ('Mirror of Princes'), a work that offers a history of the world by tracing the origins of contemporary royal lineages back to the Trojans. Claims of Trojan ancestry were common in medieval Europe, and a crucial means by which Europe's Latin 'West' articulated not only its cohesion and internal dynamics, but also its difference from the Byzantine Greek 'East'. But as well as claiming a Trojan heritage for his patrons, Godfrey also sought to establish a connection between himself and Homer, thereby constructing his own authorial identity, and positioning himself in relation to one of the major figures of literary history. The next section considers the Hollywood film *Troy* (2004). Jan begins the discussion by exploring its most overtly Homeric quality: the emphasis on glory and fame. The discussion then considers the film's identity politics. In a reversal of the medieval situation, in the early twenty-first century when the film was produced, America and the 'West' claimed a classical Greek heritage in opposition to the Trojans of the Oriental 'East'. Jan also highlights the subversive nature of the film, in which the Greeks occupy the traditional 'baddie' role, and argues that this is firmly grounded in the political upheavals of the early twenty-first century, notably the so-called 'War on Terror'.

Both of these cases explore questions of politics and cultural identity as played out in relation to the Trojan War story. Throughout history, different groups have aligned themselves variously with the Achaeans/Greeks or with the Trojans, positioning themselves as the cultural (or literal) heirs to one or other side of the conflict. In the case of the *Speculum*, this enabled a competitive jockeying for status amongst related dynasties, using the common language of Trojan ancestry to create ever more complex and innovative mythic genealogies. In the case of the film *Troy*, the common cultural assumption of alignment between America and ancient Greece allowed for a cinematic critique of contemporary government policy and a subversion of popular expectation.

Crucially, both the examples we have chosen in this chapter reflect inwards on their own 'side' of the war – the *Speculum* is concerned with the relationships between different branches of the Trojan family tree, while *Troy* offers political commentary on American foreign policy. This is not, of course, the only way that myths of the Trojan War could be incorporated into identity politics – the war could just as easily be framed as a 'clash of civilizations', and identity claims linked to one side in the war could be set up in opposition to the 'Other'. Within the ancient world, a widely discussed example of this is the classical period in Greece, at Athens in particular. Specifically, there seems to have been a dramatic shift in the portrayal of Trojans after the Persian Wars in the middle of the fifth century BCE. Whereas Trojans had previously been depicted in much the same way as the Achaeans, both iconographic and literary portrayals now tended to represent them as oriental 'Others', aligned with Persians and other non-Hellenic 'barbarians'.[1] The Trojan War therefore became a way of thinking about 'us' and 'them', with the Hellenes of the fifth century claiming a Western, European, and Achaean heritage in opposition to the Persians who could be linked with an Eastern, Asian, and Trojan heritage. This and other cases of the Trojan War being used in the oppositional construction of identity are well covered in the existing scholarly literature, and so we have opted instead to explore the use of the Trojan War tradition in other kinds of cultural identity politics.

The case studies considered in previous chapters of this book have all displayed a more or less detailed interaction with the content of the *Iliad*. In this chapter, however, the discussion considers two texts that are notably

---

[1] For this phenomenon, see above p.113 and especially n.24.

less concerned with the content of the poem. Both stem from periods when engagement with the Greek text of the *Iliad* was either rare or non-existent. At the time that Godfrey was writing, the Homeric poems were not accessible in western Europe and knowledge about the myth of Troy came entirely through other sources – the non-Homeric Trojan War tradition. And yet, the *idea* of the Homeric remained powerful, despite there being no real way of knowing what actually *was* Homeric. The early twenty-first century when the film *Troy* was produced offers a comparable, although less extreme, situation. Knowledge of both ancient Greek and the precise contents of the *Iliad* was once again limited, despite a general awareness of the Trojan War story being widespread. Then, as now, popular ideas about the Trojan War were shaped primarily by a range of other sources, including films, television programmes, and children's storybooks, rather than by the Homeric poems. Hence, while Chapter 4 explored two examples from periods where the *Iliad* occupied a central and unassailable position at the heart of the Trojan War tradition, this chapter presents the alternative view – two examples from periods when the *Iliad* was peripheral.

Naoíse: Godfrey's hall of mirrors

DE PRINCIPIO REGUM, UNDE ORTUS FUIT HERNICUS:
Principium regum, quo descendisse videris,
Et genus imperii Troianaque tempora queris:
Hec si metra geris, certiorandus eris.
Imperiale genus quod et unde sit, ecce feremus;
Que species regnum fuerit primeva, canemus.
Urget, ut instemus, Romulus atque Remus.
Gentis Hebreorum loca, tempora, regna tacemus,
Vertimur ad Grecos, gentilia gesta canemus,
Unde sit imperii linea, norma, genus.

ON THE BEGINNING OF KINGSHIP, AND FROM WHAT DESCENT
    CAME HENRY:
You ask of the beginning of kingship, and about the Trojan race
And the empire and era from where you will be seen to descend.
If you read these lines, you will be the wiser.

Look, we will tell what was the imperial race and from whence it came;
We will sing of what kind of kingship was the first.
We will consider, as suggested, Romulus and Remus.
We will touch on the place, time, and kingdom of the Hebrew people,
Turning to the Greeks, of the deeds of the people we will sing,
And from where comes the imperial line, customs, and race.

Godfrey of Viterbo, Speculum Regum 1.2[2]

Kingship begins at Troy. At least, this is what is claimed in the *Speculum Regum* ('Mirror of Princes'), a history of the world in both poetry and prose written *c.* 1183 CE.[3] Its author was Godfrey of Viterbo, a notary working for the Hohenstaufen Holy Roman Emperor Frederick I 'Barbarossa'; and the *Speculum* was addressed to Frederick's son and heir, Henry.[4] Having recounted the descent of all humanity from Noah in his first poem, Godfrey immediately launches into this programmatic statement in the second. The *Speculum*, he boasts, offers its royal reader the chance to peer into the past and to gaze at visions of kingly power that reflect his own. And the first image in Godfrey's literary mirror was that of Troy.

Godfrey was not content, however, to describe the transfer of empire through the ages from Troy until his own day. In the rest of the *Speculum*, he went on to set out a specific genealogy for his Hohenstaufen patrons, tracing their bloodlines back to the house of Priam. In itself, this project was unremarkable: twelfth-century Europe was awash with groups who either claimed Trojan ancestry, or who had Trojan origins attributed to them. They included the British, the Normans, the Franks, the Saxons, the Teutons, various cities in Italy, and, according to the Icelandic author of the *Prose Edda*, even the Norse gods.[5] Coupled with this historical mania for Trojan descent, works that

---

[2]　The Latin text of the *Speculum* quoted in this chapter is that of Waitz 1872.

[3]　From this point onwards, when dates are given in this chapter, CE is assumed unless otherwise specified.

[4]　Godfrey's position at court and his relationship with both Frederick and his son Henry are topics of debate; see Hering 2015, 55–57 and Freed 2016, 109–10. See Hausmann 1992 for the argument that Godfrey was close to the Emperor and Weber 1994 for the arguments against.

[5]　By the end of the twelfth century, as one contemporary British chronicler put it, most of the peoples of Europe claimed descent from Troy (Henry of Huntingdon, *Historia Anglorum* 7.38). British: Nennius, *Historia Britonnum* 2.10; Geoffrey of Monmouth, *Historia Regum Britanniae* 1. Normans: Dudo of St Quentin, *Historia Normannorum* 130; Guillaume de Jumièges, *Gesta Numannorum ducum* 1.14–6. Franks: Fredegar, *Chronica* 2.4–6. Saxons: Widukind: *Res gestae saxonicae sive annalium libri tres* 1.2. Teutons: see n.13 below. Italian cities but especially Venice: *Origo vicitatum italie seu venetiarum* 1.1 and Brown 1996, 13. Norse gods: Snorri Sturlusen, *Prose Edda*, Prologue 3.

more generally recounted the myths of Troy also enjoyed a blockbuster-like popularity. Chronicles, poems, and *chansons de geste* (songs of great deeds) dealing with myths of the Trojan War proliferated in the twelfth century. Written both in scholarly Latin and various vernacular languages, these often cast the Trojan tales in a romantic and chivalric light.[6]

In this section, I do not seek to explain the craze for all things Trojan in twelfth-century Europe, as this is already the subject of a rich body of scholarly literature.[7] It is worth noting, however, that interest in the Trojan War in this period was not primarily driven by a desire to create oppositional identities of 'self' and 'other'. Rather, as we shall see below, the common and shared nature of Trojan ancestry was a means by which different groups could negotiate their relationships with each other, rather than separating themselves from those with Greek ancestry. This changed only at the start of the thirteenth century with the Third Crusade, where crusaders from Western Europe sacked Constantinople. At this point, the Latin 'West' used its Trojan heritage to justify the treatment of the Greek 'East' – the sack and looting of Constantinople by the heirs of Troy portrayed as revenge for the sack and looting of Troy by the Achaean ancestors of medieval Byzantium.[8] In the twelfth century, however, the claim of a Trojan heritage was primarily used as a means of relating to others, rather than a means of distancing them.

This section focuses on two aspects of Godfrey's work that relate to the idea of a Trojan or Homeric heritage as a means of creating relationships: first,

---

[6] As Boeck puts it, there was 'a pan-European fashion for the wildly popular and ideologically powerful bestsellers with a Trojan theme' (Boeck 2015, 264). Perhaps the best known of these was Benoît de Sainte-Maure's *Roman de Troie*, written in the French vernacular around 1160. The popularity of this work was such that translations rapidly appeared in Latin, German, Dutch, Italian, Spanish, and modern Greek. These works were so common that the literary theme was given its own moniker – the 'Matter of Troy'. See Desmond 2016 for the 'Matter of Troy' in the medieval period. The simultaneous circulation of politically motivated Trojan genealogies meant that such works, although ostensibly popular and romantic, were necessarily also political (Eley 1991, Bruckner 2015).

[7] For studies of the medieval Trojan genealogies, see especially Waswo 1995 and Wolf 2008; but also Eisenhut 1983, Beaune 1991, Bouet 1995, Ewig 1998, Shawcross 2003, Plassmann 2006, and Clark 2010 (for the practice of medieval genealogy more generally, see Speigel 1999, 99–110). Similar claims to Trojan ancestry can be found in later periods of European history: see p.96 above and especially nn.76–80 for the Tudors and Early Modern England; and Tanner 1993 for the Habsburgs and the Early Modern Period in continental Europe. For wider medieval literary traditions of Trojan-themed poetry and stories, see the summaries in Jung 1996 and Desmond 2016. For the popularity of Troy in the visual art of the medieval period, see Buchthal 1971, Stones 2005, and Boeck 2015, 256–67.

[8] Beaune 1991, 237 and Shawcross 2003.

the claims of Trojan ancestry he made on behalf of his patrons; and second, the relationship he implied between himself and Homer. Godfrey of Viterbo's *Speculum Regum*, I shall argue, was a mirror not only for princes but also for poets, with Godfrey using it to reflect on his own scholarly practice and literary ambition. In both the *Speculum* and his later works, Godfrey sought to position himself within an intellectual and literary tradition – one that connected him to Homer no less than it connected his patrons to the kings of Troy.

The heirs of Troy

As evident from the passage quoted at the start of this section, in the *Speculum* Godfrey claimed Troy as the place of origin, not only for the institution of kingship in the abstract, but also for the lineage of his Hohenstaufen patrons specifically. The poem presents Godfrey's headline argument in lyrical rhyming verse. By this point, however, Godfrey has already set out the basic parameters of the argument in a prose prologue, offering a brief summary of the genealogy that he would later give at length in verse. In this summary, Godfrey highlights the key points of the genealogy. Although the relevant passage is lengthy, it bears reading in its entirety.

> Sane cum Romanorum et Theutonicorum regum et imperatorum ingenuitas ab una Troianorum regum stirpe procedat eademque Troiana progenies a primo rege Atheniensium trahat originem, ad maiorem rei evidentiam a diebus filiorum Noe post diluvium libellus iste orditur, et inde expressis omnium gestis atque nominibus per seriem generationis de patribus in filios ad reges Athenienses descendit, et ab Atheniensibus usque ad reges Troianos, scilicet Anchisem et Priamum, cognationis linea derivatur. In Priamo autem et Anchise prosapia regum in duo dividitur. Ex Anchise enim Eneas et Ascanius omnesque reges et imperatores Ytalici oriuntur usque ad Karolum regem Magnum; a Priamo autem iuniore, nepote magni Priami ex sorore, universa Theutonicorum nobilitas usque ad eundem Karolum patenter emanat. In ipso Karolo utriusque propaginis genus concurrit. Mater enim eius Berta, cum esset filia filie imperatoris Eraclii, de genere imperatorum Romanorum et Grecorum fuit, Pipinus autem pater eius, rex Theutonicorum, a genere Troiano descendit. Fuit itaque Karolus Magnus patre Theutonicus et matre Romanus.

> Indeed the nobility of the kings and emperors of the Romans and of the Teutons comes from the same root – the king of the Trojans, and this

same lineage of the Trojans takes its origin from the first king of Athens. For clarity, this little book lays out even older things, from the days of the children of Noah after the Flood. From there it explains the deeds and the names of all, going down in order through the generations, from fathers to sons down to the kings of Athens, and from those Athenians to the kings of Troy, especially Anchises and Priam, from where our lineage is derived. But from Priam and Anchises the line of kings was divided in two. From Anchises sprang Aeneas and Ascanius and all the Italian kings and emperors through to king Charlemagne; from the younger Priam, the nephew of the older Priam by his sister, clearly the entire nobility of the Teutons is descended through to the same Charlemagne. In this Charlemagne, the blood of both lines ran together: as his mother Berta was the daughter of the daughter of the emperor Heraclius, and therefore born of Roman and Greek emperors; but his father Pipin, the king of the Teutons, was descended from the Trojans. Charlemagne was therefore a Teuton by his father and a Roman by his mother.

Godfrey of Viterbo, Speculum Regum Prologue 21–22.

The culmination of the genealogy, we are told, is Charlemagne, the first Holy Roman Emperor and the founder of the Carolingian dynasty. This is perhaps unsurprising given that the Hohenstaufen dynasty celebrated Charlemagne as their ancestor.[9] Claiming Charlemagne allowed the Hohenstaufens to justify their imperial ambitions, and also served as a kick in the teeth to their neighbours and rivals, the Capetian dynasty of France. The Capetians, although they had ruled France for several generations, were sometimes characterized as usurpers who had unseated the Carolingians.[10] The Hohenstaufen appropriation of Charlemagne was therefore a direct ideological challenge to the Capetians – one of several that can be found in the pages of the *Speculum*, as we shall see below. For Godfrey, then, making Charlemagne the climax of the Trojan genealogy was a clear statement of support for the Hohenstaufen dynastic project. Godfrey claimed in no uncertain terms that Charlemagne

---

[9] For the Hohenstaufen appropriation of Charlemagne, see Latowsky 2013, 183–214. Charlemagne became most enthusiastically adopted into Hohenstaufen imperial ideology following Frederick's break with the Pope in 1160. For a Holy Roman Emperor estranged from the Church at Rome, celebrating Charlemagne was a means of promoting a non-papal vision of the Empire's past.

[10] See Hallam and Everard 2013, 176 and 242 for the increasing need by 1150 for the Capetians to connect themselves to the Carolingians.

was the true heir of Troy, making the Hohenstaufens, by extension, the rightful possessors of the Trojan kingly heritage.

Following the prologue, Book 1 of the *Speculum* comprises thirty-eight short poems recounting tales from antiquity, in particular that of the Trojan War and the transfer of Trojan power to ancient Rome (for which see below). Godfrey returns to the question of genealogy, however, in the poems of Book 2. Here, the Trojan genealogy is used for more than just the elevation of the Hohenstaufen family into a position of dynastic privilege – it is used to comment more generally on ethno-cultural distinctions within Europe.

Godfrey is careful to respect the familiar Italian claim to Trojan heritage, not only that of Rome but also those of other Italian cities.[11] He is keen, however, to place the Trojan claims of the Teutons on an equal footing. As he explains in the introductory preamble to Book 2: 'the offspring of the Trojan seed is divided in two: | One took up the crown of Rome in Italy, | the other rules the blessed Teutonic kingdom' (In duo dividimus Troiano semine prolem: | Una per Ytaliam sumpsit dyademata Rome, | Altera Theutonica regna beata fovet, *Speculum* 2.preamble). Following on from this, the first poem recounts in some detail how the younger Priam led his half of the Trojan survivors, first through Thrace and Pannonia, and then into the lands that became Germania, changing the name of the people along the way: 'the Trojan people sought for themselves the name of Germans' (Gens Troiana sibi Germanica nomina querit: *Speculum* 2.1); while the second describes how the Romans and Germans were allies, on seemingly equal terms, due to their shared blood (*Speculum* 2.2). These assertions of brotherhood between Romans and Teutons spoke to some very contemporary concerns. When Godfrey penned the *Speculum* in the early 1180s, Frederick had already fought several campaigns in Italy and waged a long and bitter war against Pope Alexander III. Frederick had reconciled with the pope only in 1177, and tensions remained until the Peace of Constance was signed between Frederick and the Italian Lombard League in 1183.[12] In this context, the conspicuous protestations of ancestral friendship between the Italians and the Germans gain an urgent new meaning.

---

[11] Roman claims to a Trojan heritage have been extensively discussed; see especially Erskine 2003 with references. For the Trojan claims made by medieval Italian cities, see n.5 above.
[12] For a biography of Frederick I, see Freed 2016.

The third poem in the book goes on to explain how the Franks got their name. According to Godfrey, they were a group of Germans who came to the aid of their Roman allies by fighting the Alans. The complete defeat of the Alans led to the name of the 'Franks' being bestowed on the group to signal their ferocity (*Speculum* 2.3). The true Franks of this story, Godfrey is at pains to stress, went on to occupy the lands around the Rhine, while the contemporary kingdom of France was a subordinate and secondary part of the realm.

> Cetera Francigene limina pauca tenent,
> Parisius patria, quondam Gaudina vocata,
> Subdita per Francos, est Francia parva vocata,
> A Francis genita sorte minore data.

> Of the other small borders occupied by the Franklings (Francigene),
> The land around Paris that was once called Gaul,
> It was subdued by the Franks, and is called 'Little Frankia',
> And was given to the French according to a lesser fate.

Godfrey of Viterbo, Speculum Regum 2.4

In his Trojan genealogy, Godfrey was thus able to denigrate the French, argue for Romano-German consanguinity, and celebrate Charlemagne. While Godfrey did not create these tales ex nihilo,[13] he nonetheless was able to bend existing traditions concerning the Trojan issue to suit the imperial rhetoric of the Hohenstaufen court.[14] Between his overtures to the Italians and insults to the French, in the *Speculum* Godfrey was proving himself to be a master of what those who study classical antiquity would call 'kinship diplomacy'.[15]

Rival Trojan genealogies

As implied in the introduction to this section, the Hohenstaufens were not the only twelfth-century dynasty for which detailed Trojan-focused genealogies

---

[13] The Trojan genealogy in the *Speculum* is known to have drawn on earlier works, chief amongst which was the *Chronica* of Frutolf of Michelsberg, composed in the eleventh century but revised and expanded by Ekkehard of Aura in the early twelfth century (for an edition of which see Pertz 1844, 155–56). Godfrey took many details of his genealogy from that of Frutolf-Ekkehard, but seems to have written this final section on the 'true' Franks in unusually scathing style. See Innes 2000 for earlier versions of the Trojan-German genealogy, and n.25 below for Godfrey's sources.

[14] For the *Speculum* and its Trojan genealogy as elements partaking of Hohenstaufen imperial ideology: Tanner 1993, 88–90 and Hering 2015, 58–62.

[15] For kinship diplomacy in antiquity, see Jones 1999 and Patterson 2010.

were written.[16] The Plantagenet kings of England and Normandy, for example, seem to have been particularly keen to capitalize on the political potential of the Troy stories.[17] But perhaps the most direct challenge to the Hohensatufen version of Trojan genealogy was that of their immediate neighbours and rivals: the Capetians of France.

While the idea of the French (or Frankish) people being of Trojan ancestry was well established by the late twelfth century,[18] a Trojan lineage had not yet been specified for their ruling dynasty, the Capetians. Less than a decade after Godfrey wrote the *Speculum*, however, the French chronicler Rigord produced the *Gesta Philippi Augusti* ('The Deeds of Philip Augustus'), extolling the great deeds of the Capetian king Philip II. The *Gesta* offered a completely different vision of the Trojan genealogy from that of the *Speculum*.[19] Rigord begins his genealogical discussion as a digression on the city of Paris, which he claims to have been named after Paris the prince of Troy. Like Godfrey, he argues that the refugee Trojans split into two main groups after the fall of the city.[20]

---

[16] As one scholar has put it, there was an 'explosive rush of ruling houses and cities to claim Trojan ancestry, to invent genealogies linking the ruler's family or the place to the sons of Priam or of Dardanus' (Waswo 1995, 286).

[17] Clark 2010, 205–6 and Mueller 2013, 24 n.18 with references. As claims of Trojan origins for both the British and Normans appear as early as the ninth century CE (see n.5 above), there was political mileage to be gained by arguing (in a way similar to Godfrey in the *Speculum*) that the two strands of Trojan blood were now united in the realm and person of the Plantagenet king (Aurell 2007, 382). These politically motivated genealogies included the *Genalogia Regum Anglorum* of Ailred of Rievaulx (Freeman 2002, 55–87), and the royal lineage recounted in the Nun of Barking's translation of the *Vita Ædwardi Regis* (MacBain 1993). Beyond genealogy, the mid-late twelfth century saw an explosion of historiography in the Plantagenet realm, all of which featured stories of Trojan descent. In Latin, these works included: Geoffrey of Monmouth's *Historia Regum Britanniae* 1; Henry of Huntingdon's *Historia Anglorum*; Alfred of Beverley's *Annales sive Historia de gestis regum Britanniae*. In general, it seems that the Plantagenets' politicized interest in history led to something of a renaissance in historical literature in the twelfth century in Britain and northern France (Damian-Grint 1999, Albu 2001). Significant amounts of historical writing also appeared in the vernacular languages, implying a broader readership for these stories than might be assumed for the Latin histories. These include a rendering of Geoffrey of Monmouth's work into French by the Norman poet Wace in the *Roman de Brut*; Wace's history of the Dukes of Normandy in his *Roman de Rou*; Benoît de Sainte-Maure's *Chronique des ducs de Normandie*; and Layamons' *Brut*. Indeed, such claims became so common that by the end of the century in Britain, historical chronicles were referred to as 'bruts' – a reference to Brutus, the supposed Trojan ancestor of the British and the standard starting point for all historical writing.

[18] Beaune 1991, Bouet 1995 and Ewig 1998.

[19] For a recent edition of and introduction to the *Gesta Philippi Augusti*, see Carpentier, Pon and Chauvin 2006.

[20] After stressing these two main stemma, Rigord also later mentions other escapees from Troy, including the descendants of Helenus the son of Priam, who lived in slavery in Greece for two centuries before being rescued by Brutus and heading to found Britain; other sons of Antenor who founded cities in northern Italy; and the descendants of Aeneas.

Post eversionem Troje multitudo magna inde fugiens, ac deinde in duos populos se dividens, alia Francionem, quondam Priami regis Troje nepotem, videlicet Hectoris filium, super se regem levavit; alia Turchum nomine, filium Troili filii Priami, secuta sit; atque ex eo, ut quidam tradunt, duos populos sumpto nomine Francos et Turchos usque hodie vocari.

After the destruction of Troy, the great mass fleeing from there split into two groups. One was brought up by Francio, who was the grandson of Priam the king of Troy and reportedly the son of Hector. The other was named for Turchus, the son of Troilus son of Priam. And so it follows that, in accordance with tradition, the two peoples assumed the names 'Franks' and 'Turks' as we call them today.

Rigord, Gesta Philippi Augusti 38[21]

From the Turkish side of the family, according to Rigord, came the Goths, the Vandals, and the Normans. The progeny of Francio initially settled close to the Danube, and then moved to the area around the Rhine under the leadership of Marcomir, the grandson of Francio and Sunno, the son of Antenor. At this time, they controlled all of Germany and Gaul right up to the Pyrenees (Rigord, *Gesta Philippi Augusti* 39). However, after refusing to pay tribute to the Romans and fighting a bitter war with them (resulting in them being dubbed the 'Franks' for their ferocity), Rigord tells us they settled permanently in Gaul.

Sed postea, Sonnone et Genebaudo ducibus in Austria remanentibus, Marcomirus, filius Priami regis Austrie, qui a Francione, nepote Priami regis Troje, per multas successorum generationes, quas hic longum esset enumerare descenderat in Galliam venit cum suis.

Afterwards, while Sunno and Genebaud remained to watch over Austria; Marcomirus the son of Priam the king of Austria, who was descended from Francio the grandson of Priam the king of Troy through so many successive generations that it would be too long to list them here, came to Gaul with his people.

Rigord, Gesta Philippi Augusti 39

Rigord stresses that the Franks are the most noble of the descendants of Troy, sprung as they were from Hector. The inhabitants of Germany, by contrast, are

---

[21] The text of Rigord used in this chapter is that of Carpentier, Pon, and Chauvin 2006.

depicted as a subordinate group, which were left behind to pay Roman tribute when the main body of Franks occupied Gaul. Their leaders, the little-known Sunno and Genebaud, are sons of a lesser line – that of Antenor.[22] Antenor not only did not belong to the Trojan royal family – he appears briefly in the *Iliad* as one of Priam's counsellors – but mythic tradition by this time had also tainted him with treason.[23] Rigord was casting genealogical aspersions on the Germans, not just directly by making them a lesser offshoot of the Franks (just as Godfrey had made the little 'Franklings' an offshoot of the Teutonic 'proper' Franks), but indirectly by implying cowardice (in the willingness to pay Roman tribute) and treachery (through Antenor).

Rigord's Trojan genealogy may not have been a direct response to Godfrey's, but it was written within a few years of it and touched upon many similar themes. The other target of the Hohenstaufen genealogical project – Charlemagne – also quickly came into the Capetians' sights. Over the next few years, the ancestry of Philip II's wife was increasingly stressed – she was said to belong to the line of Charlemagne, and so their son Louis could be said to legitimately be reclaiming his Carolingian heritage.[24] Godfrey may have been adept in 'kinship diplomacy', but he was not the only one playing the game of twelfth-century political genealogies.

Godfrey's Homer

Promoting the Hohenstaufen imperial ideology was only one of Godfrey's aims in the *Speculum*. He also had literary ambitions, as evident from the scale and scope of the planned work, in spite of that fact that the *Speculum* ultimately remained unfinished. These literary ambitions meant establishing himself within the pantheon of great writers and locating himself within the wider literary landscape. The citation and use of sources was one way of doing

---

[22] For Sunno and Genebaud, see: Carpentier, Pon and Chauvin 2006, 197, n.157.

[23] The idea of Antenor as a traitor to Troy can be found in Dionysius of Halicarnassus 1.48, but appears even more clearly in two of the main texts used in the twelfth century as sources for the Trojan War story: Dares Phrygius, *De Excidio Troiae Historia* (Antenor's treachery is at 39–42); and Dictys Cretensis, *Ephemeris Belli Troiani* (an account of Antenor's treason can be found at 5.8-12). The idea of Antenor selling out his homeland also appeared in popular literature of the twelfth century: e.g. Benoît, *Roman de Troie* lines 23, 497–25, 713.

[24] See Hering 2015, 64 for the theory of *reditus regni Francorum ad stirpem Caroli*', which became a vital tenet of Capetian ideology in the early thirteenth century.

this, and Godfrey made use of a wide range of sources in several different languages. He drew from previous historiographical works, in particular relying heavily on the *Chronicon* of Otto of Friesling; but also from wider traditions in the *chansons de geste*, vernacular chronicles such as the High German *Kaiserchronik*, and local oral traditions.[25]

The most obvious way for a twelfth-century writer to establish their position in relation to existing works was to set things out explicitly, as Godfrey's contemporary Rigord chose to do. Indeed, Rigord often named his sources in his work, arguing that his own historical authority was based on his careful and detailed study of older texts.[26] For example, Rigord cites his sources for his Trojan genealogy thus:

> Et quoniam multi solent dubitare de origine regni Francorum, quomodo et qualiter reges Francorum ab ipsis Trojanis descendisse dicantur, ideo sollicicius, prout potuimus colligere ex historia Gregori Turonensis et ex cronicis Eusebii et cronicis Hidacii et ex aliorum multorum scriptis in hac nostra historia satis lucide determinavimus.

> Because many are used to doubting the origin of the French kings, and how and in what way the French kings are said to be descended from the Trojans; therefore we have collected as well as possible details from the *History* of Gregory of Tours, the *Chronicle* of Eusebius, the *Chronicle* of Hydace, and many other texts into this, our history, and set it out with great clarity.

> Rigord, *Gesta Philippi Augusti* 38

Godfrey's approach to his sources was markedly different. He named them only rarely, and did not usually discuss their merits or failings. Instead, he usually opted for a strategy of using unattributed quotations, seemingly in the expectation that his readers would be able to pick up on the references. This seems to be the way that Godfrey made use of several ancient and late antique works including the writings of Ovid, Virgil through Servilius' commentary, Isidorus, Boethius, and the *Historia Augusta*.[27] Interestingly, although Godfrey made use of all these sources, he did not name them. Perhaps surprisingly one of the few authors that he did explicitly mention by name is Homer.

---

[25] For Godfrey's use of sources, see Waitz 1872, 4, Meyer 1933 and Dorninger 2015, 25–28.
[26] For Rigord's explicit discussion of his sources, see Carpentier, Pon and Chauvin 2006, 86–93.
[27] Boethius: Pittaluga 2004. *Historia Augusta:* Betrand, Desbordes and Callu 1986. Ovid: Meyer 1933.

This may be unexpected given that the Homeric poems were not known or available in western Europe at this time. Indeed, it was not until Petrarch commissioned a translation of the *Iliad* in the fourteenth century that knowledge about the content and details of the Homeric epics spread in Western Europe.[28] Godfrey therefore wrote about Troy in a world without Homer – or at least, a world where Homer was not in any practical way at the centre of traditions about Troy, and where it was not known precisely *what* Homer had said about Troy. This makes it all the more remarkable that a full century and a half before the *Iliad* became accessible, Godfrey wrote as if he had already consulted it.

> DE PRIAMO ET ANCHISE REGIBUS TROIANIS
> Anchisem Priamumque simul regnasse fatemur.
> Istis temporibus Troiam descripsit Homerus;
> Nos quoque tangemus, me rogat alma Venus.
> Nascitur ex Priamo Paris et laudabilis Hector,
> De quibus annecto breviter quam plurima, lector,
> Cetera que remanent magnus Homerus habet.

> OF PRIAM AND ANCHISES, THE KINGS OF THE TROJANS
> I say that Anchises and Priam ruled at the same time.
> Homer described Troy in this era.
> We may also touch on it, if I ask kindly Venus.
> From Priam was born Paris and praiseworthy Hector,
> About whom, my reader, I link up many things briefly.
> The rest which remains, great Homer has it.
>
> Godfrey of Viterbo, *Speculum Regum* 1.12 lines 1–6

Godfrey does not explicitly claim to have read Homer, but he does claim to know what was in the Homeric texts – Homer wrote of Troy in the time of Anchises and Priam. He then offers a tantalizing suggestion: he claims that, in his own poem, he has summarized the story in the interests of brevity, but implies that the reader may consult Homer for further details.[29] This is a somewhat strange conceit given that both Godfrey and his readers must have

---

[28] For Petrarch and the *Iliad*, see Graziosi 2016, 62–65.
[29] Waitz: 'For he had knowledge of Homer – Spec. 1.10 and 12 – but he could scarcely be thought to have seen a copy himself' (Etiam Homeri cognitionem habuit, Spec. I, 10.12, quem tamen vix ipse inspexisse putandus est: 1872, 4).

known this was impossible. Godfrey was not alone, however, in writing as if he had access to Homer during the twelfth century.

The *Roman de Troie* was a long poem presenting a chivalric and romantic version of the tale of Troy, written for a popular audience in the vernacular French by Benoît de St Maure around 1160.[30] Like Rigord, Benoît was careful to specify his sources for the story; and like Godfrey, he implied that he had access to the Homeric poems. Homer, he claimed, was still 'received and held in authority' (receüz | et en autorité tenuz: Benoît, *Roman de Troie*, 73–74). Benoît went on to explain that he had good historical and scholarly reasons for choosing not to use Homer as a source, despite his prestige. Homer, he argued, had created an unreliable account of the Trojan War:

> Mais ne dist pas ses livres veir,
> quar bien savons sens nuil espier
> qu'il ne fu puis de cent anz nez
> que li granz osz fu asemblez.
> N'est merveille s'il i faillit,
> qui unc n'i fu ne rein n'en vit.

> But his book does not speak truly, for we know without any doubt that he was not born even a hundred years after the great army was assembled. It is no surprise if he makes mistakes, for he was never there and saw nothing of it.

> *Roman de Troie*, 51–56[31]

Benoît's preferred source was the *De excidio Troiae historia* by Dares Phrygius, a late antique text that was widely believed to be an eyewitness account of the Trojan War.[32] His eyewitness status, Benoît asserts, made Dares a better source than Homer: 'thus each day he wrote as he had seen it with his own eyes' (chascun jor ensi l'escrivait | cum il o ses oilz le veeit: *Roman de Troie*, 105–06; text and trans. Damian-Grint 1999, 110). Like Rigord, therefore, Benoît claimed his historical reliability on the basis of using superior source material.[33]

---

[30] For Benoît and the *Roman de Troie*, see n.6 above.
[31] Text and translation from Damian-Grint 1999, 109.
[32] For Benoît, Dares, and Homer, see: Damian-Grint 1999, 109–10 and Gumpert 2001, 130.
[33] This is explicitly claimed: 'We have written and put down what Dares and Dictys said' (ço que dist Daires et Ditis | i avons si retrait e mis: *Roman de Troie*, lines 30, 303–4.

And even more explicitly than was the case with Rigord, for Benoît this did not include Homer.

Godfrey shares with Benoît the implicit suggestion that he had access to the Homeric poems, but parts ways with Benoît in his judgement of Homer. Godfrey's positive assessment of Homer is evident from the choice to name him explicitly in the text. As mentioned above, Godfrey rarely named his sources and it is significant that although he drew extensively from Dares in his Trojan genealogy, he nonetheless chose not to mention Dares' name.[34] In contrast, when Godfrey names Homer, he also seems to suggest that Homer occupied an especially elevated position – Godfrey himself may only touch on Homeric themes, apparently, if he first petitions the divine (me rogat alma Venus). Furthermore, Homer is described as 'great' (magnus). Indeed, later in the poem, Godfrey offers an even more glowing assessment of Homer.

> Iudicio veri si querimus ista fateri,
> Optima longevi rescripta probentur Homeri:
> Ytala nam tellus Grecia maior erit.

> If we seek to profess this as a true judgment,
> The excellent writings of venerable Homer would confirm
> That the land of Italy is now greater than Greece.

Godfrey of Viterbo, *Speculum Regum* 1.12, 34–36

These lines occur in a passage that describes the transfer of worldly power from ancient Greece to Italy.[35] Godfrey tells us that although the Greeks (indeed we are now dealing with the Latin term 'Graeci' rather than with Homeric Achaeans or classical Hellenes) were once thought greater than the Trojans (*Speculum* 1.12, 31), things had now changed, and that this is evident from Homer's work. Homer himself is described as 'venerable' (longevi: line 35), while his writings are 'the best' (optima: line 35). Not only did Godfrey imply that he had access to the Homeric poems therefore, but he also offered his judgement on the poems as being of particularly high quality.

However, at this point Godfrey is not really writing about Homer at all. Rather, he is writing about himself, and his own argument about the changing

---

[34] Meyer 1933, 43–55.
[35] The idea of the *translatio imperii* (the transfer of empire) was already well developed in the twelfth century and linked with ideas about the *translatio studii* (the transfer of the centres of knowledge and learning). See Stoll 2014.

seat of power. Homer is invoked only to confirm Godfrey's position, supporting his version of history and the Trojan genealogy. In the opacity of contemporary ignorance concerning Homer, Godfrey saw an opportunity. He used Homer as a mirror to reflect and authenticate his own arguments, casting Homer in his own image.

The mirror refracted

In the decade that followed the initial composition of the *Speculum*, Godfrey worked almost constantly on revising his history. The historical material of the *Speculum* was reworked into the *Memoria seculorum* ('Remembrance of the Ages'), parts of which began to circulate as early as 1185; and then eventually into a work entitled the *Pantheon*, which reached its final form around 1190. The composition of the *Pantheon* involved a fair amount of cut-and-paste, but there were also many additions and a significant change of emphasis in relation to Godfrey's Trojan material.

In particular, there is considerably less interest in Trojan genealogy and the Hohenstaufen dynasty in the *Pantheon* than in the *Speculum*. Charlemagne does not feature so prominently, and is no longer presented as the culmination of the genealogical discussion. Similarly, the fate of the Trojan survivors receives less attention, as does the division between the proper Teutonic 'Franks' and the 'Franklings' of France. Overall, Godfrey had become far less interested in the imperial ideology of the Hohenstaufen dynasty. Instead, his own literary and historical ambitions now take centre stage – as indicated by the change of title. Where the *Speculum regum* suggested looking backwards to reflect on past images of kingly power, the *Pantheon* was larger and more encyclopaedic in scope, looking outwards. It has been suggested that this change may have been partly due to the *Speculum* receiving only a lukewarm reception from the Hohenstaufens, leading Godfrey to seek patronage and recognition elsewhere. Significantly, the *Pantheon* was no longer dedicated to the Hohenstaufen heir Henry, but instead to the Pope Urban III – a personal enemy of Frederick I.[36]

---

[36] For Godfrey's working drafts, the publication date of the *Pantheon*, and the dedication to Urban III, see Weber 1994, 181–88. As Weber says: 'Godfrey did not rewrite the *Pantheon* entirely from scratch, but he nevertheless subordinated the panegyric elements of the *Speculum regum* to vast amounts of other, newer material' (1994, 188).

Although much of Godfrey's Trojan material was trimmed for the *Pantheon*, it is significant that the lines concerning Homer were retained, albeit with a slight change of emphasis. The new title given to the poem about the fall of Troy sets the tone – this is no longer a poem focusing on the kings of Troy exclusively. Instead, the poem is first and foremost concerned with chronicling the times.

CHRONICA ILIUS TEMPORIS, DE REGIBUS ET CAUSIS
    TROIANORUM:
Istis temporibus Troiam describit Homerus,
Anchisem Priamumque simul feremus,
Gestaque, tangemus, me rogat ipsa Venus.
Nascitur ex Priamo Paris et laudabilis Hector,
De quibus annecto breviter quam plurima lector,
Cetera quae remanent, magnus Homerus habet.

THE CHRONICLE OF THAT TIME, OF THE KINGS AND TROUBLES
    OF THE TROJANS:
Homer described Troy in this era,
We find that Anchises and Priam reigned at the same time;
And we will touch on their deeds, if I ask Venus herself.
Of Priam was born Paris and praiseworthy Hector,
About whom, my reader, I link up many things briefly.
The rest which remains, great Homer has it.

> Godfrey of Viterbo, *Pantheon* 7, columns 183–84[37]

The other subtle change in these lines is in the description of Venus – instead of 'kindly' (alma) Venus, Godfrey will now ask the goddess 'herself' (ipsa). In the later reference to Homer there is once again a subtle change of wording. Crucially, Godfrey has made a firmer claim on what was in the Homeric text.

Iudicio veri, si quaerimus ista fateri:
Inclyta longaevi rescripta legantur Homeri,
Itala nam tellus Graecua maior erit.

If we seek to profess this as a true judgement,
In the renowned writings of venerable Homer it is read that
That the land of Italy is now greater than Greece.

> Godfrey of Viterbo, *Pantheon* 7, column 185

---

[37] The text of the *Pantheon* used in this chapter is that of Herold 1559.

Godfrey implies, now more than before, that he has access to the writings of Homer – specifying for his own readers what could be 'read' (*legantur*) in Homer's writings. And yet, while this formulation is stronger in its claims about Homeric content, it is weaker in its claims for a Godfreidian Homer. Homer is not cited here simply to prove the arguments of Godfrey – he is here to be read in his own right. Perhaps, in this more final version of his universal history, Godfrey felt less constrained within his literary hall of mirrors.

Jan: *Troy's* Hall of Fame

Cinema in the early twenty-first century witnessed a remarkable interest in all things ancient. This began in the year 2000, when viewers flocked to see Ridley Scott's Oscar-winning epic, *Gladiator*, a film that told the story of the gladiator Maxmius Decimus Meridius and his struggles under the cruel emperor Commodus.[38] Since then, various films have centred on specific individuals from antiquity, for instance Alexander the Great (*Alexander*, 2004) and Hypatia (*Agora*, 2009), while others have focused on significant historical events, such as the Battle of Thermopylae (*300*, 2007) and the volcanic destruction of Pompeii (*Pompeii*, 2014).[39] One of the most commercially, though not always critically, successful of this roster of ancient world films is Wolfgang Petersen's 2004 epic *Troy*.[40] The film tells the story of Paris' love for Helen of Sparta, their flight to Troy and the Greeks' subsequent attack (for in twenty-first-century popular culture, Homeric Achaeans are almost universally equated with 'Greeks'; see below) on the Trojan capital. While *Troy's* screenwriter David Benioff has cautiously professed an interest in Homer's account of the

---

[38] For *Gladiator's* wider impact, see the various essays in Winkler 2004 and cf. Richards 2008, 1–2, 174–77, Berti and Morcillo 2008b, 9–10, and Elliott 2014, 4–5. On the term 'epic' in film, see Elliott 2014.

[39] For the ancient world and cinema, see variously Wyke 1997, Solomon 2001, Martin 2002, Nisbet 2006, Berti and Morcillo 2008a, Winkler 2009, Llewellyn-Jones 2009, Theodorakopoulos 2010, Blanshard and Shahabudin 2011, Paul 2013, Michelakis and Wyke 2013, Elliott 2014, and Safran and Cyrino 2015.

[40] The film earned a sizeable $497.4 million according to Box Office Mojo, eighth on the list of highest grossing films in 2004, <http://www.boxofficemojo.com/movies/?id=troy.htm>. This compares rather favourably to *Alexander's* worldwide gross of $167,298,192, or even the much more critically successful *Gladiator*, which earned $457,640,427. It is curious indeed to note how sparingly other critics and scholars remark on *Troy's* relative commercial success, albeit note Burgoyne 2011b, 7. For the film's limited critical success, see Jancovich 2014, 61–63.

Trojan War,[41] and the director Wolfgang Petersen has spoken repeatedly of his classical education,[42] the film shows limited engagement with the specific details of the text of the *Iliad*. Rather, *Troy* (modelled in part on Robert Wise's 1956 epic film *Helen of Troy*)[43] attempts to synthesize various elements of the wider Trojan War storyline, beginning with Agamemnon's overlordship of the different Bronze Age Greek communities and culminating with the fall of Troy (though omitting several details, e.g., the sacrifice of Iphigenia, Cassandra's prophetic statements on Troy's demise).[44]

Troy is not much more than a decade old, yet there has been a fairly constant flow of scholarly engagement with the film since its theatrical release. In 2007, the same year that witnessed the appearance of the extended director's cut of the film,[45] Martin Winkler oversaw an important set of essays that examined a wide range of issues, from the film's tragic dimension to the long-standing cinematic tradition of adapting the Trojan War story.[46] Since then, Jonathan Burgess has argued that the film's rationalism comes at the expense of myth, since the Trojan War story is inextricably bound up with mythological traditions.[47] Some have focused too on the significant emphasis placed on various love stories in the film, notably Paris and Helen's much more conventional romance compared to that of the *Iliad*, as well as the romance between Briseis and Achilles, the latter figure presented as a warrior *and* a lover.[48] More recently, Joanna Paul has offered a sensitive analysis of the film's particular interest in heroic κλέος (glory) and Martin Winkler has published a second edited collection, which explores

---

[41] Benioff 2014 refers to Bernard Knox, 'whose introduction to Robert Fagles' superb translation of The Iliad is probably my single favourite work of Homeric analysis'.
[42] Winkler 2007b, 5, 2015b, 23 and Kofler and Schaffenrath 2015, 87.
[43] Wieber 2005, 150 and Winkler 2007c, 206.
[44] Richards 2008, 178, cf. Nisbet 2006, 84, and Mendelsohn 2008, 116, remarking negatively on the film's debt not so much to the *Iliad*, but to the (supposedly inferior) wider Epic Cycle.
[45] I refer to this extended version of the film throughout, although my reading of the film applies equally to the original theatrical release; *contra* Weinlich 2015, 202, who argues that this extended version becomes more of a political film in the light of George Bush's prolonged military campaigns in Iraq and Afghanistan, though Weinlich does not identify *specific* aspects of the extended cut of the film that show how *Troy* 'becomes more of a political film'. In Winkler 2015b, 20, 23, Petersen comments pointedly on his preference for this cut of the film, some thirty minutes longer than the 2004 cinematic release.
[46] Tragic qualities: Ahl 2007; Trojan War in cinema: Winkler 2007a, c.
[47] Burgess 2009. Cf. Petersen's comments in Winkler 2015b, 18: 'My intent was always to tell the story as it could have happened in reality, before it was relegated by the centuries to a more mythical realm'.
[48] Roisman 2008, 141–42, Chiasson 2009, 188–95 and Winkler 2009, 219.

the director's cut edition of the film and its particular relationship with the Homeric texts.[49]

In this section, I would like to analyse in greater depth an important aspect of *Troy* that many have remarked on either implicitly or only in passing: the film's undermining of popular expectations concerning cultural ownership and the classical Greek heritage, used as a means of commenting on early twenty-first-century global geopolitics and specifically on the so-called 'War on Terror'.[50] While the film is clearly interested in tracking the fortunes of its two central heroes, Achilles and Hector,[51] as well as underlining the everlasting fame that these epic heroes attained for themselves, it does not shy away from offering a thorough critique of the Greeks' motivations for war, as well as of the effectiveness of their leaders, most notably the cartoonish villain Agamemnon. This critique has a sharp political edge, when it is considered that America and the 'West' claims a Greek cultural heritage, positioning itself as the heir to Hellenic antiquity. If the Greeks of the film stand for the twenty-first-century 'West', and the Trojans of the film stand for the peoples of the modern Middle East, then this vision of the Trojan War is an intensely political one.

The first part of this discussion will explore the film's preoccupation with fame, illustrating how various figures aspire for future glory, though, and to some extent differently from Homer's *Iliad*, they remain uncertain of the nature or intensity of that fame. It also considers the general characterization of the Greeks as opposed to the Trojans, and begins to explore the problematic portrait of the Greeks in Petersen-Benioff's film.[52] The analysis then moves on to explore the characterization of Agamemnon and his imperialistic agenda, as well as the problematic interactions between the central Greek

---

[49] Paul 2013, 70–76, cf. (less favourably) Mendelsohn 2008, 117 and Winkler 2015a.

[50] So Winkler 2007b, 4, 7–8, Rabel 2007, 190, Richards 2008, 179, Berti and Morcillo 2008b, 16, Mendelsohn 2008, 115, 117–18, Burgess 2009, 170–72 ('Agamemnon's machinations obviously represent post-9/11 American foreign policy', 172), Elliott 2014, 11, Weinlich 2015, 202, cf. Denby 2004, and French 2004. For American appeals to Homer in relation to earlier, twentieth-century conflicts, see Winkler 2007b, 2. On the importance of reading a film against its own contemporary mores and cultural assumptions, see Berti and Morcillo 2008b, 15–16. However, note too Elliott 2014, 10–11, who cautions that while a film is partly a reflection of its own present, this does not necessarily, in the case of historical films, prevent them from functioning as 'earnest attempt[s] to retell historical events' (11).

[51] On the contrasting forms of masculinity that Achilles and Hector offer in *Troy*, see Proch and Kleu 2013.

[52] In the discussion that follows, I refer to the director-writer partnership, Petersen-Benioff, since they played the most crucial role in shaping the film's narrative.

protagonists, a refraction of the Homeric poet's depiction of the Achaeans, and a clear response to the film's wider social-political context. I will propose that *Troy* – a film that responds to the wider Trojan War tradition, but is nevertheless clearly indebted to the *Iliad* – is much harsher in its critique of the Greek leadership than the Homeric account. I will also suggest that the film responds to the *Iliad*'s search for causation in unexpected ways, providing a serious challenge to our understanding of the war's purpose and its consequences. *Troy*'s bleak narrative of cynical geopolitical manoeuvrings ultimately reframes our view of the causes of the conflict, redirecting audience sympathies away from the impotent Greek forces towards the innocent people of Troy.[53]

Remembering Troy

Troy does not claim to be a faithful adaptation of the *Iliad* (the film's closing credits declare that it was 'inspired by Homer's "The Iliad"'); indeed, there are various differences between the narratives of the film and poem respectively, not the least Agamemnon's murder at the hands of Briseis (for the Homeric version of his death, see *Od.* 4.519–37, 11.405–35; cf. further discussion below), as well as Menelaus' death in a duel with Hector. Yet there are some specifically Iliadic resonances.

Notably, the film's concern with memory and remembrance strikes a familiar chord for those viewers that are familiar with the Homeric texts. Throughout the film, characters speak of their desire to achieve κλέος, that is, everlasting fame; κλέος thus becomes, as Paul puts it, 'a site of competition between heroes'.[54] At the outset of the film, for instance, the Ithacan hero Odysseus breathily muses 'Will strangers hear our names long after we are gone, and wonder who we were, how bravely we fought, how fiercely we loved?' Odysseus' concern about posterity once more comes to the fore at the climax of the film, in which he hopes that 'If they ever tell my story, let them say I walked with giants … Let them say I lived in the time of Hector, tamer of horses. Let them say I lived in the time of Achilles'. Similarly, following

---

[53] The primary focus here is on the film's extratextual contexts; it remains for others to shed additional light on *Troy*'s aesthetic sensibilities.
[54] Paul 2013, 72.

Agamemnon's decision to support Menelaus' desire to reclaim Helen, the aged king Nestor emphasizes to Agamemnon that 'this will be the greatest war the world has ever seen'. Even the film's greatest warrior Achilles is depicted as extemporizing on the heroic memory that will be afforded the Greeks; when flyting with Hector outside the temple of Apollo, Achilles observes, 'They'll be talking about this war for a thousand years'. After Hector rejects these words,[55] Achilles emphasizes that although their bodies may wither, 'our names will remain' – a line that speaks intertextually towards the famous scene in Book 9 of the *Iliad*, in which Achilles sings of the glories of men (see p.15 above).

Various critics of the film have been quick to denigrate the special emphasis that multiple characters place on future memory.[56] Perhaps the most sustained critique of all derives from the film critic Jonathan Romney, who asserted that 'The clunking irony is that a film which so harps on posterity will barely be remembered a year from now'.[57] And yet, Petersen-Benioff's emphasis on the significance of posterity for these Bronze Age heroes in fact chimes with the *Iliad*'s own frequent self-conscious references to poetic memory.[58] In both film and poem, it is the principal agents of the story such as Odysseus and Helen that are concerned with the κλέος that is conferred by their actions, rather than some Homer-like figure. And in both poem and film alike, the heroes remain uncertain of the future fame that will be attained, precisely because the Iliadic world does not appear to be occupied by bardic figures. It is not the case, therefore, that the film's special interest in glory and lasting memory is specifically un-Homeric or that the lack of a bard figure deviates away from the Iliadic tradition. That being said, the related question of what it is precisely that *Troy*'s characters hope future generations will remember when they recall their names is likely to lead to a rather different set of ideas compared to the *Iliad*.

---

[55] Paul 2013, 72 well notes, however, the contrast between *Troy* and *Iliad*'s Hector. In the former, he rejects the idea of immortal glory ('the dust from our bones will be gone'); in the latter, Hector speaks repeatedly of his desire to achieve undying personal glory (e.g. *Il.* 6.460-61; 7.91).

[56] Paul 2013, 73.

[57] Romney 2004, cf. Robey 2004 ('It's a disgrace. As an adaptation of The *Iliad*, it's a pathetic joke'); Nisbet 2006, 82–86 and Mendelsohn 2008, 112–23. For a more sardonic response to the film, see the amusing 'Troy in 15 Minutes' by 'Cleolinda Jones', <http://m15m.livejournal.com/1487.html>.

[58] Paul 2013, 73–75.

Goodies and baddies

Crucially, what *Troy*'s audiences might recall about the film's Trojans is markedly different from what they might recall about its Greeks. Thus, in turning to the presentation of the Greeks and Trojan characters in the *Iliad* and *Troy*, we can begin to detect more clearly the film's wider cultural contexts, as well as its more explicit deviations away from its Homeric source material. It has long been acknowledged that the *Iliad* draws no clear cultural or ethnic distinction between its Achaeans and its Trojans.[59] This is not to propose that the poem elides any distinction between the two sides,[60] but that the *Iliad* avoids a narrowly partisan outlook in favour of a more universalizing approach that demands sympathy for all involved. The film, in contrast, sits squarely in a cultural context that automatically equates the 'Greeks' with America and the 'West'.

Turning to Petersen-Benioff's version of the war, it is soon apparent that theirs is a much more partisan account. While Achilles' inhuman μῆνις ('wrath') is a direct response to his improper treatment at the hands of the leader Agamemnon in Book 1 of the *Iliad*, in *Troy* Achilles' anger is less clearly delineated. Agamemnon's commandeering of his γέρας ('war-prize') Briseis near the beginning of the *Iliad* is a significant episode which has eruptive consequences; in *Troy*, the seizure of Briseis does not signal a decisive change in Achilles' mental state, but merely adds to an extended list of grievances that he harbours against the king of kings. Not only are Achilles' motivations for dissent watered down, but he is also refashioned as an individualist who is disposed to irrational, even cruel acts of violence. In one particularly memorable scene, as Achilles and his Myrmidon troops outpace the other Greek contingents, landing first on the shores of Troy, he and his men raid the temple of Apollo, slaughtering the temple servants.[61] As if to underline the sacrilegious nature of the Greeks' behaviour, Achilles then decapitates the honorific statue of the sun

---

[59] Vlassopoulos 2013, 170–72 with references.

[60] The poem does certainly privilege the Achaean perspective, as indicated most clearly in the uneven space dedicated to listing the Achaean contingents and the Trojan allies in Book 2. Some scholars have argued that some subtle distinctions do emerge; see, for example, Christensen 2015.

[61] Winkler 2009, 111–12 argues that this must be the temple of Apollo Thymbraeus, which stood outside the walls of Troy. See *Il.* 10.430; *Cypria*, fr. 41; Ibycus fr. S 224 (Davies); cf. Cavallini (2015, 72–73, 79–80), providing further historical and archaeological contextualization. Chiasson 2009, 199–201 reads this scene as further proof of the gods' impotence in the world of *Troy*.

god – a shocking act of religious intolerance that bears little resemblance to the *Iliad*'s characterization of Achilles, and one that could hardly appeal even to the film's most secular audience(s), who are accustomed to living with various religions and faiths.[62] That being said, it is unlikely that audiences would express no sympathy for Achilles. The casting of Brad Pitt to play Achilles is clearly designed to appeal to one of the film's key audience demographics,[63] and the affection that he develops for Briseis in particular draws out the complexity of Achilles' character, which emphasizes his independent status amongst the Greek warriors.[64] In this way, Achilles is largely exempted from the loathsome expansionist polices adopted by the Greeks.

Perhaps the most striking disparity of all between the Homeric texts and Petersen-Benioff's film can be discerned in the latter's portrayal of Helen's husband Menelaus as an ineffectual brute who displays open contempt to his wife back at Sparta,[65] and his brother Agamemnon as an obvious 'mega-villain'[66] – an advance even on earlier Trojan War films such as Robert Wise's *Helen of Troy* (1956), in which Menelaus and numerous Greek kings are depicted as cynically debating the possibility of a campaign against the Trojans before the flight of Menelaus' wife. Indeed, the film's relentlessly negative presentation of the two sons of Atreus proves a decisive contrast with the *Iliad*, in which the two flawed leaders are given a more sympathetic reading.[67] The next

---

[62] As Winkler 2009, 112 n.58 notes, the seated Apollo figure in *Troy* recalls the god's initial appearance in the *Iliad*, in which he is depicted as being seated, shooting his terrible arrows into the Greek camp (*Il.* 1.43–52). The film took $364,031,596 in cinemas outside the USA, well over two-thirds of its total box office takings, and opened in over forty territories; cf. Iordanova (2011). On 'epic film as an international, global narrative apparatus not bound by nation or ethnicity', see Burgoyne 2011b (quote at 2).

[63] Shahabudin 2007, 109–10 notes that much of the marketing for the theatrical release centred on Brad Pitt's chiselled physique. For references to Achilles' handsomeness in the *Iliad*, see *Il.* 2.673–4; 24.629–30; cf. 1.197; 23.141.

[64] Proch and Kleu 2013, 182–87 and, cf. Wieber 2005, 158.

[65] So Winkler 2009, 230–31, who notes the clear discrepancies in Helen and Menelaus' relationship in *Troy* and the *Iliad*. In the latter, Helen in fact yearns for Menelaus (3.139–42; 6.349–351).

[66] On Agamemnon, see Burgess 2009, 171: 'The film clearly signals that the war's instigator, Agamemnon, is not sympathetic'. See too Proch and Kleu 2013, 179, who remark on the corpulent frames of Agamemnon and Menelaus – a clear contrast with the svelte, well-defined physiques of the younger heroes Hector and Achilles.

[67] Cf. Graziosi 2016, 37, who regards Agamemnon as a flawed leader in the *Iliad*. Indeed, regardless of his poisonous dispute with Achilles, Agamemnon, like Achilles, Ajax, and the *Iliad*'s other great warriors, has his own *aristeia* at 11.91–147. As the discussion below will demonstrate, 'flawed' is a less-suitable adjective to describe the wicked megalomaniac that is Agamemnon in *Troy*. Cf. too Thuc. 1.9.3, where the historian Thucydides claims that fear of Agamemnon's naval power played a signal role in the Achaeans' united expedition against Troy.

section of this discussion will thus explore further the implications of *Troy*'s unsympathetic portrayal of Agamemnon, as well as demonstrate Petersen-Benioff's more sympathetic rendering of the Trojans.

A clash of civilizations

In the popular imagination of the twenty-first century, the classical world and ancient Greece in particular belongs to the cultural heritage of the modern 'West'. From the Doric columns of the Lincoln Memorial in Washington DC to the inclusion of ancient Greek texts on the reading lists of American 'Great Books' courses;[68] from the discourse surrounding western democracy to the debates over international financial assistance for Greek national debt – the idea of the 'West' as the cultural heir of ancient Greece is both widespread and pervasive.[69] This notion is particularly true of contemporary American political discourse, preoccupied as it is with democracy.[70]

When faced with a twenty-first-century account of the Trojan War, therefore, in America and the 'West' sympathies would automatically tend to lie with the Achaeans/Greeks rather than with the Trojans. As we have seen in the previous section, this was not always the case at other points in history. The ubiquity of this assumption is evident from the sense of rupture we feel when faced with its inversion. For instance, Maureen Dowd wrote the following editorial in *The New York Times* shortly after the terrorist attacks of 9/11:

> The most famous story of the Western world, the proto-type of all tales of human conflict … is the Wooden Horse. Despite repeated warnings, the Trojans relaxed their guard and let their fortress be breached. After the Trojans feasted and fell asleep, the hidden Greeks emerged. 'Mad with murder', Homer writes, they wielded their swords and hacked men and women to 'the last thrust' … We are chilled as we learn more about how the Middle East terrorists mad with murder breached our walls.[71]

For Dowd, the paradigmatic value of the Trojan War was of special relevance following the atrocities in Manhattan. Just as the Trojans had let their guard

---

[68] Schein 2007.
[69] See most recently Hanink 2017.
[70] Goldwyn 2015 and cf. Winkler 2007b, 3 n.9.
[71] Dowd 2001.

down, the Americans too had failed to ward off their own modern-day murderous Greeks: the Middle Eastern terrorists. Readers may take issue with Dowd's depiction, which reveals perhaps rather less about the shape of the complicated political landscape in the new millennium and rather more about Dowd's own intellectual heritage, but it is nonetheless striking that Dowd equates the Americans with the Trojans. The effect is disarming for readers expecting to see a parallel developed between Americans and the Greeks. In fact, through the use of Manichean language ('terrorists mad with murder') Dowd demands that the reader perceive afresh the Greeks' deception, attacking the Trojans not through military force but, as Goldwyn notes, from within the city walls.[72]

Dowd's editorial in the *New York Times* was only one of several journalistic appeals to the Trojan War myth following 9/11. Just days before the 2003 invasion of Iraq, Nicholas Kristof observed in the very same newspaper:

> Agamemnon was the Donald Rumsfeld of his day, needlessly angering his key allies – and outraging Achilles by swiping his concubine Briseis … We Americans are the Greeks of our day, and as we now go to war, we should appreciate not only the beauty of the tale, but also the warnings within it.[73]

Like Dowd, Kristof uses the reference to the Trojan War to highlight the potentially problematic repercussions arising from US foreign policy. Kristof differs from Dowd, however, in maintaining the popular association between the modern United States and ancient Greece. The way he does this is particularly Iliadic, making an uncomplimentary comparison between the then Secretary of Defence of the United States, Donald Rumsfeld, and the Achaean leader Agamemnon, whom he characterizes as 'outraging Achilles by swiping his concubine'. And as we shall see in a moment, Kristof's negative characterization of Agamemnon chimes closely with Brian Cox's portrayal of the Mycenaean king in *Troy*.

Returning to Petersen-Benioff's *Troy*, it is clear that their film needs to be situated within its wider geopolitical context.[74] In order to understand the

---

[72] Goldwyn 2015, 245.
[73] Kristof 2003.
[74] Cf. Berti and Morcillo 2008b, 16: '[a film's] view of historical episodes transmits certain ideological tendencies, collective values and cultural conventions attested in the context in which the movie has been produced and released'.

negative portrayal of Agamemnon and the Greeks in the film, we need to understand the contemporary political situation – only then can we appreciate the political statement that the film-makers were making. The script of the film was in production in late 2001, when the world-changing events of 9/11 prompted new discussion of a 'clash of civilizations' in popular political discourse. The script was then finalized in the following year, amidst bellicose political rhetoric in the United States surrounding the 'War on Terror' and ever-rising death tolls from the occupation of Afghanistan. The spring of 2003 saw both the controversial invasion of Iraq in March, and the start of filming for *Troy* in April. The movie was released in America in the following year – 2004 – amidst spiralling levels of violence in Iraq. The entire production process of *Troy* was therefore carried out against the backdrop of the 'War on Terror'. Indeed, in one especially revealing interview, Wolfgang Petersen confirms that the Iraq War and the penumbra of events surrounding it indelibly influenced the film-making process:

> You develop such a story [for your film], and then almost the identical thing happens when you turn on the television. You can't help thinking that this Homer was a real genius, that he exactly understood us humans who apparently need wars again and again; also that someone like Agamemnon reappears again and again. Still, Homer was never interested in black–white, good–bad. Such a concept doesn't exist in reality. Only in the mind of George W. Bush ... But this direct connection between Bush's power politics and that of Agamemnon in the *Iliad*, this desire to rule the world, to trample everything underfoot that gets in your way, that became evident only during filming. Only gradually did we realize how important Homer still is today.[75]

Petersen's reflections on the film and its wider associations and relationships clearly relate to the so-called 'War on Terror'. Although he makes no direct reference to Iraq, his comments on Bush's 'power politics' and his 'desire to rule the world' recalling the behaviour of Agamemnon in the *Iliad* underline the director's view that the Greek invasion was a spurious one, which echoed (at least for Petersen) Agamemnon's immoral desire to control the Aegean Sea region.

---

[75] In Winkler 2007b, 8.

What is especially striking about Petersen's comments is the director's belief that the ancient-modern connection between Agamemnon and Bush is axiomatic, something that elides the need for interpretation. For Petersen, the contiguity between these two individuals, 'became evident … during filming', at which point he and his team came to 'realize' the significance of Homer even for a twenty-first-century audience. The effect of Petersen's comments for our understanding of his engagement with Homer is twofold: first, his ideas amplify the conception of Homer as an artistic genius, creating a poem that still resonates with audiences and reveals important truths that speak to power after 3,000 years; secondly, his comments further reinforce the 'historical' quality of *Troy*, by distancing the film from any charge of anachronism or inapposite deployment of modern ideas to ancient material.[76] The director's rhetoric insinuates that these connections between the ancient and modern material are self-evident, and came into being of their own volition once the film was in production. Agamemnon's/Bush's 'power politics' are the destructive forces that the *Iliad/Troy* magnify.

Various scenes in the film reinforce the film's emphasis on hegemonic ambitions and cynical realpolitik as vital causal factors to explain the Trojan War.[77] Prior to setting out for Troy, Agamemnon smirks to his comrade king Nestor that, by fleeing with Paris, '[Helen has] proved to be very useful'. Having been advised of the Trojans' great military strength, Agamemnon angrily retorts that 'if Troy falls … I control the Aegean', before announcing that 'I build the future, Nestor … Me!' In a heated exchange with his naïve brother, Hector reminds Paris of Priam's protracted efforts to achieve peace, underscoring both the martial conditions under which these men operate, but also the interstices between the Trojans and Greeks, the latter led by an unrepentant imperialist. Indeed, later in the film, prior to the uncanonical death of Menelaus at the hands of Hector, Agamemnon declares to his brother that 'I didn't come here for your pretty wife. I came here for Troy'. And another, further instance worth noting is Agamemnon's bilious reaction to Achilles' temporary pact with the

---

[76] I thank Jo Paul for alerting my attention to this vital aspect of Petersen's comments.

[77] Mendelsohn 2008, 115: 'Benioff has exiled Homeric heroics in favor of something that modern audiences will feel more comfortable with: global geopolitical Realpolitik'. One of the most explicit visual indicators of Agamemnon's drive for global conquest occurs near the end of the film. Stewing alone in his tent, the king repeatedly stabs Troy on a map of the world with his dagger.

Trojans, following the return of Hector's corpse to Troy; his irate response to such a suggestion ('Peace. Peace!') firmly underscores what redounds throughout the picture: Agamemnon's unrelenting imperial agenda.[78]

Given the film-makers' presentation of Agamemnon as an unremittingly sleazy, loathsome individual, his final comeuppance at the hands of Briseis is less surprising than this most un-Homeric event might have otherwise suggested.[79] Barbara Weinlich has recently explored the way that Briseis' killing of Agamemnon subscribes to the Western cultural trope of good overcoming evil, for the Homeric princess stabs the king with a ceremonial dagger in what is clearly a sacerdotal context.[80] This moralizing interpretation accords well with our reading of the film's negative approach to Agamemnon's imperial programme. Agamemnon might well have routed Troy, but his subsequent murder shines a light on the futility of the Greeks' 'victory'. Moreover, the execution of Agamemnon is a clear turning point in the narrative, enabling the film-makers initially to focus on Paris' somewhat improbable evolution from an immature naïf to a fully fledged heroic warrior by killing Achilles and, ultimately, allowing the film-makers to navigate away from the film's martial politics towards a poetics of hope, by placing strong visual emphasis on the Trojans' survival as they march away from their smouldering city.

Alongside foul Agamemnon, the film's contrasting presentation of the Greek and Trojan protagonists further underscores the moral superiority of the latter and clearly indicates where audience sympathies should lie. For instance, in a pair of scenes that offer perhaps the starkest indication of the differences between the Greeks and the Trojans, the film contrasts Agamemnon's autocratic form of rule with the Trojans' much more egalitarian system. In the first scene, several Greek kings congratulate Agamemnon for 'his' successful capture of the Trojan plain, furnishing him with a number of lavish gift offerings. Agamemnon then proceeds to sneer at Achilles, reminding the Myrmidon king that the Greeks' victory on the shores of Troy will be remembered as Agamemnon's victory. He also seizes the booty

---

[78] Note that earlier in the film, too, Agamemnon assuages his brother by observing that 'Peace is for the women and the weak. Empires are forged by war'.

[79] The similarities between Agamemnon's death in the *Odyssey* and *Troy* are just as striking as the differences: in both accounts, his murderers take vengeance on his immoral deeds; cf. Safran and Cyrino 2015, 3.

[80] Weinlich 2015, 201–02.

that Achilles and his men had plundered from Apollo's sanctuary, as well as the temple servant Briseis (the very dishonourable action that of course precipitated Achilles' anger in Book 1 of the *Iliad*). Throughout this scene, the lighting is gloomy and the atmosphere is febrile and debilitating; the lack of effective communication between the Greek leaders serves as a marked signifier of their future demise.[81] Immediately following this scene, the camera swoops to the palace of Troy, where counsellors are found seated in the round, advising Priam on their chances of success against the Greeks. Whilst each individual encourages Priam to attack, the nature of the discussion is calm and measured. The style of seating utilized by the Trojans, in which the council are sat in an oval formation at equal height, is a striking contrast with the subservient postures adopted by Agamemnon's 'allies' in the former scene, all of which suggests that it is in fact the Trojans that practice freedom of speech. Indeed, Priam's son Hector is not afraid to rally against the consensus, questioning the use of augury as an effective tool for military decision-making. The respectful nature of the Trojans' dialogue further throws into sharp relief the toxicity of the Greeks' interactions; in particular, the devastating effects of the elite's unswerving allegiance to their corrupt king Agamemnon. This in turn brings us back to Wolfgang Petersen's remarks on Bush/Agamemnon's monochromatic world view, and their shared desire for global domination; *Troy* indicates that the *Iliad*'s Achilles offers a useful vehicle through which one can discern the dissenting voices of Bush's powerless allies.[82]

Heroic ambivalence

In drawing this section to a close, it has become clear that Homer's *Iliad* is a crucial context for understanding *Troy*, a film that of course acknowledges other receptions of the Trojan War narrative, which range from other ancient world epic films to Virgil's *Aeneid*.[83] As emphasized at the outset of this section, the film is not straightforwardly an adaptation of the *Iliad*, yet it nonetheless

---

[81] Burgess 2009, 172 notes the way that Achilles interacts more readily with the Trojans Priam and Briseis than he does with his fellow Greeks.

[82] On the widespread opposition to the Iraq War in Western Europe, see Dumbrell 2005, 33.

[83] Benioff 2014: 'Dozens of different versions of the War have been told, and my script ransacks ideas from several of them'.

constitutes a valuable reception of the Trojan War tradition, which is, as we
have sought to demonstrate throughout this study, inextricably bound up with
the Homeric poems. Petersen-Benioff radically transform major elements of
Homer's Trojan War narrative, not least Agamemnon and Menelaus' early
deaths, and the successful flight of multiple Trojans (as well as the non-Trojan
Helen).[84] As many others have noted, *Troy*'s story is also an obsessively secular
one, almost entirely eradicating the gods from the action, and presenting an
uncompromisingly human vision of the conflict, its causes and its effects.[85]
The lack of a divine architecture, and the story's grounding within a strictly
human sphere were clearly of paramount importance to Petersen (the director
says as much in a recent interview with the classicist Martin Winkler).[86] These
revisions will no doubt have appealed to the film's production company Warner
Bros. Pictures, who were no doubt buoyed by the phenomenal fiscal success of
recent epic 'historical' films like Ridley Scott's *Gladiator*, not to mention Peter
Jackson's *Lord of the Rings* trilogy.[87]

The fissures that exist between *Troy* and *Iliad* are nonetheless provocative. I
have argued here that alongside the need to develop an aesthetic appreciation
of *Troy* as a film whose narrative is not heavily indebted to the ancient texts,
the film must be situated within its broader historical, political, cultural, and
commercial context. While *Troy* should not to be understood as an explicit
commentary on any one war, this analysis has shown how the film participates
in a wider dialogue on the moral underpinnings of George Bush's so-called
'War on Terror'.[88] Didactic appeals to the classical past were made immediately
following the attack on the Twin Towers; the escalating military response of
the United States went hand in hand with a widening public discourse on
the lessons to be learnt from, amongst others, the fall of Priam's Troy, or even

---

[84] On the film's transformation of established story patterns, see further Wieber 2005 and Winkler 2005, 418–20.
[85] Scully 2007, 120, Burgess 2009, 169, and Winkler 2009, 218. As Fitton 2007, 103 observes, however, the gods are still revered by various characters and statuary representing the divine features throughout the film; cf. too Benioff 2014 and Latacz 2007, 42. For a different view again, see Chiasson 2009, 197, who argues that the gods *do* exist in the film, but 'as utterly debased versions of their Homeric counterparts ... powerless both to punish the humans who are disrespectful to them and to protect the humans who revere them'.
[86] Winkler 2015b, 18.
[87] Winkler 2007b, 3–4. Indeed, Petersen himself has acknowledged the impact of *Gladiator* on the American film industry: 'It became so successful that all of a sudden these projects were popping up that dealt with the times of 2,000 years ago–3,000 years ago, in our case' (in Winkler 2007b, 4).
[88] Ahl 2007, 167 and cf. Rabel 2007, 186: '[*Troy* is] a dialogue with the past about the present'.

Athens' tyrannical treatment of its allies during the Peloponnesian War. Most notably, this American production might well have challenged many amongst its initial audience. In some ways conventional – Achilles kills Hector, Troy burns to smithereens – the film also rewrites the character and fortunes of its "Western" protagonists, the Greeks – and clearly for the worse. They are the invading force, blindly following a leader who induces either silent acquiescence or moral indolence amongst the majority of the Greek leaders. And given the film's heavy-handed emphasis on Agamemnon's hegemonic agenda, what audience would accept the idea that the Greeks' campaign was an honourable attempt to recover Helen, a woman who freely chooses to abscond with her insipid lover Paris (a prettified Orlando Bloom) and one who is patently miserable in her hometown of Sparta, where her bellicose husband takes visible delight in multiple paramours.[89] The Greek leaders also suffer a fate worse than that of the Trojans; while a good number of the latter flee, marching on to found a new home, many amongst the Greeks' chief leaders (Agamemnon, Menelaus, Achilles, and Ajax) are killed by Trojans.[90] It is only the wily Odysseus who is left to perorate about the great deeds at Troy, wistfully hoping that later generations will sing of 'Hector, breaker of horses', as well as glorious Achilles. The phrase 'Hector, breaker of horses' is of course a Homeric one and is found repeatedly throughout the *Iliad*. And, strikingly, ἱπποδάμοιο ('breaker of horses') is the final word of the poem (*Il.* 24.884), just as the phrase occupies a central place in Odysseus' closing sentiments in the film *Troy*.

Troy demands that we ask ourselves some hard questions. What was the point of the Greeks' (or the US) invasion? And why did the Greeks (or the Americans) so unswervingly follow boastful Agamemnon (or Bush/Rumsfeld) – a bona fide 'baddie' in film parlance? These ominous lines of enquiry are particularly redolent in a post-Chilcot age,[91] more than a decade after the film's release, when western intervention in the Middle East looks to be increasingly feeble and new actors in the theatre of war (especially Trump, Russia, and ISIS)

---

[89] Similarly Roisman 2008, 140–41 and Winkler 2009, 225. Particularly revealing in this context are Helen's soothing words to Paris following his retreat from the duel with Menelaus: '[Menelaus] lived for fighting. And I hated him from the day I married him until the day he died'.

[90] Cf. Ahl 2007, 175: 'in the world of mainstream epic the future lies with the conquered Trojans, not with the conquering Greeks'.

[91] Here I refer to the British government's Iraq inquiry (or Chilcot report), published in July 2016. The report submitted a damning verdict on the British government's involvement before, during, and after the Iraq War.

have both reinvigorated the rhetoric of an East-versus-West conflict whilst simultaneously destabilizing political realities of conflict on the ground. As the twenty-first century progresses, it becomes increasingly difficult to draw clear lines of equivalence between modern actors and the Trojan War myth, and the sense of cultural heritage and legacy is even more difficult to pin down. The seeds of this process – the deconstruction of the 'clash of civilizations' model – can be seen in *Troy*.

Conclusion: Memorial

And
MENESTHES
ANCHIALOS
AMPHIUS
TLEPOLEMOS
COERANUS
CHROMIUS
ALCASTOR
ALCANDER
HALIUS
PYRTANIS
NOEMON
TEUTHRAS
ORESTES
TRECHUS
OENOMAUS
HELENUS
ORESBIUS
PERIPHAS
And
Oswald, *Memorial* p.25

The title of this epilogue takes its name from a poem by Alice Oswald, *Memorial: An Excavation of the Iliad*, published in 2011.[1] The poem begins

---

[1] The focus here is on the written version of Oswald's poem; for her live oral performances and the audio publication of *Memorial*, see Harrop 2013, cf. Minchin 2015, 206, n.17, 210, n.26, 216–20, Schein 2016, 156–61, and cf. Hardwick 2016, 24–25, a brief but elegant treatment. For many, Oswald's poem is perhaps the most significant and distinctive poetic reception of the *Iliad* since Christopher Logue's *War Music*, for which see Greenwood 2007 and Reynolds 2011, 219–34, 247–48 and Schein 2016, 161–65.

with a list of 200 names, each printed on a separate line in bold capital letters. These are the names of fallen soldiers, both Achaean and Trojan, starting with the Achaean Protesilaus, the first to die on the beaches of Troy, and running through to the Trojan Hector, whose death sealed the fate of his city. This stark list of the fallen evokes archaic Greek catalogue poetry (most obviously the lists of Achaeans and the Trojan allies in Book 2 of the *Iliad*),[2] as well as ancient epigrammatic funeral monuments,[3] and, perhaps more familiarly for Oswald's twenty-first-century audience, modern war memorials.[4] As the poem continues, it opens out into a string of individual 'obituaries', interspersed with formulaic lines and simile doublets.[5] The poem is therefore not a narrative, or a retelling of the Troy story. Instead, it is what its title suggests – a literary memorial, a verbal monument commemorating the war dead. Indeed, in the published preface to the poem, Oswald herself described it as 'a kind of oral cemetery'.[6] *Memorial* differs from Iliadic poetry, then, in that while both are concerned with commemoration,[7] *Memorial* has little interest in *klea andrōn* (see above pp.17–19).

The key lies in the individual obituaries provided for the fallen warriors. One such passage is that of Lycaon, which picks up on and transmutes the events of *Iliad* 21, 34–135.

> Laothoe, one of Priam's wives
> Never saw her son again he was washed away
> Now she can't look at the sea she can't think about
> The bits unburied being eaten by fishes
> He was the tall one the conscientious one

---

[2] Minchin 2001.
[3] Minchin 2015, 205. On the interactions between the Homeric poems and early Greek epigrams, see Petrovic 2016.
[4] Harrop 2013, 80 and Schein 2016, 156.
[5] We do not discuss Oswald's complex engagement with Homeric poetics in this conclusion. Nonetheless, the poem's use of repetition and simile are particularly interesting (Harrop 2013, 79). In many cases (e.g. the case of Ophelestes, Oswald 2011, 71), Oswald repeats, not half-line formulaic phrases as in the *Iliad*, but longer-verse-length similes. These longer repeated passages serve to slow the pace of the poem, encouraging deeper reflection on the death being described before moving on to the next soldier. Of course, Oswald also employs thoroughly modern poetics. Strikingly, the name of each dead individual is fully capitalized, making innovative use of print medium (Harrop 2013, 79). As Seth Schein has recently illustrated, these passages often take particular moments from their original Iliadic context and refract them in order to present new perspectives (Schein 2016, 157–58).
[6] Oswald 2011, 2.
[7] In the preface to the poem, Oswald articulates her interest in ancient lament poetry (Oswald 2011, 1). For lament poetry in the *Iliad*, see pp.19–23 above.

Who stayed out late pruning his father's fig trees
Who was kidnapped who was ransomed
Who walked home barefoot from Arisbe
And rested for twelve days and was killed
LYCAON killed Lycaon unkilled Lycaon
Bending down branches to make wheels
Lycaon kidnapped Lycaon pruning by moonlight
Lycaon naked in a river pleading for his life
Being answered by Achilles No.

Oswald, *Memorial* p.69

For all its Iliadic resonances, this is no Homeric death scene. Gone, for example, is Achilles' lengthy exposition on Patroclus' death and his own inevitable fate:[8] instead, Lycaon's death is seen through the eyes of his mother rather than those of his killer. At the heart of the passage are the dead man's family relationships, personal memories, and domestic details; with the result that the poem celebrates the life that has been lost as much as it mourns the loss of life.[9] Poignancy comes from the inclusion of small, quiet details; such as in the example of Pandarus, who 'had a wife at home ... He was captain of Zelea and he and his men | Used to drink the black raw water from the river'.[10] The pathos is heightened yet further by the inclusion of obituaries written in the form of appeals to the deceased in the second person, as in the case of Socus: 'Your father is a rich man a breeder of horses | And your house has deep decorated baths'.[11] For Oswald, the deaths of minor heroes are major events, and every human life is worthy of commemoration.[12]

While the content of the poem may serve as a literary memorial for Iliadic heroes, its form is a meditation on both the processes and practices of memorialization more generally. How do we choose to remember? How do we

---

[8] *Il.* 21.97–113. Here, Achilles makes a nod to the extra-Iliadic tradition that he will be fatally wounded by the archer Paris: 'there will be a dawn or evening or midday when my life shall be extinguished by somebody with Ares' strength, whether he strikes me by the launch of a spear or the arrow from its bow-string' (ἔσσεται ἢ ἠὼς ἢ δείλη ἢ μέσον ἦμαρ | ὁππότε τις καὶ ἐμεῖο Ἄρῃ ἐκ θυμὸν ἕληται | ἢ ὅ γε δουρὶ βαλὼν ἢ ἀπὸ νευρῆφιν ὀϊστῷ, *Il.* 21.111–13).

[9] Schein 2016, 158.

[10] Oswald 2011, 22.

[11] Oswald 2011, 42. In the published preface, Oswald claims: 'The *Iliad* is a vocative poem. Perhaps even (in common with lament) it is invocative'. The same might also be said of *Memorial*.

[12] For example, Hardwick 2016, 24 notes that Oswald's Protesilaus acquires 'the memorial that he does not achieve in Homer'.

create a memory of a person, a thing, or an event? Oswald's poem demonstrates that we 'do' memorialization by creating links – by forging connections and analogies between our own experience and the thing being memorialized.[13] In other words, memorialization is achieved in the same way that traditions are created – through dialogue. Memorialization is the making of tradition.

The subject and the process of memorialization

Oswald's *Memorial* commemorates more than either the legions of Homeric dead or the processes of memorialization and tradition-making. It commemorates the poem of the *Iliad* itself. Just as Oswald uses names, lists, anecdotes, repetition, and comparison to create connections between the reader and the deceased, these same techniques also serve to create a connection between *Memorial* and the *Iliad*.

Similar processes are at work in the other examples we have discussed in this book. In each case, we began by investigating how our examples both used and innovated on the *Iliad* in order to create their own unique representation of the Trojan War. In each case, we also found that the opposite line of enquiry could also be pursued – how our examples used and innovated on the Trojan War story in order to create their own unique *Iliad*. This is more obvious in some cases than others. In the first choral ode of the *Troades*, for example, Euripides deliberately presents his audience with an alternative *Iliad* from a Trojan perspective. Less explicitly, Petersen-Benioff's *Troy* seeks to 'out-Homer' Homer as a vehicle for *kleos*, offering a kind of extended 'Director's Cut' of the *Iliad*, padded out with outtakes and extra scenes. Similarly, Herodotus and Schliemann both look to present their own more complete version of the *Iliad*, aiming at a higher level of historical truth which they claimed as the privilege of their own respective genres. On a smaller scale, Godfrey of Viterbo sought to create Homer and the *Iliad* in his own image, as a reflection of his own arguments. Shakespeare also looked to create an *Iliad* for his own times in the *Troilus and Cressida*, expanding and elaborating on what he would have seen

---

[13] There is an extensive literature on the creation of memory and memorialization in historiography. For a brief summary, see Hutton 2013.

as the key theme of the poem – argument. More subtly, Rossetti's painting of Helen (literally) points to other possible *Iliad*s, while Euthymides' amphora (literally) punctures the frame of the Iliadic narrative.

As might already be evident, when referring to these 'other *Iliad*s' we do not necessarily mean a wholesale denial or replacement of the Homeric poem. Instead, these new *Iliad*s represent a conceptual challenge to the Homeric *Iliad* and its place at the core of the Trojan War tradition. In very different ways, all of these works question the *Iliad*'s centrality, and signal the possibility of other narratives. So, for instance, Herodotus' *Histories* propose that Helen was never at Troy – a rival narrative that he suggests has its roots in the Homeric account. And in the case of the film *Troy*, the Trojan War is transformed into a wholly cynical affair, a manifestation of one man's imperial megalomania. Just as Hesiod does in the *Contest of Homer and Hesiod* (for which see the Introduction), these later Iliadic receptions engage in a form of competitive dialogue with Homer. The story of the Trojan War may be the subject that they are dialoguing *about*; but for our purposes, this is less significant than the related issues of (1) who and what they are dialoguing *with* and (2) *how* this dialogue is carried out.

The first of these issues – who/what is being dialogued *with* – is key. In all the cases we have explored, later contributions to the Trojan War tradition have engaged directly with Homer's *Iliad*. This seems to have been true not only at moments when the Homeric poems were an essential part both of the wider cultural milieu and were critical to the way in which the Trojan War story was conceived (as is the case for Rossetti, Euripides, Herodotus and Schliemann), but also at times when their cultural status was less pronounced and they did not dominate contemporary understandings of the myth (as for Euthymides and Shakespeare), and even during periods when there was little or no engagement with the Greek text of the *Iliad* (as it was for Godfrey and, to a lesser extent, Petersen-Benioff). This is not to say that these works do not engage with non-Homeric elements of the Trojan War tradition (indeed, we have highlighted wide-ranging intertextual nexuses for all of our case studies) – only that in all cases, sustained and deliberate engagement with Homer's *Iliad* is evident. The *Iliad* seems to dominate the Trojan War tradition utterly.

The second of these issues – *how* the dialogue is carried out – is also significant. Our case studies seem to suggest three qualitatively different modes of engagement. The first, and perhaps the most intuitive, is engagement with specific details of the Iliadic narrative. This emerged perhaps most notably in the quest for historical truth in the work of Herodotus and Schliemann, but also in the peri-Iliadic games of Euthymides and the scholarly claims of Godfrey. In each of these cases, particular Iliadic features and points of narrative detail were explored. Alternative *Iliad*s were presented by the revision of Iliadic details or the inclusion of supplementary material. The second mode of engagement centres around Iliadic or Homeric themes. This was evident in the cases of Rossetti, Euripides, and Shakespeare, for all of whom Iliadic ideas about narrative, argument, and speech acts were crucial, opening the door to alternative *Iliad*s by the destabilizing of authoritative speech and the presentation of contrasting perspectives. In the third and final mode of engagement, the central point of reference was even more abstracted – the very idea of a central text at the core of the wider tradition. Most obviously, this can be seen in Euripides' claim to redefine the concept of the Iliadic by offering a Trojan-centred memorial song for Troy, but it is also evident in Petersen-Benioff's attempts to occupy the Homeric space of recounting *klea andrōn*, as well as *Memorial's* rejection of *klea andrōn* through the foregrounding of lament.

It is worth noting that these three qualitatively different modes of dialogue do not map directly onto historical circumstances, i.e. the contemporary position of the *Iliad* within the Trojan War tradition. The specifics of the Iliadic text were just as important to Godfrey in the twelfth century – even though he had to invent them – as they were to Schliemann in the nineteenth century, when he could rely on his audience's familiarity with its detail. Similarly, Euripides' idea of an inverted *Iliad* is not a sign of ignorance of Homeric poetry in late fifth century BCE Athens, although Petersen-Benioff's notion of replicating epic glories might be predicated on precisely such unawareness amongst *Troy*'s mainstream audience.[14] The ways we talk to Homer are not determined, it seems, in a direct and straightforward way by the practicalities of our access to his work.

---

[14] Of course, it is still possible to detect a more extensive engagement with the *Iliad* in non-academic contexts. A notable example is Eric Shanower's *Age of Bronze* comic book series, in which Shanower engages with the *Iliad*, as well as various literary and archaeological sources, in order to present a holistic account of the Trojan War; see further Shanower 2011 and Sulprizio 2011.

The *Iliad* and the Trojan War tradition

In this book, we set out to investigate the position of the *Iliad* within the wider Trojan War tradition; and we have unsurprisingly reached the conclusion that it is central. But this centrality takes an unexpected form. It is partly about content and themes, as we might have anticipated; but it is also about the poem in the abstract, and the very concept of a central text in the tradition. The centrality of the *Iliad* in the Trojan War tradition, then, is the result of individual receptions engaging *both* with the *Iliad*'s text *and* with the *Iliad*'s status.

In short, the centrality of the *Iliad* to the wider Trojan War tradition is partly due to the metapoetics of that tradition, where each new contribution must not only talk to the same core text, but must position itself in relation to the very *idea* of there being a core text. Part of what holds the *Iliad* at the centre of the wider tradition is the very discussion of its centrality. Perhaps counterintuitively, the challenge to Iliadic centrality implied by these discussions does not serve to destabilize that centrality, but rather to confirm it. While everyone is trying to present a new *Iliad*, the *Iliad* remains the standard by which each new *Iliad* is judged.

Perhaps it is time, then, to redefine what we mean by the 'Trojan War tradition'. Implied in this term (and, indeed, in the explicit framing of this entire book project) is the assumption that the story of the Trojan War is the crucial defining feature of the wider tradition and that the *Iliad* was simply an important instantiation of the story within this tradition. As we saw in Chapter 1, this was certainly the case at the time during which the *Iliad* was being composed and in the early phases of its circulation. For centuries, it seems that there was indeed a broad set of traditions concerning the Trojan War, manifested not only in Greek poetry but also in social and cult practices at the city of Troy itself, and perhaps also in various Anatolian literatures (see pp.8–9 above). The *Iliad* itself is aware of this wider tradition, making reference at various points to poets, poetry, and narrative. This metapoetic consciousness was by no means unique around the time of its composition – the *Odyssey* has a similar interest, as do contemporary Mesopotamian poems such as the *Erra and Ishum*. Unlike the *Erra*, however, the *Iliad* made no claim to centrality within the wider tradition. It made no claim to being a unique 'story-entity'.

Instead it explicitly acknowledges that at this point, the Trojan War tradition was dispersed and decentralized.

This was no longer the case in the late sixth century, when Euthymides painted the arming of Hector on his amphora. The *Iliad* had already come to occupy a privileged position within the wider Trojan War tradition, exercising a centripetal force that meant it was increasingly difficult to engage with the story without engaging with some of the details of the Homeric poem (the first mode of dialogic reception, as identified above). When Euripides and Herodotus wrote a century later, the *Iliad*'s place at the heart of the tradition was firmly established with a solidity only further cemented by these authors' attempts to challenge it (the third mode of dialogic reception), by elaborating on its themes (the second mode) and disputing its details (the first mode). By this point, there was no 'wider' Trojan War tradition independent of the *Iliad*. By this, we mean it was impossible to conceive of the Trojan War without engaging in some way with the *Iliad* (even if only to reject or embellish it). The tradition was already held together, not just by the common theme of the Trojan War, but also by the very process of dialogic reception with the text of the *Iliad*.

This is most clearly demonstrated by the work of Godfrey and his contemporaries in the twelfth century CE, who found it impossible to escape the shadow of Homer (the third mode of engagement) despite having no access to actual Homeric poetry. While in practical terms the *Iliad* was completely absent from the Trojan War tradition, in conceptual terms it remained at the tradition's core. It still held this central position four centuries later in the time of Shakespeare, although there was a growing awareness of the Homeric texts at this time'; enabling the second and third modes). The same was true of in the nineteenth century in the time of Rossetti and Schliemann, when knowledge of the text was widespread (allowing for all three modes of dialogic reception once more). In the twenty-first century, for Petersen and Benioff, being a part of the Trojan War tradition meant not just talking about the Trojan War, but also talking about the making of tradition itself (the third mode).

As we mentioned in our Introduction to this book, dialogic processes of reception are central to the forging of story traditions. And as we saw in Chapter 1, the *Iliad* and other contemporary poems engaged in these processes in innovative and sophisticated ways, seeking to locate themselves within a rich landscape of wider poetic traditions. Perhaps the metapoetic qualities of the *Iliad* fundamentally transformed the nature of the Trojan War tradition – it became a tradition defined not just by its subject (the Trojan War) but also by its process (metapoetic engagement). As a result of the *Iliad*, writing about the Trojan War means unavoidably writing about the Trojan War tradition.

This brings us finally to the cover image of our book, in which Rembrandt imagines the philosopher Aristotle resting his hand reflectively on a bust of Homer. The painting might recall for some Aristotle's discourses on the *Iliad* and *Odyssey* in his *Poetics*, but it is also a representation of dialogue between the two authors. Although the stone bust of Homer does not, of course, literally talk to Aristotle, Homeric poetry has nonetheless spoken to and provoked him. But Aristotle is not depicted here engaging with particular aspects of Homeric poetry (the first mode of dialogic reception), or even with Homeric themes (the second mode of dialogic reception). Rather, he is pictured engaging with the more abstract idea of Homer as a conceptual centre and core of his own literary tradition (the third mode of dialogic reception). This is Aristotle responding to Homer as a cultural icon, to Homer's iconic status, and to the concept as well as the physical reality of Homer set up on a pedestal. But this is also an image which triangulates Rembrandt's own relationship with the classical tradition[15] – a commentary on and response to precisely the dialogue that it depicts. We, like Rembrandt, must each figure out our own position on the dialogical relationship in front of us, locating ourselves in the wider tradition.

*   *   *

---

[15] Rembrandt showed considerable interest in depicting Homer (Golahny 2003, 122–29). This particular image was commissioned as a portrait of Aristotle, and it is significant that it is actually an image of Aristotle contemplating Homer – that is, Aristotle's wider intellectual tradition and his place within it.

Did it work then, this whole dialogue thing?

It depends what we were trying to achieve.

Perhaps it's less about where we got to in the end, and more about the doing of it.

The process?

The process. Talking to each other.

Talking to everyone else too. One small part of a very long, very wide-ranging, ongoing conversation. In fact, I think that...

References

Aerts, W. (2012), 'Troy in Byzantium', in J. Kelder, G. Uslu and Ö. F. Şerifoğlu (eds), *Troy. City, Homer, Turkey*, 98–103, Istanbul: W. Books.

Ahl, F. (2007), '*Troy* and Memorials of War', in M. M. Winkler (ed), *Troy: From Homer's Iliad to Hollywood Epic*, 163–85, Malden and Oxford: Wiley-Blackwell.

Albu, E. (2001), *The Norman in Their Histories: Propaganda, Myth and Subversion*, Woodbridge: Boydell and Brewer.

Alexander, C. (2009), *The War That Killed Achilles: The True Story of Homer's Iliad and the Trojan War*, New York: Penguin Group.

Amerasinghe, C. W. (1973), 'The Helen Episode in the *Troades*', *Ramus*, 2: 99–106.

Anderson, M. J. (1997), *The Fall of Troy in Early Greek Poetry and Art*, Oxford: Clarendon Press.

Anon. (1874), 'Discoveries at Troy', *The London Quarterly Review*, 136: 287–301.

Antonaccio, C. M. (1995), *An Archaeology of Ancestors. Tomb Cult and Hero Cult in Early Greece*, Lanham: Rowman and Littlefield.

Armstrong, I. (2012), 'The Pre-Raphaelites and Literature', in E. Prettejohn (ed), *The Cambridge Companion to the Pre-Raphaelites*, 13–31, Cambridge: Cambridge University Press.

Arnold, M. J. (1984), '"Monsters in Love's Train": Euripides and Shakespeare's "Troilus and Cressida"', *Comparative Drama*, 18 (1): 38–53.

Arthur, M. B. (1981), 'The Divided World of *Iliad* VI', in H. Foley (ed), *Reflections of Women in Antiquity*, 19–44, New York: Routledge.

Asheri, D. (2007),. 'General Introduction', in D. Asheri, A. Lloyd and A. Corcella (eds), *A Commentary on Herodotus Books I–IV*, 1–56, trans. O. Murray and A. Moreno, Oxford: Oxford University Press.

Aslan, C. C. (2002), 'Ilion before Alexander: Protogeometric, Geometric, and Archaic Pottery from D9', *Studia Troica*, 12: 81–129.

Aslan, C. C. (2011), 'A Place of Burning: Hero or Ancestor Cult at Troy', *Hesperia*, 80: 381–429.

Aslan, C. C. and C. B. Rose (2013), 'City and Citadel at Troy from the Late Bronze through the Roman Period', in S. Redford and N. Ergin (eds), *Cities and Citadels in Turkey: From the Iron Age to the Seljuks*, 7–38, Leuven: Peeters.

Aurell, M. (2007), 'Henry II and Arthurian Legend', in C. Harper-Bill and N. Vincent (eds), *Henry II. New Interpretation*, 362–94, Woodbridge: Boydell and Brewer.

Austin, N. (1994), *Helen of Troy and Her Shameless Phantom*, Ithaca: Cornell University Press.

Ayo, N. (1984), 'Prolog and Epilog: Mythical History in Herodotus', *Ramus*, 13: 31–47.

Azoulay, V. (2014), *Les Tyrannicides d'Athènes: vie et mort de deux statues. L'Univers historique*, Paris: Editions Seuil.

Bachvarova, M. R. (2016a), 'The Destroyed City in "World History"', in M. R. Bachvarova, D. Dutsch and A. Suter (eds), *The Fall of Cities in the Mediterranean: Commemoration in Literature, Folk-Song, and Liturgy*, 36–78, Cambridge: Cambridge University Press.

Bachvarova, M. R. (2016b), *From Hittite to Homer. The Anatolian Background of Ancient Greek Epic*, Cambridge: Cambridge University Press.

Bakker, E. J. (2002), 'The Making of History: Herodotus' *Historiês Apodexis*', in E. J. Bakker, I. J. F. de Jong and H. van Wees (eds), *Brill's Companion to Herodotus*, 3–32, Leiden: Brill.

de Bakker, M. (2012), 'Herodotus' Proteus: Myth, History, Enquiry and Storytelling', in E. Baragwanath and M. de Bakker (eds), *Myth, Truth, and Narrative in Herodotus*, 107–26, Oxford: Oxford University Press.

Bal, M. (1985), *Narratology: Introduction to the Theory of Narrative*, trans. C. Van Boheemen, London and Toronto: University of Toronto Press.

Baragwanath, E. (2008), *Motivation and Narrative in Herodotus*, Oxford: Oxford University Press.

Baragwanath, E. (2012), 'The Mythic Plupast in Herodotus', in J. Grethlein and C. Krebs (eds), *Time and Narrative in Ancient Historiography. The 'Plupast' from Herodotus to Appian*, 3–56, Cambridge: Cambridge University Press.

Baragwanath, E. and M. de Bakker (2012a), 'Introduction', in E. Baragwanath and M. de Bakker (eds), *Myth, Truth, and Narrative in Herodotus*, 1–56, Oxford: Oxford University Press.

Baragwanath, E. and M. de Bakker, eds (2012b), *Myth, Truth, and Narrative in Herodotus*, Oxford: Oxford University Press.

Baragwanath, E. and E. Foster (2017), 'Introduction: Clio and Thalia', in E. Baragwanath and E. Foster (eds), *Clio and Thalia. Attic Comedy and Historiography*, 1–30, Newcastle upon Tyne: *Histos* Supplement 6.

Barker, E. (2009), *Entering the Agon: Dissent and Authority in Homer, Historiography and Tragedy*, Oxford and New York: Oxford University Press.

Barlow, S. A., ed (1986), *Euripides. Trojan Women*, Warminster: Aris and Phillips.

Barney, R. (2006), 'The Sophistic Movement', in M. L. Gill and P. Pellegrin (eds), *A Companion to Ancient Philosophy*, 77–97, Oxford: Wiley-Blackwell.

Barringer, T. and E. Prettejohn, eds (1999), *Frederic Leighton: Antiquity Renaissance Modernity*, New Haven and London: Yale University Press.

Beaune, C. (1991), *The Birth of an Ideology. Myths and Symbols of Nation in Late-Medieval France*, Berkeley: University of California Press.

Beazley, J. D. (1963), *Attic Red-Figure Vase-Painters*, 2nd edn, Oxford: Oxford University Press.

Beckman, G. (2009), 'Hurro-Hittite Epic', in J. M. Foley (ed), *A Companion to Ancient Epic*, 255–63, Oxford: Wiley-Blackwell.

Bednarz, J. P. (2001), *Shakespeare and the Poets' War*, New York: Columbia University Press.

Benioff, D. (2014), 'Web Access ... David Benioff', *BBC*, 28 October. Available online: http://www.bbc.co.uk/films/webaccess/david_benioff_1.shtml (8 February 2017).

Bennet, J. (2007), 'Representations of Power in Mycenaean Pylos: Script, Orality, Iconography', in F. Lang, C. Reinholdt and J. Weilhartner (eds), *Stefanos Aristeios. Archaeologische Forschungen zwischen Nil und Istros. Festschrift für Stefan Hiller zum 65. Gerburtstag*, 11–22, Vienna: Phoibos Verlag.

Bergren, A. (2008), *Weaving Truth: Essays on Language and the Female in Greek Thought*, Washington, DC: Center for Hellenic Studies.

Berti, I. and M. G. Morcillo, eds (2008a), *Hellas on Screen. Cinematic Receptions of Ancient History, Literature and Myth*, Stuttgart: Franz Steiner.

Berti, I. and M. G. Morcillo (2008b), 'Introduction', in I. Berti and M. G. Morcillo (eds), *Hellas on Screen. Cinematic Receptions of Ancient History, Literature and Myth*, 9–20, Stuttgart: Franz Steiner.

Betrand, C., O. Desbordes and J.-P. Callu (1986), 'L'*Histoire Auguste* et l'historiographie médiévale', *Revue d'Histoire des Textes*, 14 (5): 97–130.

Bevington, D., ed (1998), *Troilus and Cressida. The Arden Shakespeare*, London: Bloomsbury Publishing.

Blake, J. (2015), *International Cultural Heritage Law*, Oxford: Oxford University Press.

Blanshard, A. J. L. and K. Shahabudin, eds (2011), *Classics on Screen: Ancient Greece and Rome on Film*, London: Bristol Classical Press.

Blondell, R. (2009), '"Third Cheerleader from the Left": From Homer's Helen to Helen of *Troy*', *Classical Receptions Journal*, 1 (1): 4–22.

Blondell, R. (2010), 'Refractions of Homer's Helen in Archaic Lyric', *American Journal of Philology*, 131 (3): 349–91.

Blondell, R. (2013), *Helen of Troy: Beauty, Myth, Devastation*, Oxford and New York: Oxford University Press.

Bloom, H., ed (1991), *Odysseus/Ulysses*, New York: Chelsea House.

Boardman, J. (1975), *Athenian Red Figure Vases. The Archaic Period. A Handbook*, London: Thames and Hudson.

Boardman, J. (1976), 'The Kleophrades Painter at Troy', *Antike Kunst*, 19 (1): 3–18.

Bodi, D. (1991), *The Book of Daniel and the Poem of Erra*, Göttingen: Vandenhoeck and Ruprecht.

Boeck, E. N. (2015), *Imagining the Byzantine Past. The Perception of History in the Illustrated Manuscripts of Skylitzes and Manasses*, Cambridge: Cambridge University Press.

Boedeker, D. (1988), 'Protesilaos and the End of Herodotus' *Histories*', *Classical Antiquity*, 7 (1): 30–48.

Boedeker, D. (2001), 'Heroic Historiography: Simonides and Herodotus on Plataea', in D. Boedeker and D. Sider (eds), *The New Simonides. Contexts of Praise and Desire*, 120–34, Oxford: Oxford University Press.

Boedeker, D. (2012), 'Speaker's Past and Plupast: Herodotus in the Light of Elegy and Lyric', in J. Grethlein and C. Krebs (eds), *Time and Narrative in Ancient Historiography. The 'Plupast' from Herodotus to Appian*, 17–34, Cambridge: Cambridge University Press.

Böhr, E. (2006), 'Oltus', in H. Cancik and H. Schneider (eds), *Brill's New Pauly*. Available online: http://referenceworks.brillonline. com/entries/brill-s-new-pauly/oltus-e830060?s.num=39&s.start=20 (1 May 2017).

Boitani, P., ed (1989), *The European Tragedy of Troilus*, Oxford: Clarendon Press.

Bouet, P. (1995), 'De l'origine troyenne des Normands', *Cahier des Annales de Normandie*, 26 (1): 401–13.

Braden, G. (2017), 'Classical Greek Tragedy and Shakespeare', *Classical Receptions Journal*, 9: 103–99.

Branscome, D. (2013), *Textual Rivals: Self-Presentation in Herodotus' Histories*, Ann Arbor: University of Michigan Press.

Braswell, B. K. (1971), 'Mythological Innovation in the *Iliad*', *Classical Quarterly*, 21 (1): 16–26.

Briggs, J. C. (1981), 'Chapman's Seaven Bookes of the Iliades: Mirror for Essex', *Studies in English Literature, 1500–1900*, 21: 59–73.

Brillet-Dubois, P. (2015), 'A Competition of *choregoi* in Euripides' *Trojan Women*. Dramatic Structure and Intertextuality', *Lexis*, 33: 168–80.

Brilliante, C. (1983), 'Episodi Iliadici nell'arte figurate e conoscenza dell'Iliade nella Grecia arcaica', *Rheinisches Museum für Philologies*, 126 (2): 97–125.

Brontë, A. ([1848] 1996), *The Tenant of Wildfell Hall*, London: Penguin Classics.

Brown, P. F. (1996), *Venice and Antiquity: The Venetian Sense of the Past*, New Haven: Yale University Press.

Bruckner, M. T. (2015), 'Remembering the Trojan War: Violence Past, Present and Future in Benoît de Sainte-Maure's *Roman de Troie*', *Speculum*, 90 (2): 366–90.

Buchthal, H. (1971), *Historia Troiana: Studies in the History of Medieval Secular Illustration*, London: Warburg Institute.

Bullen, J. B. (2011), *Rossetti: Painter and Poet*, London: Frances Lincoln.

Burgess, J. S. (2009), 'Achilles' Heel: The Historicism of the Film *Troy*', in K. Myrsiades (ed), *Reading Homer: Film and Text*, 163–85, Teaneck: Fairleigh Dickinson University Press.

Burgoyne, R., ed (2011a), *The Epic Film in World Culture*, New York and London: Routledge.

Burgoyne, R. (2011b), 'Introduction', in R. Burgoyne (ed), *The Epic Film in World Culture*, 1–16, New York and London: Routledge.

Burian, P. (2010), 'Introduction', in P. Burian and H. A. Shapiro (eds), *The Complete Euripides, Volume 1*, 153–77, Oxford and New York: Oxford University Press.

Burrow, C. (2013), *Shakespeare and Classical Antiquity*, Oxford: Oxford University Press.

Cagni, L. (1969), *l'Epopea di Erra*, Studi Semitici 34, Rome: Instituto de Studi del Vicino Oriente.

Cagni, L. (1974), *The Poem of Erra*, Malibu: Undena Publications.

Caine, B. (1978), 'John Stuart Mill and the English Women's Movement', *Historical Studies*, 18 (70): 52–67.

Caine, B. (1997), *English Feminism, 1780–1980*, Oxford: Oxford University Press.

Calder, III, W. M. (1980), 'Wilamowitz on Schliemann', *Philologus*, 124 (1–2): 146–51.

Calder, III, W. M. (1972), 'Schliemann on Schliemann: A Study in the Use of Sources', *Greek, Roman, and Byzantine Studies*, 13 (3): 335–53.

Carey, C. (2000), 'Old Comedy and the sophists', in D. Harvey and J. Wilkins (eds), *The Rivals of Aristophanes: Studies in Old Athenian Comedy*, 419–36, London: Duckworth.

Carey, C. (2016), 'Homer and Epic in Herodotus' Book 7', in A. Efstathiou and I. Karamanou (eds), *Homeric Receptions across Generic and Cultural Contexts*, 71–89, Berlin and Boston: De Gruyter.

Carpentier, É., G. Pon and Y. Chauvin, eds (2006), *Rigord. Histoire de Philippe Auguste*, Paris: CNRS Editions.

Cartledge, P. and E. Greenwood (2002), 'Herodotus as a Critic: Truth, Fiction, Polarity', in E. J. Bakker, I. J. F. de Jong and H. van Wees (eds), *Brill's Companion to Herodotus*, 351–71, Leiden: Brill.

Castriota, D. (2005), 'Feminizing the Barbarian and Barbarizing the Feminine. Amazons, Trojans, and Persians in the Stoa Poikile', in J. M. Barringer and J. M. Hurwit (eds), *Periclean Athens and Its Legacy. Problems and Perspectives*, 89–102, Austin: University of Texas Press.

Cavallini, E. (2015), 'In the Footsteps of Homeric Narrative: Anachronisms and Other Supposed Mistakes in *Troy*', in M. M. Winkler (ed), *Return to Troy. New Essays on the Hollywood Epic*, 65–89, Leiden: Brill.

Chiasson, C. C. (2009), 'Redefining Homeric Heroism in Wolfgang Petersen's *Troy*', in K. Myrsiades (ed), *Reading Homer: Film and Text*, 186–207, Teaneck: Fairleigh Dickinson University Press.

Chiasson, C. C. (2012), 'Herodotus' Prologue and the Greek Poetic Tradition', *Histos*, 6: 114–43.

Christensen, J. P. (2015), 'Trojan Politics and the Assemblies of *Iliad* 7', *Greek, Roman, and Byzantine Studies*, 55 (1): 25–51.

Cingano, E. (2009), 'The Hesiodic Corpus', in F. Montanari, C. Tsagalis and A. Rengakos (eds), *Brill's Companion to Hesiod*, 91–130, Leiden: Brill.

Clader, L. L. (1976), *Helen. The Evolution from Divine to Heroic in Greek Epic Tradition*, Leiden: Brill.

Clark, F. N. (2010), 'Reading the "First Pagan Historiographer": Dares Phrygius and Medieval Genealogy', *Viator*, 41 (2): 203–26.

Clarke, K. (2008), *Making Time for the Past: Local History and the Polis*, Oxford: Oxford University Press.

Clarke, M. (2004), 'Manhood and Heroism', in R. Fowler (ed), *The Cambridge Companion to Homer*, 74–90, Cambridge: Cambridge University Press.

Clarke, M. J., B. G. F. Currie and R. O. A. M. Lyne, eds (2006), *Epic Interactions: Perspectives on Homer, Virgil, and the Epic Tradition Presented to Jasper Griffin by Former Pupils*, Oxford: Oxford University Press.

Clay, D. (2010), 'An Essay on Euripides' *Trojan Women*', in S. Esposito (ed), *Odysseus at Troy: Sophocles' Ajax and Euripides' Hecuba and Trojan Women*, 233–55, Newburyport: Focus Publishing.

Cline, E. H. (2013), *The Trojan War: A Very Short Introduction*, Oxford: Oxford University Press.

Cobet, J. (2002), 'The Organization of Time in the *Histories*', in E. J. Bakker, I. J. F. de Jong and H. van Wees (eds), *Brill's Companion to Herodotus*, 387–412, Leiden: Brill.

Collins, D. (2005), *Master of the Game. Competition and Performance in Greek Poetry*, Cambridge, MA: Harvard University Press.

Croally, N. T. (1994), *Euripidean Polemic: The Trojan Women and the Function of Tragedy*, Cambridge: Cambridge University Press.

Cruise, C. (2012), 'Pre-Raphaelite Drawing', in E. Prettejohn (ed), *The Cambridge Companion to the Pre-Raphaelites*, 47–61, Cambridge: Cambridge University Press.

Cyrino, M. S. (2007), 'Helen of *Troy*', in M. M. Winkler (ed), *Troy: From Homer's Iliad to Hollywood Epic*, 131–47, Malden and Oxford: Wiley-Blackwell.

Cyrino, M. S. and M. E. Safran, eds (2015), *Classical Myth on Screen*, New York: Palgrave Macmillan.

Dalley, S. (2000), *Myths from Mesopotamia*, Oxford: Oxford University Press.

Damian-Grint, P. (1999), *The New Historians of the Twelfth-Century Renaissance*, Woodbridge: Boydell and Brewer.

Davidson, J. (1999–2000), 'Euripides, Homer and Sophocles', *Illinois Classical Studies*, 24/25: 117–28.

Davidson, J. (2001), 'Homer and Euripides' *Troades*', *Bulletin of the Institute of Classical Studies*, 45 (1): 65–79.

Davies, M. and P. J. Finglass, eds (2014), *Stesichorus: The Poems*, Cambridge: Cambridge University Press.

De Shong Meador, B. (2000), *Inanna: Lady of the Largest Heart. Poems of the Sumerian High Priestess Enheduanna*, Austin: University of Texas Press.

De Shong Meador, B. (2009), *Princess, Priestess, Poet: The Sumerian Temple Hymns of Enheduanna*, Austin: University of Texas Press.

Demetriou, T. and T. Pollard (2017), 'Homer and Greek Tragedy in Early Modern England's Theatres: An Introduction', *Classical Receptions Journal*, 9: 1–35.

Denby, D. (2004), 'Heroes: Wolfgang Petersen's *Troy*', *The New Yorker Magazine*, 17 May. Available online: http://www.newyorker.com/magazine/2004/05/17/heroes-4 (16 February 2017).

Derderian, K. (2001), *Leaving Words to Remember: Greek Mourning and the Advent of Literacy*, Leiden: Brill.

Desmond, M. (2016), 'Trojan Itineraries and the Matter of Troy', in R. Copeland (ed), *The Oxford History of Classical Receptions in English Literature. Volume I: 800–1558*, 251–64, Oxford: Oxford University Press.

Dickinson, J. (2012), *Court Politics and the Earl of Essex, 1589–1601*, London: Pickering and Chatto.

Donnelly, B. (2015), *Reading Dante Gabriel Rossetti: The Painter as Poet*, Burlington: Ashgate.

Dorninger, M. E. (2015), 'Modern Readers of Godfrey', in T. Foerster (ed), *Godfrey of Viterbo and His Readers. Imperial Tradition and Universal History in Late Medieval Europe*, 13–36, London and New York: Routledge.

Dover, K. (2001), 'Who Was to Blame?', in D. Stuttard and T. Shasha (eds), *Essays on Trojan Women*, 1–9, London: Actors of Dionysos.

Dowd, M. (2001), 'Liberties; Old Ruses, New Barbarians', *New York Times*, 19 September. Available online: http://www.nytimes.com/2001/09/19/opinion/liberties-old-ruses-new-barbarians.html (3 May 2017).

Dué, C. (2002), *Homeric Variations on a Lament by Briseis*, London: Rowman and Littlefield.

Dué, C. (2005), 'Homer's Post-Classical Legacy', in J. M. Foley (ed), *A Companion to Ancient Epic*, 397–414, Oxford: Wiley-Blackwell.

Dué, C. (2006), *The Captive Woman's Lament in Greek Tragedy*, Austin: University of Texas Press.

Dumbrell, J. (2005), 'Bush's War: The Iraq Conflict and American Democracy', in A. Danchev and J. Macmillan (eds), *The Iraq War and Democratic Politics*, 33–44, London and New York: Routledge.

Dunn, F. M. (1996), *Tragedy's End: Closure and Innovation in Euripidean Drama*, New York and Oxford: Oxford University Press.

Dyce, A. (1821), *Select Translations from the Greek of Quintus Smyrnaeus*, Oxford: W. Baxter.

Easterling, P. E. (1997), 'Form and Performance', in P. E. Easterling (ed), *The Cambridge Companion to Greek Tragedy*, 151–77, Cambridge: Cambridge University Press.

Edmunds, L. (2015), *Stealing Helen: The Myth of the Abducted Wife in Comparative Perspective*, Princeton and Oxford: Princeton University Press.

Efstathiou, A. and I. Karamanou, eds (2016), *Homeric Receptions across Generic and Cultural Contexts*, Berlin and Boston: De Gruyter.

Eisenhut, W. (1983), 'Spätantike Troja-Erzählungen – mit einem Ausblick auf die mittelalterliche Troja-Literatur', *Mittellateinisches Jahrbuch*, 18: 1–28.

Eley, P. (1991), 'The Myth of Trojan Descent and Perceptions of National Identity: The Case of Eneas and the Roman de Troie', *Nottingham Medieval Studies*, 35: 27–41.

Elliott, A. B. R., ed (2014a), *The Return of the Epic Film: Genre, Aesthetics and History in the 21st Century*, Edinburgh: Edinburgh University Press.

Elliott, A. B. R. (2014b), 'Introduction: The Return of Epic', in A. B. R. Elliott (ed), *The Return of the Epic Film: Genre, Aesthetics and History in the 21st Century*, 1–16, Edinburgh: Edinburgh University Press.

Elmer, D. F. (2013), *The Poetics of Consent: Collective Decision Making and the* Iliad, Baltimore: Johns Hopkins University Press.

Elsner, J. (2010), 'Reflections on the "Greek Revolution" in Art: From Changes in Viewing to the Transformation of Subjectivity', in S. Goldhill and R. Osborne (eds), *Rethinking Revolutions through Ancient Greece*, 68–95, Cambridge: Cambridge University Press.

Eph'al, I. (2005), 'Esarhaddon, Egypt, and Shubria: Politics and Propaganda', *Journal of Cuneiform Studies*, 55: 99–111.

Erskine, A. (2001), *Troy between Greece and Rome. Local Tradition and Imperial Power*, Oxford and New York: Oxford University Press.

Erskine, A. (2003), *Troy between Greece and Rome*, Oxford: Oxford University Press.

Ewig, E. (1998), 'Troja und die Franken', *Rheinische Vierteljahrsblätter*, 62: 1–16.

Fantuzzi, M. and C. Tsagalis, eds (2015), *The Greek Epic Cycle and Its Ancient Reception: A Companion*, Cambridge: Cambridge University Press.

Farron, S. (1979), 'The Portrayal of Women in the *Iliad*', *Acta Classica*, 22: 15–31.

Fehling, D. (1989), *Herodotus and His 'Sources': Citation, Invention and Narrative Art*, trans. J. G. Howie, Leeds: Francis Cairns.

Finkelberg, M. (1990), 'A Creative Oral Poet and the Muse', *American Journal of Philology*, 111 (3): 293–303.

Finkelberg, M. (2007), 'More on ΚΛΕΟΣ ΑΦΘΙΤΟΝ', *Classical Quarterly*, 57 (2): 341–50.

Finkelberg, M. (2011), 'Homer and His Peers: Neoanalysis, Oral Theory, and the Status of Homer', *Trends in Classics*, 3 (2): 197–208.

Fitton, J. L. (2007), '*Troy* and the Role of the Historical Advisor', in M. M. Winkler (ed), *Troy: From Homer's Iliad to Hollywood Epic*, 99–106, Malden and Oxford: Wiley-Blackwell.

Flack, L. C. (2015), *Modernism and Homer: The Odysseys of H.D., James Joyce, Osip Mandelstam, and Ezra Pound*, Cambridge: Cambridge University Press.

Fletcher, R. and J. Hanink, eds (2016), *Creative Lives in Classical Antiquity: Poets, Artists and Biography*, Cambridge: Cambridge University Press.

Foley, J. M. (2010), 'Reading Homer through Oral Tradition', in K. Myrsiades (ed), *Approaches to Homer's* Iliad *and* Odyssey, 15–41, Oxford and New York: Peter Lang.

Ford, A. (1992), *Homer: The Poetry of the Past*, Ithaca: Cornell University Press.

Ford, A. (2002), *The Origins of Criticism: Literary Culture and Poetic Theory in Classical Greece*, Princeton: Princeton University Press.

Fornara, C. W. (1971), *Herodotus: An Interpretative Essay*, Oxford: Clarendon Press.

Fornara, C. W. (1981), 'Herodotus' Knowledge of the Archidamian War', *Hermes*, 109 (2): 149–56.

Foster, B. R. (1991), 'On Authorship in Akkadian Literature', *Istituto Universitario Orientali di Napoli Annali*, 51: 17–32.

Foster, B. R. (2005), *Before the Muses. An Anthology of Akkadian Literature*, 3rd edn, Bethesda: CDL Press.

Fowler, R. L. (1996), 'Herodotos and His Contemporaries', *Journal of Hellenic Studies*, 116: 62–87.

Fowler, R. L., ed (2004a), *The Cambridge Companion to Homer*, Cambridge: Cambridge University Press.

Fowler, R. L. (2004b), 'The Homeric Question', in R. L. Fowler (ed), *The Cambridge Companion to Homer*, 220–32, Cambridge: Cambridge University Press.

Fowler, R. L. (2011), '*Mythos* and *Logos*', *Journal of Hellenic Studies*, 131: 45–66.

Fredeman, W. E., ed (2003), *The Correspondence of Dante Gabriel Rossetti 3. The Chelsea Years 1863–1867: Prelude to the Crisis I*, Woodbridge: Boydell and Brewer.

Freed, J. B. (2016), *Frederick Barbarossa: The Prince and the Myth*, New Haven and London: Yale University Press.

Freeman, E. (2002), *Narratives of a New Nation: Cistercian Historical Writing in England, 1150–1220*, Turnhout: Brepols.

French, P. (2004), 'Review of *Troy*', *Guardian*, 16 May. Available online: https://www.theguardian.com/film/2004/may/16/philipfrench (12 February 2017).

Friis Johansen, K. (1967), *The Iliad in Early Greek Art*, Copenhagen: Munksgard.

Gadamer, H. G. (1975), *Truth and Method*, trans. G. Barden and J. Cumming, New York: Seabury.

Garcia, L. F. (2013), *Homeric Durability: Telling Time in the Iliad*, Washington, DC: Center for Hellenic Studies.

Garvie, A. (2001), 'Euripides' *Trojan Women*: Relevance and Universality', in D. Stuttard and T. Shasha (eds), *Essays on Trojan Women*, 45–60, London: Actors of Dionysos.

Gellie, G. (1986), 'Helen in the *Trojan Women*', in J. H. Betts, J. T. Hooker and J. R. Green (eds), *Studies in Honour of T. B. L. Webster*, Vol. 1, 114–21, Bristol: Bristol Classical Press.

George, A. R. (2003), *The Babylonian Gilgamesh Epic. Introduction, Critical Edition and Cuneiform Texts*, Oxford: Oxford University Press.

George, A. R. (2007), 'The Gilgameš Epic at Ugarit', *Aula Orientalis*, 25 (2): 237–54.

George, A. R. (2013), 'The Poem of Erra and Ishum: A Babylonian Poet's View of War', in H. N. Kennedy (ed), *Warfare and Poetry in the Middle East*, 39–71, London: I. B. Tauris.

Georges, P. (1994), *Barbarian Asia and the Greek Experience: From the Archaic Period to the Age of Xenophon*, Baltimore and London: Johns Hopkins University Press.

Gilbert, J. (2002), 'The Sophists', in C. Shields (ed), *The Blackwell Guide to Ancient Philosophy*, 27–50, Malden: Wiley-Blackwell.

Gilbert, J. L. (2012), 'Repetition and the Death Drive in *Gilgamesh* and Medieval French Literature', *KASKAL. Rivista di Storia, Ambiente e Cultura del Vicino Oriente Antico*, 9: 136–55.

Gleadle, K. (2001), *British Women in the Nineteenth Century*, New York: Palgrave-Macmillan.

Gleadle, K. and S. Richardson, eds (2000), *Women in British Politics 1760–1860: The Power of the Petticoat*, New York: St Martin's Press.

Goff, B. (2009), *Euripides: Trojan Women*, London: Duckworth.

Goldhill, S. (1986), *Reading Greek Tragedy*, Cambridge: Cambridge University Press.

Goldhill, S. (1997), 'The Language of Tragedy: Rhetoric and Communication', in P. E. Easterling (ed), *The Cambridge Companion to Greek Tragedy*, 127–50, Cambridge: Cambridge University Press.

Goldhill, S. (2011), *Victorian Culture and Classical Antiquity: Art, Opera, Fiction, and the Proclamation of Modernity*, Princeton and Oxford: Princeton University Press.

Goldwyn, A. J. (2015), 'Achaeans, Athenians and Americans in the Post-9/11 Era: Comparing Empires in *The New York Times*', in A. J. Goldwyn (ed), *The Trojan Wars and the Making of the Modern World*, 245–58, Uppsala: Uppsala University Library.

Gould, J. (1989), *Herodotus*, London: Weidenfeld and Nicolson.

Graf, F. (1993), *Greek Mythology. An Introduction*, Baltimore: Johns Hopkins University Press.

Graver, M. (1995), 'Dog-Helen and Homeric Insult', *Classical Antiquity*, 14 (1): 41–61.

Grayson, A. K. and J. Novotny (2012), *Royal Inscriptions of Sennacherib, King of Assyria (704–681 B.C.): Volume 3, Royal Inscriptions of the Neo-Assyrian Period (RINAP)*, Winona Lake: Eisenbrauns.

Graziosi, B. (2002), *Inventing Homer: The Early Reception of Epic*, Cambridge: Cambridge University Press.

Graziosi, B. (2016), *Homer*, Oxford: Oxford University Press.

Graziosi, B. and E. Greenwood, eds (2007), *Homer in the Twentieth Century*, Oxford: Oxford University Press.

Graziosi, B. and J. Haubold, eds (2010), *Homer: Iliad. Book VI*, Cambridge: Cambridge University Press.

Green, P. (1999), 'War and Morality in Fifth-Century Athens: The Case of Euripides' *Trojan Women*', *Ancient History Bulletin*, 13 (3): 97–110.

Greenwood, E. (2007), 'Logue's Tele-Vision: Reading Homer from a Distance', in B. Graziosi and E. Greenwood (eds), *Homer in the Twentieth Century*, 145–76, Oxford: Oxford University Press.

Gregory, J. (1991), *Euripides and the Instruction of the Athenians*, Ann Arbor: University of Michigan Press.

Grethlein, J. (2009), 'How Not to Do History: Xerxes in Herodotus' *Histories*', *American Journal of Philology*, 130 (2): 195–218.

Grethlein, J. (2010), *The Greeks and Their Past*, Cambridge: Cambridge University Press.

Griffin, J. (1977), 'The Epic Cycle and the Uniqueness of Homer', *Journal of Hellenic Studies*, 97: 39–53.

Griffin, J. (2001), 'The *Trojan Women*', in D. Stuttard and T. Shasha (eds), *Essays on Trojan Women*, 61–73, London: Actors of Dionysos.

Gumpert, M. (2001), *Grafting Helen. The Abduction of the Classical Past*, Madison: University of Wisconsin Press.

Hall, E. (1989), *Inventing the Barbarian: Greek Self-Definition through Tragedy*, Oxford: Oxford University Press.

Hall, E. (2008), *The Return of Ulysses: A Cultural History of Homer's* Odyssey, Baltimore: Johns Hopkins University Press.

Hall, E. (2010), *Greek Tragedy: Suffering under the Sun*, Oxford: Oxford University Press.

Hall, J. M. (2002), *Hellenicity. Between Ethnicity and Culture*, Chicago: University of Chicago Press.

Hallam, E. M. and J. Everard (2013), *Capetian France, 987–1328*, London: Routledge.

Halliwell, S. (2011), *Between Ecstasy and Truth: Interpretations of Greek Poetics from Homer to Longinus*, Oxford: Oxford University Press.

Hammer, P. E. J. (1999), *The Polarisation of Elizabethan Politics: The Political Career of Robert Devereux, 2nd Earl of Essex, 1587–1597*, Cambridge: Cambridge University Press.

Hanink, J. (2017), *The Classical Debt: Greek Antiquity in an Era of Austerity*, Cambridge: Harvard University Press.

Hardwick, L. (2016), 'Homer, Repetition and Reception', in A. Efstathiou and I. Karamanou (eds), *Homeric Receptions across Generic and Cultural Contexts*, 15–27, Berlin and Boston: De Gruyter.

Harris, O. J. T. and C. Cipolla. (2017), *Archaeological Theory in the New Millennium. Introducing Current Perspectives*, London and New York: Routledge.

Harrison, T. (2000), *Divinity and History. The Religion of Herodotus*, Oxford: Clarendon Press.

Harrop, S. (2013), 'Speech, Silence and Epic Performance: Alice Oswald's *Memorial*', *New Voices in Classical Reception Studies*, 8: 79–91.

Haubold, J. (2000), *Homer's People: Epic Poetry and Social Formation*, Cambridge: Cambridge University Press.

Haubold, J. (2007), 'Xerxes' Homer', in E. Bridges, E. Hall and P. J. Rhodes (eds), *Cultural Responses to the Persian Wars: Antiquity to the Third Millennium*, 47–63, Oxford: Oxford University Press.

Haubold, J. (2013), *Greece and Mesopotamia. Dialogues in Literature*, Cambridge: Cambridge University Press.

Hausmann, F. (1992), 'Gottfried von Viterbo: Kapellan und Notar, Magister, Geschichsschreiber, un Dichter', in A. Haverkamp (ed), *Friedrich Barbarossa: Handlungsspielräume und Wirkungsweisen des staufischen Kaisers*, 603–21, Stuttgart: Jan Thorbecke Verlag.

Haywood, J. L. T. (2013), 'Intertext and Allusion in Herodotus' *Histories*: Authority, Proof, Polemic', PhD diss., University of Liverpool, Liverpool.

Hedreen, G. (2009), 'Iambic Caricature and Self-Representation as a Model for Understanding Internal References among Red-Figure Vase-Painters and Potters of the Pioneer Group', in D. Yatromanolakis (ed), *An Archaeology of Representations, Ancient Greek Vase-Painting and Contemporary Methodologies*, 200–39, Athens: Institut du livre A. Kardamitsa.

Hedreen, G. (2016), *The Image of the Artist in Archaic and Classical Greece*, Cambridge: Cambridge University Press.

Herold, J. B. (1559), *Pantheon, siove Universitatis libri qui chronici appellantur XX, omnes omnium secuoru et gentium, tam sacras quam prophanas Historias completentes: per Gottofridum Viterbensem*, Basilieae: Iaocobi Parci.

Hering, K. (2015), 'Godfrey of Viterbo: Historical Writing and Imperial Legitimacy at the Early Hohenstaufen Court', in T. Foerster (ed), *Godfrey of Viterbo and His Readers. Imperial Tradition and Universal History in Late Medieval Europe*, 47–66, London and New York: Routledge.

Heuck Allen, S. (1999), *Finding the Walls of Troy: Frank Calvert and Heinrich Schliemann at Hisarlik*, Berkeley and Los Angeles: University of California Press.

Hobden, F. (2013), *The Symposion in Ancient Greek Society and Thought*, Cambridge: Cambridge University Press.

Holloway, R. (1992), 'Why Korai?', *Oxford Journal of Archaeology*, 11 (3): 267–73.

Hoppin, J. C. (1917), *Euthymides and His Fellows*, Cambridge, MA: Harvard University Press.

Hornblower S. (1991), *A Commentary on Thucydides. Volume I: Books I–III*, Oxford: Clarendon Press.

Horrocks, G. C. (1980), 'The Antiquity of the Greek Epic Tradition: Some New Evidence', *The Proceedings of the Cambridge Philological Society*, 206: 1–11.

Howard, R. R. (1972), *The Dark Glass: Vision and Technique in the Poetry of Dante Gabriel Rossetti*, Athens, OH: Ohio University Press.

Hunter, R. L. (2004), 'Homer and Greek Literature', in R. L. Fowler (ed), *The Cambridge Companion to Homer*, 235–53, Cambridge: Cambridge University Press.

Hunter, V. (1982), *Past and Process in Herodotus and Thucydides*, Princeton and Guildford: Princeton University Press.

Hurwit, J. M. (1999), *The Athenian Acropolis. History, Mythology, and Archaeology form the Neolithic Era to the Present*, Cambridge: Cambridge University Press.

Hutton, P. H. (2013), 'Memory: Witness, Experience, and Collective Meaning', in N. Partner and S. Foot (eds), *The Sage Handbook of Historical Theory*, 354–77, London: Sage.

Innes, M. (2000), 'Teutons or Trojans? The Carolingians and the Germanic Past', in
   Y. Han and M. Innes (eds), *The Uses of the Past in the Early Middle Ages*, 227–49,
   Cambridge: Cambridge University Press.

Iordanova, D. (2011), '"Rise of the Rest": Globalizing Epic Cinema', in R. Burgoyne
   (ed), *The Epic Film in World Culture*, 101–23, London: Routledge.

Irwin, E. (2013), '"The *hybris* of Theseus" and the Date of the *Histories*', in B. Dunsch
   and K. Ruffing (eds), *Source References in Herodotus – Herodotus' Sources:
   Conference in Memoriam Detlev Fehling. Classica et Orientalia* 6, 7–84, Wiesbaden:
   Harrassowitz Verlag.

Iser, W. (1978), *The Act of Reading: A Theory of Aesthetic Response*, Baltimore and
   London: The Johns Hopkins University Press.

Jakobsen, T. (1987), *The Harps that Once … Sumerian Poetry in Translation*, New
   Haven and London: Yale University Press.

Jancovich, M. (2014), '"There's Nothing so Wrong with a Hollywood Script that a
   Bunch of Giant CGI Scorpions Can't Solve": Politics, Computer Generated Images
   and Camp in the Critical Reception of the Post-*Gladiator* Historical Epics', in A. B.
   R. Elliott (ed), *The Return of the Epic Film: Genre, Aesthetics and History in the 21st
   Century*, 57–73, Edinburgh: Edinburgh University Press.

Jenkyns, R. (1980), *The Victorians and Ancient Greece*, Oxford: Wiley-Blackwell.

Jones, C. P. (1999), *Kinship Diplomacy in the Ancient World*, Cambridge, MA:
   Harvard University Press.

de Jong, I. J. F. (1999), 'Aspects narratologiques des *Histoires* d'Hérodote', *Lalies*, 19:
   217–75.

de Jong, I. J. F. (2006), 'The Homeric Narrator and His Own *kleos*', *Mnemosyne*, 59 (2):
   188–207.

de Jong, I. J. F. (2012), 'The Helen *Logos* and Herodotus' Fingerprint', in E.
   Baragwanath and M. de Bakker (eds), *Myth, Truth, and Narrative in Herodotus*,
   127–42, Oxford: Oxford University Press.

Jonker, G. (1995), *The Topography of Remembrance: The Dead, Tradition, and
   Collective Memory in Mesopotamia*, Leiden: Brill.

Jung, M.-R. (1996), *La Légende de Troie en France au moyen âge: analyse des versions
   françaises et bibliographe raisonée des manuscrits*, Basel: Francke.

Karamanou, J. (2016), 'Euripides' "Trojan Trilogy" and the Reception of the Epic
   Tradition', in A. Efstathiou and I. Karamanou (eds), *Homeric Receptions across
   Generic and Cultural Contexts*, 355–67, Berlin and Boston: De Gruyter.

Keesling, C. M. (2005), 'Patrons of Athenian Votive Monuments of the Archaic and
   Classical Periods. Three Studies', *Hesperia*, 74 (3): 395–426.

Kelder, J., G. Uslu and Ö. F. Şerifoğlu, eds (2012), *Troy. City, Homer, Turkey*, Istanbul:
   W. Books.

Kelly, A. (2015), 'Stesichorus' Homer', in P. J. Finglass and A. Kelly (eds), *Stesichorus in Context*, 21–44, Cambridge: Cambridge University Press.

Kennedy, G. (1986), 'Helen's Web Unraveled', *Arethusa*, 19: 5–14.

Kim, L. (2010), *Homer Between History and Fiction in Imperial Greek Literature*, Cambridge: Cambridge University Press.

Knauer, G. N. (1964), *Die Aeneis und Homer*, Göttingen: Vandenhoeck and Ruprecht.

Knight, V. (1995), *The Renewal of Epic: Responses to Homer in the Argonautica of Apollonius*, Leiden: Brill.

Köchly, H. A. T. (1843), *De lacunis in Quinto Smyrnaeo quaestio*, Dresden: E. Blochmann.

Kofler, W. and F. Schaffenrath (2015), 'Petersen's Epic Technique: *Troy* and Its Homeric Model', in M. M. Winkler (ed), *Return to Troy: New Essays on the Hollywood Epic*, 86–107, Leiden and Boston: Brill.

Korfmann, M. (1997), *A Guide to Troia*, Istanbul: Ege Yayınları.

Korfmann, M., ed (2006), *Troia. Archäologie eines Siedlungshügels und seiner Landschaft*, Mainz: Philipp von Zabern.

Kovacs, D. (1997), 'Gods and Men in Euripides' Trojan Trilogy', *Colby Quarterly*, 33 (2): 162–76.

Kristof, N. (2003), 'Cassandra Speaks', *New York Times*, 18 March. Available online: http://www.nytimes.com/2003/03/18/opinion/cassandra-speaks.html (10 February 2017).

Kullmann, W. (1984), 'Oral Poetry Theory and Neoanalysis in Homeric Research', *Greek, Roman, and Byzantine Studies*, 25 (4): 307–24.

Lambert, W. G. (1957), 'Ancestors, Authors and Canonicity', *Journal of Cuneiform Studies*, 11: 1–14.

Lambert, W. G. (1962a), 'A Catalogue of Texts and Authors', *Journal of Cuneiform Studies*, 16: 59–77.

Lambert, W. G. (1962b), 'The Fifth Tablet of the Era Epic', *Iraq*, 24 (2): 119–25.

Lambert, W. G. and A. R. Millard (1969), *Atra-ḫasīs. The Babylonian Story of the Flood*, Oxford: Clarendon Press.

Latacz, J. (2007), 'From Homer's Troy to Petersen's *Troy*', M. M. Winkler (ed), *Troy: From Homer's Iliad to Hollywood Epic*, 27–42, Malden and Oxford: Wiley-Blackwell.

Latacz, J., T. Greub, P. Blome and A. Wieczorek, eds (2008), *Homer: Der Mythos von Troia in Dichtung und Kunst*, Munich: Hirmer Verlag.

Lateiner, D. (1989), *The Historical Method of Herodotus*, Toronto and London: University of Toronto Press.

Latowsky, A. A. (2013), *Emperor of the World. Charlemagne and the Construction of Imperial Authority*, 800–1229, Ithaca: Cornell University Press.

Lauriola, R. (2015), 'Trojan Women', in R. Lauriola and K. N. Demetriou (eds), *Brill's Companion to the Reception of Euripides*, 44–99, Leiden and Boston: Brill.

Lee, K. H., ed (1976), *Euripides. Troades*, Basingstoke: Macmillan.

Leichty, E. (2011), *The Royal Inscriptions of Esarhaddon, King of Assyria (680–669 BC)*, Winona Lake: Eisenbrauns.

Llewellyn-Jones, L. (2009), 'Hollywood's Ancient World', in A. Erskine (ed), *A Companion to Ancient History*, 564–79, Chichester and Malden: Wiley-Blackwell.

Lloyd, A. B. (1976), *Herodotus Book II: Commentary 1–98*, Leiden: Brill.

Lloyd, A. B. (1988), *Herodotus, Book II: Commentary 99–182*, Leiden: Brill.

Lloyd, A. B. (1990), 'Herodotus on Egyptians and Libyans', in G. Nenci and O. Reverdin (eds), *Hérodote et les peoples non grecs*. Entretiens sur l'antiquité Classique 35, 215–44, Geneva: Fondation Hardt.

Lloyd, A. B. (2007), 'Book II', in D. Asheri, A. B. Lloyd and A. Corcella (eds), *A Commentary on Herodotus Books I–IV*, 219–378, Oxford: Oxford University Press.

Lloyd, M. (1992), *The Agon in Euripides*, Oxford: Oxford University Press.

Lloyd-Jones, H. (1999), 'The Pride of Halicarnassus', *Zeitschrift für Papyrologie und Epigraphik*, 124: 1–14.

Longman, T. (1991), *Fictional Akkadian Autobiography: A Generic and Comparative Study*, Winona Lake: Eisenbrauns.

Lowenstam, S. (2008), *As Witnessed by Images. The Trojan War Tradition in Greek and Etruscan Art*, Baltimore: Johns Hopkins University Press.

Luraghi, N. (2001), 'Local Knowledge in Herodotus' *Histories*', in N. Luraghi (ed), *The Historian's Craft in the Age of Herodotus*, 138–60, Oxford and New York: Oxford University Press.

Luraghi, N. (2006), 'Traders, Pirates, Warriors. The Proto-History of Greek Mercenary Soldiers in the Eastern Mediterranean', *Phoenix*, 60: 21–47.

MacBain, W. (1993), 'Anglo-Norman Women Hagiographers', in I. Short (ed), *Anglo-Norman Anniversary Essays*, 235–50, London: Anglo-Norman Text Society.

Macleod, C. W. (1983), 'Homer on Poetry and the Poetry of Homer', in O. Taplin (ed), *Collected Essays*, 1–15, Oxford: Oxford University Press.

MacNeice, L. E. R. (2002), *Collected Poems*, ed. E. R. Dodds, Boston and London: Faber and Faber.

Mac Sweeney. N. (2018), *Troy: Myth, Site, Icon*, London: Bloomsbury.

Maguire, L. (2009), *Helen of Troy: From Homer to Hollywood*, Chichester and Malden: Wiley-Blackwell.

Marchand, S. (1996), *Down from Olympus. Archaeology and Philhellenism in Germany, 1750–1970*, Princeton: Princeton University Press.

Marillier, H. C. (1899), *Dante Gabriel Rossetti: An Illustrated Memorial of His Art and Life*, London: George Bell and Sons.

Marincola, J. (1994), 'Plutarch's Refutation of Herodotus', *The Ancient World*, 25 (2): 191–203.

Marincola, J. (1997), *Authority and Tradition in Ancient Historiography*, Cambridge and New York: Cambridge University Press.

Marincola, J. (2006), 'Herodotus and the Poetry of the Past', in C. Dewald and J. Marincola (eds), *The Cambridge Companion to Herodotus*, 13–28, Cambridge: Cambridge University Press.

Markovitis, S. (2006), *The Crisis of Action in Nineteenth-Century English Literature*, Columbus: Ohio State University Press.

Marsh, J. (2001), 'Annie Miller', in J. Berk Jiminez (ed), *Dictionary of Artists' Models*, 374–75, Oxford and New York: Routledge.

Marshall, C. W. (2011), 'Homer, Helen, and the Structure of Euripides' *Trojan Women*', in J. Davidson and D. Rosenbloom (eds), *Greek Drama IV: Texts, Contexts, Performance*, 31–46, Oxford: Aris and Phillips.

Martin, F. (2002), *L'Antiquité au Cinéma*, Paris: Dreamland.

Martin, R. P. (1989), *The Language of Heroes: Speech and Performance in the Iliad*, Ithaca: Cornell University Press.

Martin, R. P. (2009), 'Read on Arrival', in R. L. Hunter and I. Rutherford (eds), *The Wandering Poets of Ancient Greece*, Cambridge: Cambridge University Press.

Martindale, C. (1993), *Redeeming the Text: Latin Poetry and the Hermeneutics of Reception*, Cambridge: Cambridge University Press.

Martindale, C. and A. B. Taylor, eds (2004), *Shakespeare and the Classics*, Cambridge: Cambridge University Press.

Mastronarde, D. J. (2010), *The Art of Euripides. Dramatic Technique and Social Context*, Cambridge and New York: Cambridge University Press.

McGann, J. (2000), *Dante Gabriel Rossetti and the Game That Must Be Lost*, New Haven and London: Yale University Press.

McGann, J., ed (2003), *Dante Gabriel Rossetti: Collected Poetry and Prose*, New Haven and London: Yale University Press.

McKinsey, M. (2002), 'Classicism and Colonial Retrenchment in W. B. Yeats's "No Second Troy"', *Twentieth Century Literature*, 48 (2): 174–90.

Mendelsohn, D. (2008), *How Beautiful It Is and How Easily It Can Be Broken: Essays*, New York: HarperCollins.

Meridor, R. (2000), 'Creative Rhetoric in Euripides' *Troades*: Some Notes on Hecuba's Speech', *Classical Quarterly*, 50 (1): 16–29.

Meyer, L. (1933), *Les Légendes des Matières de Rome, de France, et de Bretagne dans le 'Pantheon' de Godefroi de Viterbe*, Paris: Editions de Boccard.

Michalowski, P. (1996), 'Sailing to Babylon, Reading the Dark Side of the Moon', in J. S. Cooper and G. M. Schwartz (eds), *The Study of the Ancient Near East in the 21st Century*, 177–94, Winona Lake: Eisenbrauns.

Michelakis, P. and M. Wyke, eds (2013), *The Ancient World in Silent Cinema*, Cambridge and New York: Cambridge University Press.

Michelini, A. N. (1987), *Euripides and the Tragic Tradition*, Madison: University of Wisconsin Press.

Minchin, E. (2001), *Homer and the Resources of Memory: Some Applications of Cognitive Theory to the Iliad and the Odyssey*, Oxford: Oxford University Press.

Minchin, E. (2015), '"Translation" and Transformation: Alice Oswald's Excavation of the *Iliad*', *Classical Receptions Journal*, 7 (2): 202–22.

Moles, J. (1993), 'Truth and Untruth in Herodotus and Thucydides', in C. Gill and T. P. Wiseman (eds), *Lies and Fiction in the Ancient World*, 88–121, Austin: University of Texas Press.

Moles, J. (2002), 'Herodotus and Athens', in E. J. Bakker, I. J. F. de Jong and H. van Wees (eds), *Brill's Companion to Herodotus*, 33–52, Leiden: Brill.

Momigliano, A. (1966), 'The Place of Herodotus in the History of Historiography', *Studies in Ancient Historiography*, 127–42, London: Weidenfeld and Nicolson.

Montanari, F. (2012), 'Introduction: The Homeric Question Today', in F. Montanari, A. Rengakos and C. Tsagalis (eds), *Homeric Contexts: Neoanalysis and the Interpretation of Oral Poetry*, 1–10, Berlin and Boston: De Gruyter.

Moorehead, C. (1994), *The Lost Treasures of Troy*, London: Weidefeld and Nicholson.

Morris, S. P. (1989), 'A Tale of Two Cities: The Miniature Frescos from Thera and the Origins of Greek Poetry', *American Journal of Archaeology*, 93 (4): 511–35.

Morrison, J. V. (1992), 'Alternatives to the Epic Tradition: Homer's Challenges in the *Iliad*', *Transactions of the American Philological Association*, 122: 61–71.

Mossman, J. M. (1995), *Wild Justice: A Study of Euripides' Hecuba*, Oxford: Clarendon Press.

Mossman, J. M. (2005), 'Women's Voices', in J. Gregory (ed), *A Companion to Greek Tragedy*, 352–65, Oxford: Wiley-Blackwell.

Moyer, I. S. (2002), 'Herodotus and an Egyptian Mirage: The Genealogies of the Theban Priests', *Journal of Hellenic Studies*, 122: 70–90.

Moyle, F. (2009), *Desperate Romantics: Private Lives of the Pre-Raphaelites*, London: John Murray.

Mueller, A. (2013), *Translating Troy: Provincial Politics in Alliterative Romance*, Columbus: Ohio State University Press.

Munson, R. V. (2001), *Telling Wonders: Ethnographic and Political Discourse in the Work of Herodotus*, Ann Arbor: University of Michigan Press.

Munson, R. V. (2007), 'The Trouble with the Ionians: Herodotus and the Beginning of the Ionian Revolt (5.28–38.1)', in E. Irwin and E. Greenwood (eds), *Reading Herodotus: A Study of the Logoi in Book 5 of Herodotus' Histories*, 146–67, Cambridge and New York: Cambridge University Press.

Munson, R. V. (2012), 'Herodotus and the Heroic Age: The Case of Minos', in E. Baragwanath and M. de Bakker (eds), *Myth, Truth, and Narrative in Herodotus*, 195–212, Oxford: Oxford University Press.

Munteanu, D. L. (2010–2011), 'The Tragic Muse and the Anti-Epic Glory of Women in Euripides' *Troades*', *The Classical Journal*, 106 (2): 129–47.

Murnaghan, S. (1987), *Disguise and Recognition in the* Odyssey, Princeton: Princeton University Press.

Myres, J. L. (1958), *Homer and His Critics*, London: Routledge and Kegan Paul.

Nagy, G. (1979), *The Best of the Achaeans: Concepts of the Hero in Archaic Greek Poetry*, Baltimore: Johns Hopkins University Press.

Nagy, G. (1990), *Pindar's Homer: The Lyric Possession of an Epic Past*, Baltimore and London: Johns Hopkins University Press.

Nagy, G. (1992), 'Homeric Questions', *Transactions of the American Philological Association*, 122: 17–60.

Nagy, G. (1996), *Homeric Questions*, Austin: University of Texas Press.

Nagy, G. (2009), *Homer the Classic*, Washington, DC: Center for Hellenic Studies.

Nappi, M. (2013), 'Texte et tissage dans l'épopée homérique: Hélène et Pénélope au miroir du poète?', in F. Bort and V. Dupont (eds), *Texte, Texture, Textile*, 41–55, Dijon: Éditions Universitaires de Dijon.

Nappi, M. (2015), 'Women and War in the *Iliad*: Rhetorical and Ethical Implications', in J. Fabre-Serris and A. Keith (eds), *Women and War in Antiquity*, 34–51, Baltimore: Johns Hopkins University Press.

Neer, R. T. (2002), *Style and Politics in Athenian Vase-Painting, The Craft of Democracy, ca. 530–460 B.C.E.*, Cambridge: Cambridge University Press.

Neitzel, H. (1975), *Homer-Rezeption bei Hesiod. Interpretation ausgewaehlter Passagen*, Bonn: Bouvier Verlag H. Grundmann.

Neville, J. W. (1977), 'Herodotus on the Trojan War', *Greece and Rome*, 24 (1): 3–12.

Nisbet, G. (2006), *Ancient Greece in Film and Popular Culture*, Exeter: Bristol Phoenix Press.

Noegel, S. M. (2009), 'Mesopotamian Epic', in J. M. Foley (ed.), *A Companion to Ancient Epic*, 233–45, Oxford: Wiley-Blackwell.

Noegel, S. M. (2011), '"Wordplay" in the Song of Erra', in W. Heimpel and G. Frantz-Szabó (eds), *Strings and Threads. A Celebration of the Work of Anne Draffkorn Kilmer*, 161–94, Winona Lake: Eisenbrauns.

Nutall, A. D. (2004), 'Action at a Distance: Shakespeare and the Greeks', in C. Martindale and A. B. Taylor (eds), *Shakespeare and the Classics*, 209–40, Cambridge: Cambridge University Press.

Ober, J. (1996), *The Athenian Revolution. Essays on Ancient Greek Democracy and Political Theory*, Princeton: Princeton University Press.

Ober, J. (2007), '"I Besieged that Man." Democracy's Revolutionary Start', in K. Raaflaub, J. Ober, and R. Wallace (eds), *Origins of Democracy in Ancient Greece*, 83–104, Berkeley and Los Angeles: University of California Press.

Osborne, R. (2009), *Greece in the Making, 1200-479 BC*, 2nd edn, London and New York: Routledge.

Osborne, R. (2010), 'When Was the Athenian Democratic Revolution?', in S. Goldhill and R. Osborne (eds), *Rethinking Revolutions through Ancient Greece*, 10–28, Cambridge: Cambridge University Press.

Osborne, R. (2011), *The History Written on the Classical Greek Body*, Cambridge: Cambridge University Press.

Osborne, R. (2014), *Greek History. The Basics*, Abingdon and New York: Routledge.

Osborne, R. (forthcoming), 'Homeric Imagery', in L. Nevett and J. Whitley (eds), *An Age of Experiment: Classical Archaeology Transformed, 1976-2014*, Cambridge: McDonald Institute.

Oshima, T. (2014), *Babylonian Poems of Pious Sufferers. Ludlul Bēl Nēmeqi and the Babylonian Theodicy*, Tübingen: Mohr Siedbeck.

Oswald, A. (2011), *Memorial: An Excavation of the Iliad*, London: Faber and Faber.

Paglia, C. (1990), *Sexual Personae: Art and Decadence from Nefertiti to Emily Dickinson*, London and New Haven: Yale University Press.

Pallantza, E. (2005), *Der Troische Krieg in der nachhomerischen Literatur bis zum 5. Jh. v. Chr.*, Stuttgart: Steiner.

Pantelia, M. C. (2002), 'Helen and the Last Song for Hector', *Transactions of the American Philological Association*, 132 (1/2): 21–27.

Papageorgiou, N. (2004), 'Prodicus and the *Agon* of the *Logoi* in Aristophanes' *Clouds*', *Quaderni Urbinati di Cultura Classica*, 78 (3): 61–96.

Pappas, A. (2012), 'More than Meets the Eye: The Aesthetics of (Non)sense in the Ancient Greek Symposium', in I. Sluiter and R. M. Rosen (eds), *Aesthetic Value in Classical Antiquity*, 71–112, Leiden: Brill.

Parry, A. M., ed (1971), *The Making of Homeric Verse: The Collected Papers of Milman Parry*, Oxford: Clarendon Press.

Patterson, L. E. (2010), *Kinship Myth in Ancient Greece*, Austin: University of Texas Press.

Paul, J. (2013), *Film and the Classical Epic Tradition*, Oxford: Oxford University Press.

Pearsall, D. (2015), 'Chaucer's Criseyde and Shakespeare's Cressida: Transformations in the Reception History of the Troy Story', in A. J. Goldwyn (ed), *The Trojan Wars and the Making of the Modern World*, 35–50, Uppsala: University of Uppsala.

Pelliccia, H. (1992), 'Sappho 16, Gorgias' *Helen*, and the Preface to Herodotus' *Histories*', *Yale Classical Studies*, 29: 63–84.

Pelling, C. (2006), 'Homer and Herodotus', in M. J. Clarke, B. G. F. Currie and R. O. A. M. Lyne (eds), *Epic Interactions. Epic Interactions: Perspectives on Homer, Virgil, and the Epic Tradition Presented to Jasper Griffin by Former Pupils*, 75–104, Oxford: Oxford University Press.

Pertz, G. H. (1844), *Monumenta Germanicae Historica. Tomus VI*, Hannover: Impensis Bibliopolii Aulici Hahniani.

Petrovic, A. (2016), 'Archaic Funerary Epigram and Hector's Imagined *Epitymbia*', in A. Efstathiou and I. Karamanou (eds), *Homeric Receptions across Generic and Cultural Contexts*, 45–58, Berlin and Boston: De Gruyter.

Phillips, R. (1996), *Mapping Men and Empire: A Geography of Adventure*, London: Routledge.

Pittaluga, S. (2004), 'Boezio, Goffredo da Viterbo e la ruota della Fortuna', in A. Bihrer and E. Stwin (eds), *Nova de veteribus. Mittel- und neulateinische Studien für Paul Gerhard Schmidt*, 504–11, Leipzig: K. G. Saur Verlag.

Plassmann, A. (2006), *Origo gentis: Identitäts- und Legitimitätsstiftung in früh- und hochmittelalterlichen Herkunfstserzählungen*, Berlin: De Gruyter.

Pollard, T. (2012), 'What's Hecuba to Shakespeare?', *Renaissance Quarterly*, 65: 1060–90.

Pollock, G. (1988), *Vision and Difference: Femininity, Feminism and Histories of Art*, London and New York: Routledge.

Poole, A. (1976), 'Total Disaster: Euripides' *The Trojan Women*', Arion, 3 (3): 257–87.

Porter, B. N. (2003), *Trees, Kings, and Politics: Studies in Assyrian Iconography*, Göttingen: Vandenhoeck and Ruprecht.

Powell, B. (1997), 'Homer and Writing', in I. Morris and B. Powell (eds), *A New Companion to Homer*, 3–31, Leiden: Brill.

Power, T. (2016), 'Literature in the Archaic Age', in M. Hose (ed), *A Companion to Greek Literature*, 58–76, Oxford: Wiley-Blackwell.

Presson, R. K. (1953), *Shakespeare's 'Troilus and Cressida' and the Legends of Troy*, Madison: University of Wisconsin Press.

Prettejohn, E. (1997), *Rossetti and His Circle*, London: Tate Gallery Publishing.

Prettejohn, E. (1998), *Interpreting Sargent*, London: Tate Gallery Publishing.

Prettejohn, E. (2012), 'The Painting of Dante Gabriel Rossetti', in E. Prettejohn (ed), *The Cambridge Companion to the Pre-Raphaelites*, 103–15, Cambridge: Cambridge University Press.

Priestley, J. M. (2014), *Herodotus and Hellenistic Culture: Literary Studies in the Reception of the Histories*, Oxford and New York: Oxford University Press.

Proch, C. and M. Kleu (2013), 'Models of Masculinities in *Troy*: Achilles, Hector and Their Female Partners', in A.-B. Renger and J. R. Solomon (eds), *Ancient Worlds in Film and Television: Gender and Politics*, 175–94, Leiden and Boston: Brill.

Purves, A. (2010), *Space and Time in Ancient Greek Narrative*, Cambridge: Cambridge University Press.

Purvis, J., ed (1995), *Women's History: Britain, 1850–1945*, London: Routledge.

Rabel, R. J. (2007), 'The Realist Politics of *Troy*', in M. M. Winkler (ed), *Troy: From Homer's Iliad to Hollywood Epic*, 186–201, Malden and Oxford: Wiley-Blackwell.

Rabinowitz, N. S. (2016), 'Trojan Women', in L. McClure (ed), *A Companion to Euripides*, 199–213, Oxford: Wiley-Blackwell.

Raubitschek, A. E. (1949), *Dedications from the Athenian Akropolis. A Catalogue of Inscriptions of the Sixth and Fifth Centuries B.C.*, Cambridge, MA: Archaeological Institute of America.

Redfield, J. (2001), 'The Proem of the *Iliad*: Homer's Art', in D. L. Cairns (ed), *Oxford Readings in Homer's Iliad*, 456–77, Oxford and New York: Oxford University Press.

Reiner, E. (1960), 'Plague Amulets and House Blessings', *Journal of Near Eastern Studies*, 19 (2): 148–55.

Rengakos, A. (1993), *Der Homertext und die hellenistischen Dichter*, Stuttgart: Franz Steiner Verlag.

Reynolds, M. (2011), *The Poetry of Translation: From Chaucer and Petrarch to Homer and Logue*, Oxford: Oxford University Press.

Rhodes, P. J. (2007), 'The Impact of the Persian Wars on Classical Greece', in E. Bridges, E. Hall and P. J. Rhodes (eds), *Cultural Responses to the Persian Wars. Antiquity to the Third Millennium*, 31–46, Oxford: Oxford University Press.

Richards, J. (2008), *Hollywood's Ancient Worlds*, London: Continuum Books.

Richardson, E. (2013), *Classical Victorians: Scholars, Scoundrels and Generals in Pursuit of Antiquity*, Cambridge: Cambridge University Press.

Richardson, N. J. (1987), 'The Individuality of Homer's Language', in J. M. Bremer, I. J. F. de Jong and J. Kalff (eds), *Homer, Beyond Oral Poetry: Recent Trends in Homeric Interpretation*, 165–84, Amsterdam: B. R. Grüner.

Richardson, N. J. (1993), *The Iliad: A Commentary. Vol. 6: Books 21–24*, Cambridge: Cambridge University Press.

Reynolds, D. F. (1995), *Heroic Poets, Poetic Heroes. The Ethnography of Performance in an Arabic Oral Epic Tradition*, Ithaca and London: Cornell University Press.

Robertson, M. (1992), 'The Pioneers in Context', in I. Wehgartner (ed), *Euphronios und Seine Zeit. Kolloquium in Berlin 19./20. April 1991*, 132–39, Berlin: Antikensammlung Museen Preussischer Kukturbesitz.

Robey, T. (2004), 'Review of *Troy*', *The Daily Telegraph*, 26 August. Available online: http://www.telegraph.co.uk/culture/film/filmreviews/10484545/Troy-review -original-Telegraph-review.html (16 February 2017).

Roisman, H. M. (2006), 'Helen in the *Iliad*; *Causa Belli* and Victim of War: From Silent Weaver to Public Speaker', *American Journal of Philology*, 127 (1): 1–36.

Roisman, H. M. (2008), 'Helen and the Power of Erotic Love: From Homeric Contemplation to Hollywood Fantasy', *College Literature*, 35 (4): 127–50.

Röllig, W. (2009), 'Aspekte der Archivierung und Kanonisierung von Keilschriftliteratur im 8./7. Jh. v. Chr.', in J. Schaper (ed), *Die Textualisierung der Religion*, 35–49, Tübingen: Mohr Siebeck Gmbh and Co.

Rollinger, R. (2001), 'The Ancient Greeks and the Impact of the Ancient Near East: Textual Evidence and Historical Perspective (ca. 750–650 B.C.)', in R. M. Whiting (ed), *Mythology and Mythologies: Methodological Approaches to Intercultural Influences. Proceedings of the Second Annual Symposium of the Assyrian and Babylonian Intellectual Heritage Project Held at Paris, France, 4–7 October 1999*, 233–64, Helsinki: Eisenbrauns.

Rollinger, R. (2007), 'Überlegungen zur Frage der Lokalisation von Jawan in neuassyrischer Zeit', *State Archives of Assyria Bulletin*, 16: 63–91.

Rollinger, R. (2009), 'Near Eastern Perspectives on the Greeks', in G. Boys-Stones, B. Graziosi, and P. Vasunia (eds), *The Oxford Handbook of Hellenic Studies*, 32–47, Oxford: Oxford University Press.

Rollinger, R. (2011), 'Der Block aus dem Osten: "Griechen" in vorderasiatischen Quellen des 8. und 7. Jahrhunderts v. Chr. – eine Zusammenschau', in H. Matthäus, N. Oettinger and S. Schroder (eds), *Der Orient und die Anfänge Europas: Kulturelle Beziehungen von der Späten Bronzezeit bis sur Frühen Eisenzeit*, 267–82, Wiesbaden: Harrassowitz Verlag.

Romney, J. (2004), 'Review of *Troy*', *The Independent*, 16 May. Available online: http://www.independent.co.uk/arts-entertainment/films/reviews/troy-15-563392.html (16 February 2017).

Rose, C. B. (2014), *The Archaeology of Greek and Roman Troy*, New York and Cambridge: Cambridge University Press.

Rose, P. W. (2013), *Class in Archaic Greece*, Cambridge: Cambridge University Press.

Ruijgh, C. J. (1985), 'Le mycénien et Homère', in A. Morpurgo-Davies and Y. Duhoux (eds), *Linear B: A 1984 Survey. Proceedings of the Mycenaean Colloquium of the VIIIth Congress of the International Federations of the Societies of Classical Studies (Dublin, 27th August–1st September 1984)*, 143–90, Leuven: Peeters.

Russo, J. (1992), 'Homer's Style: Nonformulaic Features of an Oral Aesthetic', *Oral Tradition*, 9 (2): 371–89.

Rutherford, I. (2009), 'Hesiod and the Literary Traditions of the Near East', in F. Montanari, C. Tsagalis and A. Rengakos (eds), *Brill's Companion to Hesiod*, 9–35, Leiden: Brill.

Safran, M. E. and M. S. Cyrino (2015), 'Introduction: Cinemyths: Classical Myth on Screen', in M. S. Cyrino and M. E. Safran (eds), *Classical Myth on Screen*, 1–11, New York: Palgrave Macmillan.

Saïd, S. (2011a), *Homer and the Odyssey*, Oxford and New York: Oxford University Press.

Saïd, S. (2011b), 'Homer, or How to Create a World Writer', in J. Dominique (ed), *Currents in Comparative Romance Languages and Literatures: Foundational Texts of World Literature*, 29–45, New York: Peter Lang.

Saïd, S. (2012), 'Herodotus and the "Myth" of the Trojan War', in E. Baragwanath and M. de Bakker (eds), *Myth, Truth, and Narrative in Herodotus*, 87–106, Oxford: Oxford University Press.

Sammons, B. (2012), 'History and *Hyponoia*: Herodotus and Early Literary Criticism', *Histos*, 6: 52–66.

Sasson, J. M. (2009), 'Comparative Observations on the Near Eastern Epic Traditions', in J. M. Foley (ed), *A Companion to Ancient Epic*, 215–32, Oxford: Wiley-Blackwell.

Schefold, K. (1992), *Gods and Heroes in Late Archaic Greek Art*, Cambridge: Cambridge University Press.

Schein, S. L. (1984), *The Mortal Hero: An Introduction to Homer's Iliad*, Berkeley, Los Angeles and London: University of California Press.

Schein, S. L. (2007), '"Our Debt to Greece and Rome": Canon, Class and Ideology', in L. Hardwick and C. Stray (eds), *A Companion to Classical Receptions*, 75–85, Malden and Oxford: Wiley-Blackwell.

Schein, S. L. (2016), *Homeric Epic and Its Reception: Interpretive Essays*, Oxford and New York: Oxford University Press.

Schein, S. L. (forthcoming), 'The *Iliad* as Princes' Mirror in Chapman's Translation and Shakespeare's *Troilus and Cressida*', in J. J. H. Klooster and B. van den Berg (eds), *Homer and the Good Ruler. The Reception of Homeric Epic as Princes' Mirror through the Ages*, Leiden: Brill.

Scherer, M. (1963), *The Legends of Troy in Art and Literature*, London: Phaidon.

Schliemann, H. (1874), *Trojanischer Alterthümer. Bericht über die Ausgrabungen in Troja*, Leipzig: F. A. Brockhaus.

Schliemann, H. (1875), *Troy and Its Remains. A Narrative of the Researches and Discoveries Made on the Site of Ilium, and in the Trojan Plain*, ed. P. Smith, London: John Murray.

Scodel, R. (1980), *The Trojan Trilogy of Euripides. Hypomnemata 60*, Göttingen: Vandenhoeck and Ruprect.

Scodel, R. (2002), *Listening to Homer: Tradition, Narrative, and Audience*, Ann Arbor: University of Michigan Press.

Scully, S. (2007), 'The Fate of Troy', in M. M. Winkler (ed), *Troy: From Homer's Iliad to Hollywood Epic*, 119–30, Malden and Oxford: Wiley-Blackwell.

Segal, C. (1993), *Euripides and the Poetics of Sorrow*, London and Durham: Duke University Press.

Segal, C. (1994), *Singers, Heroes, and Gods in the Odyssey*, Ithaca and London: Cornell University Press.

Shahabudin, K. (2007), 'From Greek Myth to Hollywood Story: Explanatory Narrative in *Troy*', in M. Winkler (ed), *Troy: From Homer's Iliad to Hollywood Epic*, 107–18, Malden and Oxford: Wiley-Blackwell.

Shanower, E. (2011), 'Twenty-First-Century Troy', in G. Kovacs and C. W. Marshall (eds), *Classics and Comics*, 195–206, Oxford and New York: Oxford University Press.

Shapiro, H. A. (1994), 'Chapter 2: Homer's *Iliad*: The Trojan War', in H. A. Shapiro (ed), *Myth into Art: Poet and Painters in Classical Greece*, 11–43, London and New York: Routledge.

Shawcross, T. (2003), 'Re-inventing the Homeland in the Historiography of Frankish Greece: The Fourth Crusade and the Legend of the Trojan War', *Byzantine and Modern Greek Studies*, 27: 120–52.

Shepard, A. and S. D. Powell, eds (2004), *Fantasies of Troy. Classical Tales and the Social Imaginary in Medieval and Early Modern Europe*, Toronto: Centre for Reformation and Renaissance Studies.

Silk, M. (2004), 'Shakespeare and Greek Tragedy: Strange Relationship', in C. Martindale and A. B. Taylor (eds), *Shakespeare and the Classics*, 241–57, Cambridge: Cambridge University Press.

Skinner, J. (2012), *The Invention of Greek Ethnography: From Homer to Herodotus*, Oxford: Oxford University Press.

Smith, A. (1996), *The Victorian Nude: Sexuality, Morality and Art*, Manchester and New York: Manchester University Press.

Smith, H. L. (1998), *The British Women's Suffrage Campaign, 1866–1928*, Harlow: Pearson.

Smith, P. (1875), 'Preface', in H. Schliemann, *Troy and Its Ruins*, iii–xxiv, London: John Murray.

Solomon, J. (2001), *The Ancient World in the Cinema*, rev. and expanded edn., New Haven and London: Yale University Press.

Solomon, J. R. (2007), 'The Vacillations of the Trojan Myth: Popularization & Classicization, Variation & Codification', *International Journal of the Classical Tradition*, 14 (3/4): 482–534.

Sommer, M. (2007), 'Networks of Commerce and Knowledge in the Iron Age: The Case of the Phoenicians', *Mediterranean Historical Review*, 22 (1): 97–111.

Sonstroem, D. (1970), *Rossetti and the Fair Lady*, Middletown: Wesleyan University Press.

Sotiriou, M. (1998), *Pindarus Homericus*, Göttingen: Vandenhoeck and Ruprecht.

Sowerby, R. (1992), 'Chapman's Discovery of Homer', *Translation and Literature*, 1 (1): 26–51.

Spencer-Longhurst, P. (2000), *The Blue Bower: Rossetti in the 1860s*, London: Scala Publishers.

Spiegel, G. M. (1999), *The Past as Text: The Theory and Practice of Medieval Historiography*, Baltimore and London: Johns Hopkins University Press.

Spitzner, E. F. H. (1839), *Observationes criticae et grammaticae in Quinti Smyrnaei Posthomerica*, Leipzig: Weidmann.

Squire, M. and V. Platt (2017), 'Framing the Visual in Greek and Roman Antiquity: An Introduction', in M. Squire and V. Platt (eds), *The Frame in Classical Art. A Cultural History*, 3–99, Cambridge: Cambridge University Press.

Stadter, P. (2004), 'From the Mythical to the Historical Paradigm: The Transformation of Myth in Herodotus', in J. M. Candau Morón, F. J. González Ponce and G. Cruz Andreotti (eds), *Historia y Mito: El Pasado Legendario Como Fuente de Autoridad*, 31–46, Málaga: Centro de Ediciones de la Diputación Provincial de Málaga.

Stewart, A. (2008), 'The Persian and Carthaginian Invasions of 480 B.C.E. and the Beginning of the Classical Style: Part 2, The Finds from Other Sites in Athens, Attica, Elsewhere in Greece, and on Sicily; Part 3, The Severe Style: Motivations and Meaning', *American Journal of Archaeology*, 112 (4): 581–615.

Stoll, J. (2014), 'Imagining Troy: Fictions of Translation in Medieval French Literature', PhD diss., King's College, London.

Stones, A. (2005), 'Seeing the Walls of Troy', in B. Dekeyzer and J. van den Stock (eds), *Manuscripts in Transition: Recycling Manuscripts, Texts and Images. Proceedings of the International Congress Held in Brussels (5–9 November 2002)*, 161–78, Leuven: Peeters.

Strauss, B. (2006), *The Trojan War: A New History*, New York: Simon and Schuster.

Stray, C. (1998), *Classics Transformed: Schools, Universities, and Society in England, 1830–1960*, Oxford: Clarendon Press.

Stray, C., ed (2007), *Remaking the Classics: Literature, Genre and Media in Britain, 1800–2000*, London: Duckworth.

Struve, J. T. (1864), *Novae curae in Quinti Smyrnaei Posthomerica*, St. Petersburg, Riga and Leipzig: Eggers und Socios, Samuel Schmidt, Leopold Voss.

Suk Fong Jim, T. (2014), *Sharing with the Gods. Aparchai and Dekatai in Ancient Greece*, Oxford: Oxford University Press.

Sulprizio, C. (2011), '*Eros* Conquers All: Sex and Love in Eric Shanower's *Age of Bronze*', in G. Kovacs and C. W. Marshall (eds), *Classics and Comics*, 207–20, Oxford and New York: Oxford University Press.

Surtees, V. (1971), *The Paintings and Drawings of Dante Gabriel Rossetti (1828–1882). A Catalogue Raisonné, Vol. 1*, Oxford: Clarendon Press.

Suter, A. (2003), 'Lament in Euripides' *Trojan Women*', *Mnemosyne*, 56 (1): 1–27.

Suzuki, M. (1989), *Metamorphoses of Helen: Authority, Difference, and the Epic*, Ithaca: Cornell University Press.

Swift, L. A. (2010), *The Hidden Chorus: Echoes of Genre in Tragic Lyric*, Oxford: Oxford University Press.

Swinburne, A. C. (1875), *Essays and Studies*, London: Chatto and Windus.

Tanner, M. (1993), *The Last Descendant of Aeneas. The Habsburgs and the Mythic Image of the Emperor*, New Haven: Yale University Press.

Taplin, O. (1992), *Homeric Soundings: The Shaping of the* Iliad, Oxford: Clarendon Press.

Tatlock, J. S. P. (1915), 'The Siege of Troy in Elizabethan Literature. Especially in Shakespeare and Heywood', *Proceedings of the Modern Language Association*, 30 (4): 673–770.

Thalmann, W. G. (1988), 'Thersites: Comedy, Scapegoats, and Heroic Ideology in the *Iliad*', *Transactions of the American Philological Association*, 118: 1–28.

Theodorakopoulos, E. (2010), *Ancient Rome and the Cinema: Story and Spectacle in Hollywood and Rome*, Exeter: Bristol Phoenix Press.

Thomas, R. (2000), *Herodotus in Context: Ethnography, Science and the Art of Persuasion*, Cambridge: Cambridge University Press.

Thomas, R. (2001), 'Herodotus' *Histories* and the Floating Gap', in N. Luraghi (ed), *The Historian's Craft in the Age of Herodotus*, 198–210, Oxford and New York: Oxford University Press.

Thompson, D. (2004), *The Trojan War: Literature and Legends from the Bronze Age to the Present*, Jefferson: McFarland and Co., Inc.

Topper, K. (2012), *The Imagery of the Athenian Symposium*, Cambridge: Cambridge University Press.

Torrance, I. (2013), *Metapoetry in Euripides*, Oxford: Oxford University Press.

Traill, D. A. (1995), *Schliemann of Troy: Treasure and Deceit*, New York: St Martin's Press.

Trigger, B. G. (1989), *A History of Archaeological Thought*, Cambridge: Cambridge University Press.

Tsagalis, C. (2008), *The Oral Palimpsest: Exploring Intertextuality in the Homeric Epics*, Washington, DC: Center for Hellenic Studies.

Turner, F. M. (1981), *The Greek Heritage in Victorian Britain*, New Haven and London: Yale University Press.

Van de Mieroop, M. (2004), *A History of the Ancient Near East, ca. 3000–323 BC*, Oxford: Blackwell.

Van Dongen, E. (2011), 'The 'Kingship in Heaven'-Theme of the Hesiodic *Theogony*: Origin, Function, Composition', *Greek, Roman and Byzantine Studies*, 51 (2): 180–201.

Van Erp Taalman Kip, A. M. (1987), 'Euripides and Melos', *Mnemosyne*, 40 (3/4): 414–19.

Vandiver, E. (1991), *Heroes in Herodotus: The Interaction of Myth and History*, Frankfurt am Main and New York: Peter Lang.

Vandiver, E. (2012), '"Strangers are from Zeus": Homeric *Xenia* at the Courts of Proteus and Croesus', in E. Baragwanath and M. de Bakker (eds), *Myth, Truth, and Narrative in Herodotus*, 143–66, Oxford: Oxford University Press.

Visvardi, E. (2011), 'Pity and Panhellenic Politics: Choral Emotion in Euripides' *Hecuba* and *Trojan Women*', in D. M. Carter (ed), *Why Athens?: A Reappraisal of Tragic Politics*, 269–91, Oxford: Oxford University Press.

Vlassopoulos, K. (2013), *Greeks and Barbarians*, Cambridge: Cambridge University Press.

Vogelzang, M. E. (1990), 'Patterns Introducing Direct Speech in Akkadian Literary Texts', *Journal of Cuneiform Studies*, 41: 50–70.

von Bothmer, D. (1981), 'The Death of Sarpedon', in S. L. Hyatt (ed), *The Greek Vase*, 63–80, Latham: Hudson-Mohawk Associates.

von Wilamowitz-Moellendorff, U. (1884), *Homerische Untersuchungen*, Berlin: Weidmannche Buchhandlung.

von Wilamowitz-Moellendorff, U. (1916), *Die Ilias und Homer*, Berlin: Weidmannche Buchhandlung.

Waitz, G., ed (1872), *Gotofridi Viterbiensis opera. Monumenta Germaniae Historica, Scriptores, Vol. 22*, Hannover: Hahn.

Wasko, J. (1987), 'The Web of Eroticism in Rossetti's "Troy Town," "Eden Bower," and "Rose Mary"', *Papers on Language and Literature*, 23 (3): 333–44.

Waswo, R. (1995), 'Our Ancestors, the Trojans: Inventing Cultural Identity in the Middle Ages', *Exemplaria*, 7 (2): 269–90.

Watkins, C. (1986), 'When they Came from Steep Wilusa', in M. J. Mellink (ed), *Troy and the Trojan War: A Symposium Held at Bryn Mawr College, October 1984*, 45–62, Bryn Mawr: Bryn Mawr College.

Waugh, E. (1928), *Rossetti: His Life and Works*, London: Duckworth.

Weber, L. J. (1994), 'The Historical Importance of Godfrey of Viterbo', *Viator*, 25: 153–95.

Węcowski, M. (2004), 'The Hedgehog and the Fox: Form and Meaning in the Prologue of Herodotus', *Journal of Hellenic Studies*, 124: 143–64.

Węcowski, M. (2014), *The Rise of the Greek Aristocratic Banquet*, Oxford and New York: Oxford University Press.

Weinlich, B. P. (2015), 'A New Briseis in *Troy*', in M. M. Winkler (ed), *Return to Troy: New Essays on the Hollywood Epic*, 191–202, Leiden and Boston: Brill.

West, M. L. (1997), *The East Face of Helicon: West Asiatic Elements in Greek Poetry and Myth*, Oxford: Oxford University Press.

West, M. L. (2011), *The Making of the Iliad: Disquisition and Analytical Commentary*, Oxford and New York: Oxford University Press.

West, M. L. (2013), *The Epic Cycle: A Commentary on the Lost Troy Epics*, Oxford and New York: Oxford University Press.

West, S. (2002), 'Demythologisation in Herodotus', *Xenia Toruniensia*, 6: 1–48.

West, S. (2004), 'Herodotus and Lyric Poetry', *Letras Clássicas*, 8: 79–91.

Westenholz, J. G. (1997), *Legends of the Kings of Akkade: The Texts*, Mesopotamian Civilizations 7, Winona Lake: Eisenbrauns.

Wieber, A. (2005), 'Vor Troja nichts neues? Moderne Kinogeschichten zu Homers *Ilias*', in M. Lindner (ed), *Drehbuch Geschichte: Die antike Welt im Film*, 137–62, Münster: LIT Verlag.

Williams, D. (1991), 'The Drawing of the Human Figure on Early Red Figure Vases', in D. Buitron-Oliver (ed), *New Perspectives in Early Greek Art*, 285–301, Washington DC: National Gallery of Art.

Winkler, M. M., ed (2004), *Gladiator: Film and History*, Malden and Oxford: Wiley-Blackwell.

Winkler, M. M. (2005), 'Neo-Mythologism: Apollo and the Muses on the Screen', *International Journal of the Classical Tradition*, 11 (3): 383–423.

Winkler, M. M., ed (2007a), *Troy: From Homer's Iliad to Hollywood Epic*, Malden and Oxford: Wiley-Blackwell.

Winkler, M. M. (2007b), 'Editor's Introduction', in M. M. Winkler (ed), *Troy: From Homer's Iliad to Hollywood Epic*, 1–19, Malden and Oxford: Wiley-Blackwell.

Winkler, M. M. (2007c), 'The Trojan War on the Screen: An Annotated Filmography', in M. M. Winkler (ed), *Troy: From Homer's Iliad to Hollywood Epic*, 202–15, Malden and Oxford: Wiley-Blackwell.

Winkler, M. M. (2009), *Cinema and Classical Texts: Apollo's New Light*, Cambridge: Cambridge University Press.

Winkler, M. M., ed (2015a), *Return to Troy: New Essays on the Hollywood Epic*, Leiden and Boston: Brill.

Winkler, M. M. (2015b), 'Wolfgang Petersen on Homer and *Troy*', in M. M. Winkler (ed), *Return to Troy: New Essays on the Hollywood Epic*, 16–26, Leiden and Boston: Brill.

Wohl, V. (2015), *Euripides and the Politics of Form*, Princeton and Oxford: Princeton University Press.

Wolf, K. (2008), *Troja – Metamorphosen eies Mythos: Französiche, englische ud italienische Überlieferungen des 12. Jahrhunderts im Vergleich*, Berlin: De Gruyter.

Wood, C. (1983), *Olympian Dreamers: Victorian Classical Painters, 1860–1914*, London: Constable.

Wood, C. (1999), *Victorian Painting*, London: Weidenfeld and Nicolson.

Wood, C. (2000), *The Pre-Raphaelites*, London: Seven Dials.

Wood, M. (1986), *In Search of the Trojan War*, London: British Broadcasting Corporation.

Wright, M. (2010), 'The Tragedian as Critic: Euripides and Early Greek Poetics', *Journal of Hellenic Studies*, 130: 165–84.

Wyke, M. (1997), *Projecting the Past: Ancient Rome, Cinema, and History*, New York and London: Routledge.

Yeats, W. B. (1910), *The Green Helmet and Other Poems*, Dundrum: Cuala Press.

Young, A. M. (1948), *Troy and Her Legend*, Pittsburgh: University of Pittsburgh Press.

Index